HUMOR IN MIDDLE EASTERN CINEMA

CONTEMPORARY APPROACHES
TO FILM AND MEDIA SERIES

A complete listing of the books in this series can be found online at wsupress.wayne.edu

General Editor
Barry Keith Grant, Brock University

Advisory Editors
Robert J. Burgoyne, University of St. Andrews
Caren J. Deming, University of Arizona, Patricia B. Erens
School of the Art Institute of Chicago
Peter X. Feng, University of Delaware
Lucy Fischer, University of Pittsburgh
Frances Gateward, California State University, Northridge
Tom Gunning , University of Chicago
Thomas Leitch, University of Delaware
Walter Metz, Southern Illinois University

HUMOR IN MIDDLE EASTERN CINEMA

EDITED BY
GAYATRI DEVI AND NAJAT RAHMAN

Wayne State University Press
Detroit

© 2014 by Wayne State University Press, Detroit, Michigan 48201. All rights reserved. No part of this book may be reproduced without formal permission.

18 17 16 15 14   5 4 3 2 1

Library of Congress Control Number: 2014936563

ISBN 978-0-8143-3937-4 (paperback)
ISBN 978-0-8143-3938-1 (ebook)

Designed and typeset by Bryce Schimanski
Composed in Gentium

CONTENTS

Introduction 1
GAYATRI DEVI AND NAJAT RAHMAN

1. Humor, Loss, and the Possibility for Politics in Recent Palestinian Cinema 31
NAJAT RAHMAN

2. Strategies of Subversion in Ben Ali's Tunisia: Allegory and Satire in Moncef Dhouib's *The TV Is Coming* 56
ROBERT LANG

3. Satiric Traversals in the Comedy of Mehrān Modiri: Space, Irony, and National Allegory on Iranian Television 79
CYRUS ALI ZARGAR

4. Ethnic Humor, Stereotypes, and Cultural Power in Israeli Cinema 104
ELISE BURTON

5. The Laughter of Youssef Chahine 126
NAJAT RAHMAN

6. Comedic Mediations: War and Genre in *The Outcasts* 145
SOMY KIM

7. Humor and the Cinematic Sublime in Kiarostami's *The Wind Will Carry Us* 161
GAYATRI DEVI

8. America the Oppressively Funny: Humor and
   Anti-Americanisms in Modern Turkish Cinema 188
   PERIN GUREL

9. Laughter Across Borders: The Case of the Bollywood
   Film *Tere Bin Laden* 214
   MARA MATTA

Bibliography 239
Filmography 257
Contributors 259
Index 263

HUMOR IN MIDDLE EASTERN CINEMA

INTRODUCTION

GAYATRI DEVI AND NAJAT RAHMAN

It would not be inaccurate to postulate that the Middle East is both a materially real topography as well as a highly conflicted *topoi*, in many cases an imagined construct, an ethical goal and destination both from within and without, a landscape as well as a representation. Like literature and other creative arts, cinema in the Middle East is heavily involved in exploring this *topoi* of representation, both by locally produced cinema, as well as by the Middle Eastern diaspora. The Middle East is valorized in a certain way in Hollywood films via certain specific genres, such as adventure stories, pop history pieces, international espionage thrillers, terrorist dramas, terrorist thrillers; themes, such as Islamic fundamentalism, martyrdom, censorship, and the status of women, to note those most popular in the West; and repeated tropes, such as the desert, the wilderness, the border, and the harem.[1] Popular images conjured up by the term Middle East include aerial views of the region—often as a target or a surveillance space—filled with congested cities, narrow alleys, colorful markets, men in military fatigues, security police, rocket launchers, infinite stretches of the desert, dust, sandstorms and armored vehicles.[2] Many of these cinematic representations have acquired hegemonic status in our media-moderated cultural conversations with and about the Middle East. The film industries in the Middle East, particularly those of Egypt, Iran, Turkey, Morocco, Algeria, and, most recently, Palestine, have explored and continue to respond in creative ways to these hegemonic narratives about the Middle East largely authored by the

West, and ideologically dispersed through Hollywood. The present volume brings together a collection of essays on Middle Eastern films that engage with some of these hegemonic and counter-hegemonic narratives about the region, perceived through the apertures of comedy and humor, and a stated interest in abiding by the region and its people.

The geopolitical boundaries of the region known as the Middle East span multiple countries that are home to the ancient civilizations of Mesopotamia, Sumeria, Babylon, the Persians, the Ottomans, and the Nile Valley; multiple races and ethnicities; at least four major languages, Arabic, Persian, Turkish, and Hebrew, along with many minor languages and dialects; and three major religions, Islam, Christianity, and Judaism, and a minor one, Zoroastrianism. The geopolitical borders of the region known as the Middle East has not always had the same identical coordinates through the course of the history of this region. Both "middle" and "east" are relative terms. For the purposes of this book, the Middle East includes the nations of Egypt, Jordan, Kuwait, Lebanon, Syria, Palestine, Israel, Iraq, or the Mashriq; Morocco, Algeria, Tunisia, and Libya, or the Maghreb; Saudi Arabia and the Gulf countries; as well as the non-Arab nations of Iran and Turkey. In our own times, particularly, since the 2001 World Trade Center attacks in New York City, Pakistan, Afghanistan, and the Indian subcontinent—generally part of South Asia and historically not identified with the geopolitical Middle East—have, nevertheless, entered into the discourse on matters Middle Eastern as well.[3] Apart from Iran and Turkey, whose political and sociocultural histories follow a path of development from empire to monarchy and republic, and, to a smaller extent, Egypt, most of the Middle Eastern nations have seen their political borders significantly redrawn in the twentieth century as a result of colonization by Western European powers, primarily Britain and France. Viewed from both within the region and from the outside, anti-imperialist revolutions, anti-monarchy rebellions, nationalist uprisings, reformist upheavals, civil wars, foreign invasions and occupations, and democracy movements all feature prominently in the history and cultural identity of this region, from the mid-1800s to the present day. If we are to search for a common denominator that unites these countries despite the great variety of

INTRODUCTION

cultures, ethnicities, languages, religions, and other vectors of lived private and public identities, we might identify their shared experience in the politically vested presence of the imperial and neocolonial powers of Western Europe, specifically these powers' often tragic encroachment, invasion, occupation, and sometimes obliteration of many aspects of what constitutes life in this region.

The second shared denominator would be the prominence of the Middle Eastern diaspora in the discourse on matters Middle Eastern throughout the world, including the West, a fact that emphasizes the substantial reach and hold of the historical patterns of eviction, migration, settlement, and return that have characterized human movement in this region from ancient to modern times. In the twentieth and twenty-first centuries, advances in mass media, including journalism, radio, television, and film, and the worldwide reach of telecommunications and the Internet, have radically altered and augmented the relationship between each nation and its diaspora. That interrelationship in the Middle Eastern context is directly relevant to our understanding of the causes and effects of transnationalism, national identity discourses, state-citizen relations, globalization, and even conflict, refugee crisis, and disarmament.

Though cinema was a late nineteenth-century colonial import to the region, it was by no means a radical new addition, a cultural disruption, or an injection of modernity into a traditional culture. Cinema, as the quintessential Western art form, is often regarded as an index of modernity, particularly when the context is colonial and the target society is regarded as primitive or exotic, the Other. However, as Viola Shafik has argued in her groundbreaking work on cultural identity and Arab cinema, "The idea of cinema as an alien cultural element, implanted in an 'authentic,' quasi-virgin Arab culture, has to be questioned in the same way as the notion of cultural 'authenticity.'"[4] Shafik effectively disproves the contention of both European as well as Arab apologists that Arab cinema is a lesser imitation of Western models by declaring the very notion of the "purity" of the "traditional" Arab society as nothing more than a self-serving myth, regardless of origin. Shafik argues for demystifying the idea of a monocultural traditional Arab society:

> The countries of North Africa and the Middle East have never formed a closed and secluded cultural environment. . . . The culture of the region must be considered as the result of a dynamic relation of power, formed along several axes: first the relation between syncretic popular culture and elitist high culture; second, between the different regional 'cultures' of various peoples and ethnic groups, religions, and languages; and third, between the indigenous culture as a whole and the influences that stem from other cultural environments. Even apparently 'authentic' movements like present-day fundamentalism or nationalism do not invalidate this model. Despite the parameters of Arabic language and Islam having, since national independence, been pushed increasingly into the foreground to serve as a starting-point for cultural purification and preservation, the idea of a pure Arab-Muslim culture is a myth.[5]

The films discussed in the present volume represent a Middle East that is culturally diverse and dynamic. Our inference stems from our longstanding interest in Middle Eastern comedy films, where a merry disruption of norms seems to uncover repressed content of a serious nature that goes to the heart of structural and representational questions regarding individual and cultural identity. Humor in these films seems to be a powerful means with which to transcend the representational obligations of the "political unconscious,"[6] and the preferred aesthetic and authentic way to renegotiate and rearticulate dimensions of life that have been repressed, replaced, and negated by the political unconscious. In other words, humor might be an idiom to rescue these films from being reduced to national allegories, although the films clearly take up the national in complex ways, perhaps owing to humor's inherently aporetic nature, and perhaps stemming from its refusal to be analogized with a category other than itself. The films discussed here, some genre comedies, others feature films, in general evoke a distinct and lingering sense of both low and high humor, parody and satire, emancipation and melancholia, though some might not fit the conventional definition of comedy. The essays herein examine humor in recent Middle Eastern cinema, including from the

INTRODUCTION

Middle Eastern diaspora. In many of these films, humor seems to open into politics in its preoccupation with communal life and freedom, but it does not always service the political.

A long tradition of humor exists in Middle Eastern (especially Egyptian) cinema, despite the sometimes solemn subjects, where the comic and the tragic intermingle. How does Middle Eastern cinema highlight the stakes and the place of humor in art and in life? What is its relation to the political, to representation, to art? Humor implies a relation to power: it intimidates, humiliates, corrects. Can humor in cinematic art be "emancipatory"? If the comical is characterized by "mechanical inelasticity," as Henri Bergson has argued, then what are its limits for any intervention or transformation? If it signals a certain aesthetic, in sharing with it the principles of equality, expressiveness, freedom, and *indifference,* it also signals a certain *anesthetic* in its momentary deadening of feeling in its appeal to intelligence rather than to emotion.[7] Is laughter bound to be aporetic? For Bergson, "Laughter is the indication of an effort which suddenly encounters a void."[8] Andrew Horton also indicates that the comic can be "conservative or subversive or even both at once, depending on the audience and context."[9]

We seek to present a substantial interdisciplinary analysis of the theory and modalities of humor in contemporary Middle Eastern cinema, of the role and impact of humor on selected films in the last few decades, and of the context of a predominant cultural phenomenon that is for the most part yet to be analyzed. Research on humor in the Middle Eastern context can contribute new theoretical understanding of the relation between the aesthetic and the political. Through the innovative (if provisional) dismantling of a familiar regime of representation that humor introduces, the cinematic works push through humor and beyond humor to reconfigure the relation of the senses. In pushing through humor, it pushes the limits of the aesthetic. Humor also "celebrates the human capacity to endure rather than to aspire and suffer."[10] Other theorists have also noted the necessity of humor for human survival.[11]

Humor serves as a critical lens through which to assess daily life. Such humor has received warm welcome from audiences, and there are no indications that such engagement with humor is fading out.

One also notes a proliferation of other cultural forms incorporating humor in television shows, cartoons, and the Internet. Given the presence of humor in Middle Eastern cultural production, we seek to account for its recent return through aesthetic, philosophical, and historical approaches.

Notwithstanding the long tradition of comedic literature in the Arabic tradition, there are very few studies devoted to the study of humor in this modern cultural production. Studies tend to focus on the classical literary tradition (from texts of early Islam to *The Thousand and One Nights* to the works of Al Hariri and Al Jahiz, and so on).[12] Nonetheless, studies of the contemporary period tend to be more in Arabic than English or French and favor single-author studies. While several recent publications attest to the growing interest in humor in the Middle East, one notes as most important Mustafa Bayyumi's *Al Fukahah inda Najib Mahfouz* (1994) or Joseph Sadan's *Al-Adab al-Arabi al-Hazil wa-Nawadir al Thuqala* (1983).[13]

This volume engages new theoretical perspectives on the absurd as an aesthetic category, the aesthetic and the political, and, to a lesser extent, transnationalism. The essays draw on the substantial body of theories and philosophies regarding humor, most importantly those of Longinus, Henri Bergson, Sigmund Freud, and Northrop Frye, among others. Theories of humor are also considered in relation to theories of aesthetics and politics, mainly those of Immanuel Kant, Mikhail Bakhtin, Fredric Jameson, Michel Foucault, Jacques Rancière, and Gilles Deleuze and Félix Guattari.[14] Further, we investigate the definition of humor in its particular Middle Eastern context, the relation of the local practice to an international one, and the relation of the different modalities to one another, as well as to the dominant poetic and narrative traditions from which they ensue.

Concerned with the theory, history, aesthetic practice, and politics of humor, this volume represents a significant and innovative contribution to the cultural and aesthetic artifacts of a region primarily known through documentary footage as a region of conflict and violence. It is the first of its kind in English to substantially chart the development of the multifarious strain of humor in Middle Eastern cinematic art. This artistic production allows us to assess the extent to which humor can be understood as an act of political subjectivity, a process of subjectification that exposes politics as a disruption of what can be seen, heard, and said as a reconfiguration of the sensible, as conceived by Rancière (2010). Humor has long been politically charged. While one cannot altogether deny its political dimension in the name of its aesthetic value, one cannot continue to consider it simply as oppositional.

"Laughter," writes Mikhail Bakhtin,

> has a deep philosophical meaning, it is one of the essential forms of the truth concerning the world as a whole, concerning history and man; it is a peculiar point of view relative to the world; the world is seen anew, no less (and perhaps more) profoundly than when seen from the serious standpoint. Therefore, laughter is just as admissible in great literature, posing universal problems, as seriousness. Certain essential aspects of the world are accessible only to laughter.[15]

Comedy, by definition, is an impure art form. Bakhtin's assertions above notwithstanding, it is also, in canonical criticism, classified as a lowbrow art form, as opposed to tragedy, that highbrow form, which, theoreticians from Aristotle to Hegel to Nietzsche and Walter Benjamin have discussed as a fundamental constituent of myth, aesthetics, history, and philosophy. We present here a few of the theorists who have informed our own engagement with the subject. They complicate the scope, function, and potential of humor in widely disparate ways. The essays reflect many of these theoretical positions.

The impulse to laugh, a ubiquitous effect of comedy, rises out of our recognition of many unequal, incongruous, asymmetrical, sometimes absurd configurations of circumstances, character, and plot that create a mental state we might call amusement. In the Western canonical writing on humor, there are two rather diametrically opposed schools of thought on the nature of amusement as produced by comic events. Though we do not find generic classifications of the "laughable" into humor, joke, wit, comedy, satire, parody, and so on in Plato's dialogue with Protarchus in *Philebus,* he nevertheless censures humor on the ground that there is no such category as "innocent" laughter. Plato defines the category of the "ridiculous," the traditionally designated object of humor as a perception that produces a mixture of pain and pleasure in the eyes of the beholder, regardless of the object's relation to the beholder. Plato admits that "laughter is pleasant, and on these occasions we both feel malice and laugh."[16]

That laughter is partly painful because of its connection to the human soul via malice is an idea that we find surfacing in the works of other theoreticians of humor such as Søren Kierkegaard, George Santayana, and Sigmund Freud. The Danish philosopher Kierkegaard portrayed incongruity as the necessary foundation upon which life is sustained; to him, this definition of incongruity stems from his preoccupation with the religious individual (the only category of human beings that interests him) who cannot be known for what he is by anyone else. This gap or contradiction is comical since it conceals rather than reveals, or reveals only obliquely: "The comical is present in every stage of life (only the relative positions are different), for wherever there is life, there is contradiction, and wherever there is contradiction, the comical is present . . . and wherever one is justified in ignoring the pain, because it is non-essential."[17] Kierkegaard postulates that the comical is always a relation, not merely the perception of the ridiculous in something or someone, but the perception of a contradiction, which involves the acknowledgment of a relation between the subject and the object, and that as a relation it adheres closely to ethical expectations as in any other form of human interaction. Kierkegaard used the comical as a spiritual device to express his hidden relation to God (he called humor his "incognito"), but he demonstrates how humor might be used as a strategy to preserve and exalt one's sense of self, instead of allowing external authority to destroy it.

Likewise, George Santayana unequivocally revives the paradoxical relationship between pain and laughter first noted by Plato, as noted above. For Santayana, it is not possible to ignore pain in any context of laughter. Indeed, pain is essential to it. Comic laughter for Santayana is the least aware since "the incongruity and degradation" that it engenders, "as such, always remain unpleasant."[18] Wit, likewise, for Santayana, "belittles one thing and dignifies another; and its comparisons are often as flattering as ironical."[19] However, Santayana regarded the malicious or destructive character of intelligence as not intrinsic since "all that can be changed by the exercise of intelligence is our sense of the unity and homogeneity of the world."[20] When intelligence and reason are mixed with generous emotion, even that of sentiment, Santayana argues that wit leaves the dry bed of repartees and satire: "The mood is transmuted; the mind takes an upward flight, with a sense of liberation from the convention it dissolves, and of freer motion in the vagueness beyond. The disintegration of our ideal here leads to mysticism, and because of this effort towards transcendence, the brilliancy becomes sublime."[21]

The Greek rhetorician Longinus connected the rhetorical devices of comedy with the effects of the sublime in his essay *On the Sublime*, where he observed "actions and feelings which come close to sweeping us off our feet serve as an excuse and a lenitive for any kind of daring phraseology."[22] As an example, Longinus picks a couplet with a comic comparison: "The field he had was smaller than a letter," thereby proving that "even when they reach the point of being actually incredible, the shafts of comedy also seem plausible from their very laughability."[23]

In the eighteenth century, Immanuel Kant made two separate but related observations, one about humor and the other about the sublime, both of which remain pertinent to an aesthetic approach to film genres to this day. Kant's theory of humor broadly belongs to the "incongruity" school of humor theories. Laughter is a sudden transformation of a strained expectation into nothing, Kant said in his *Third Critique*. To illustrate his point, Kant tells the following joke of an Indian at the table of an Englishman in Surat who, when he saw a bottle of ale opened and all the beer turned into froth and overflowing, testified to his great astonishment with many exclamations. When the Englishman asked him, "What is there in this to astonish you so much?" he answered, "I am not at all astonished that it should flow out; but I do wonder how you ever got it in."[24] We might be able to read aggression into this joke, but the joke is much more than mere aggression. There is a free play of thought here that fascinates and eventually overwhelms us with our inability to reason it out. Humorous disposition, Kant writes, is "the talent of being able voluntarily to put oneself into a certain mental disposition, in which everything is judged quite differently from the ordinary method (reversed, in fact), and yet, in accordance with certain rational principles in such a frame of mind."[25] Kant's theory of the sublime, likewise, revisits the triumph of the rational and moral principles when confronted by the formless and the mighty; both the sublime and humor share the indestructible adaptations of the human mind.

Freud, in his *Jokes and Their Relation to the Unconscious* (1905), analyzed and contrasted all manifestations of the mental state of amusement occasioned by humor—jokes, wit, the comic, smut, and so on. Freud, like Santayana, distinguished between jokes and wit, comic and humor, and in each case he identified a different deployment of our psychic energy. He argued that we summon psychic energy for a specific task, which is then discovered not to be needed; and thus it is "saved" or "economized" and "released" in the form of muscular movement known as laughter. The comic saves us energy of thought; jokes and wit conserve the energy used to repress hostile, sexual, aggressive feelings; and humor preserves the energy of wasting any negative emotions like fear and pity. In a later essay titled *Humor* (1928), Freud revised some of his earlier findings about humor, not in a theoretical leap, but in an expansion of the central idea. The relation produced by "tendentious" laughter, Freud argued, is essentially aggressive and leads to neuroses and repression and eventual destruction of the ego. The German adjective "tendenzios," from the German substantive "tendenz," has become the naturalized English word "tendentious," which Freud uses to refer to jokes with a purpose and that are likely to provoke or elicit conflict. Humor, on the other hand, Freud observes, is tendentious laughter that does not leave the ground of mental sanity and that counters aggression without destruction of the ego of the subject. Not everyone possesses the humorous point of view, Freud notes; it is the triumph of the pleasure principle, "the ego's victorious assertion of its own invulnerability. It refuses to be hurt by the arrows of reality or to be compelled to suffer."[26] "By its repudiation of the possibility of suffering," Freud notes, humor "takes its place in the great series of methods devised by the mind of man for evading the compulsion to suffer."[27] Humor is rebellious and is the loftiest of mind's defensive devices, according to Freud. The humorous point of view, in his terminology, incorporates a strong super-ego pacifying the ego intimidated by conflict. The humorous point of view requires the creation of a benign authority within ourselves that protects or vaccinates us against destructive authority from the outside.

When we move from philosophical, aesthetic, and psychological theories of humor to an exploration of its mimetic aspects, one of the most useful definitions of comedy for our purposes in the cinematic arts comes from the literary critic Northrop Frye. At least since the theater of Aristophanes, laughter has touched on politics, art, and society. Since then, too, comedy has been inextricably connected to the human condition, to life, to death. In his influential study of modes and genres, *Anatomy of Criticism* (1957), Frye points out that the fundamental structural requirement of a comedy includes a young man who desires a young woman who is thwarted in this desire by some opposition, usually a paternal figure, and that near the end of the play some twist in the plot enables the hero to have his will.[28] In such a plot twist, Frye points out that the movement of comedy is from one kind of society to another.[29] At the beginning of the play the obstructing characters are in charge of the play's society, and the audience recognizes that they are usurpers.[30] At the end of the play the device in the plot that brings hero and heroine together causes a new society to crystallize around the hero, and the moment when this crystallization occurs is the point of the resolution in the action, the comic discovery, *anagnorisis* or *cognition*.[31] In the cinematic arts as well, this structure of a comedy remains more or less the same, with the crucial genre difference between the tragic and the comic contained in the emphasis on "character" in tragedy and on "society" in comedy. Frye, moreover, directs our attention to that fact that when comedy moves toward a "happy ending," it sounds like a moral judgment, but that this judgment is a social one.[32]

Frye points out that the moral judgment in a comedy is always against the absurd, and not the wickedly villainous.[33] The oppositional or blocking characters in a comedy are absurd; the ethos of conflict in a comedy is serious enmity, but not hatred.[34] Humor is thus instrumental in creating the ethos of a comedy in presenting the villains or the blocking characters as bound in "ritual bondage,"[35] or a certain mechanical inflexibility of spirit, a lack of imagination, that renders them slaves to an obsessive habit, belief, or other social structures.

Humor becomes the aesthetic diagnosis of such deadening conditions of ritual bondage.

The impure content of comedy, the humorous aesthetic, might be read as a powerful and tendentious corrective not only to socially condemned vices, as in the case of the targets of conventional satirical realism, but also to affectations of authenticity, purity, proportionality, symmetry, and other extreme and essentialist positions that are perceived to be "good," "moral," "desirable" and so on; but they may equally be seen as mere ritualistic bondage lacking imagination, through the aperture of humor. Thus humor, paradoxically enough, depending on the social network within which it operates, may be seen to be fundamentally at odds with even desirable states in life, if rigidity is involved. Thus laughter and humor have a moral and ethical dimension to them, not only in giving us permission to laugh at what is socially perceived to be "immoral," but also by endorsing our inclination to laugh at what sometimes societies consider moral and good, driven as it is by an exigency that is always inclusive, aesthetic, and ethical. The films we discuss in this volume all concern themselves with inequalities, incongruities, disproportions, and asymmetries. We explore the limits of the humorous perspective as an ethical alternative to deal with the imperfections of life.

But all of the above is the minority report on humor, which, by and large, wears either the Aristotelian mask of "painless ridicule" or sides with aggressive social laughter in the service of social conformity. Plato's student, Aristotle, initiated a school of thought regarding humor, which confidently asserted that humor is a "painless mask," or *gelos*. Aristotle's critique of comedy addresses the ostensible lack of a moral dimension in comic texts. In his extant definition of comedy (Umberto Eco based *The Name of the Rose* on the missing original fragment), Aristotle argued that "comedy, as we have said, is an imitation of people who are worse than average. Their badness, however, is not of every kind. The ridiculous, rather, is a species of the ugly; it may be defined as a mistake or unseemliness that is not painful or destructive."[36] This Aristotelian adage has become the accepted wisdom regarding the psychosocial mechanism of humor in many circles. For instance, the rhetorician Cicero and the philosophers Hobbes and Descartes have all turned to this "superiority" the-

INTRODUCTION

ory of humor, where someone's misfortune, or even disaster, brings on unapologetic laughter with no subjective identification with the object of laughter. In other words, the Aristotelian school of humor theorists does not see either a moral provision afforded to the comic, nor an ethical exigency animating its execution of humor. Retrospectively, we might call such callous characters the objects of satire in the higher comedies.

Thus comedy as a genre, and humor as a mode to perceive conflict in the Aristotelian sense, may be equated with the master-slave dialectic in their lack of ability to instantiate any substantial social change or movement, or to render visible the workings of the effect of the conflict on the psyches of those subjected to it. Here, the relation between the one who laughs and the one being laughed at, in other words, the deployment of the concept of the "ridiculous," may be likened to the social relation between the one who commands and the one who obeys—the master and the slave. The ridiculous as a laughable category is dependent on the masters suppressing the subjectivity of the slaves, which is the only way in which such laughter can possess an appeal. The lowest kind of laughter is one where the discourse context completely obliterates the subjectivity and self-consciousness of the slaves; they offer no resistance to being laughed at, and no attempt is made from their side to transform their relation to their oppressors. For this transformation to take place, acknowledging the ground of pain in laughter is essential, which Plato recognized and Aristotle dismissed. Hegel in the *Phenomenology of the Spirit* explained the role and responsibility of the slave to change the social conditions of his existence:

> Generally speaking, it is the Slave, and only he, who can realize a progress, who can go beyond the given and—in particular—the given that he himself is. On the one hand, as I just said, possessing the idea of Freedom and not being free, he is led to transform the given (social) conditions of his existence—that is—to realize a historical progress. Furthermore—and this is the important point—this progress has a meaning for him which it does not and cannot have for the Master.[37]

What Bakhtin identified as the great "centrifugal"[38] power of language may be applied to comedy and humor as well, in its anarchic potential to propel outward, to disrupt inside-out the Aristotelian social order organized from top-down. The disruption made through laughter in such contexts echoes the Hegelian uprising of the slave against the master. The films discussed in this edition all examine the various ways in which the humorous aesthetic triumphs over the rigid bondage of overbearing social roles, norms, and structures.

Plato's awareness of pain intermingled with pleasure and Aristotle's dismissal of a moral consciousness to laughter are both relevant to Henri Bergson, whose theory of humor outlines a form of pessimism and which can nevertheless be transformed into a source of authentic acts of freedom. Bergson's *Laughter: An Essay on the Meaning of the Comic* is pertinent to examining a body of cinematic art that could be considered an art of experience as well as of expression, for Bergson proposes that the comic has to also be considered within "the nature of art" and its relation to life, including to politics. According to Bergson, the comic cannot be entirely situated in either the realm of art or of life. Akin to artifice, it is this fluctuating space between art and life, a space of "in-between."[39] It is utilitarian insofar as it aims for improvement, and it is aesthetic insofar as the comical emerges from a certain freedom, "when the society and the individual freed from the worry of self-preservation, begin to regard themselves as works of art."[40] And yet, what happens when there is no such fundamental social or political freedom? Seriousness may signal the burden of choice, the weight of what is most profound in life. Seriousness for him is an indication of freedom.[41] In *A Theory of Parody: The Teachings of Twentieth-Century Art Forms,* Linda Hutcheon presents the example of parody, with its ironic distance and inversion, as a conduit for freedom: "The ironic distance afforded by parody has made imitation a means of freedom."[42] And yet the source of parody may well be anchored in loss: "Parody . . . is one of the ways in which modern artists have managed to come to terms with the weight of the past."[43]

While laughter signals "a slight revolt on the surface of social life," it nonetheless focuses our attention on mechanical gestures rather than on intentional acts, on missed freedoms.[44] It is precisely the "breakdown" of these gestures into free acts that the films under discussion open up and that we consider in this volume.

Laughter, which is not necessarily subject to will, and which is fundamentally *human,* as Bergson has noted,[45] is more significantly a response to a certain mechanism that we witness or that we elicit. The comical is characterized first and foremost by "*mechanical inelasticity,*" whether "introduced into nature" or into "regulation of society."[46] He writes: "A really living life should never repeat itself.... This deflection of life towards the mechanical is here the real cause of laughter."[47] So we laugh when someone living resembles something mechanical or when something mechanical is at the heart of someone living. Ultimately, all humans are prone to rigid habits that turn them against themselves and others.[48]

Laughter, then, which can signal a certain aesthetic, in sharing with it the principles of equality, expressiveness, distance, and *indifference,* also signals a certain *anesthetic* in that it appeals to intelligence, not to emotion. Bergson speaks of an "*absence of feeling* which usually accompanies laughter," a laughter that "demands something like a momentary anesthesia of the heart."[49] Indifference and a social environment are prerequisites for it, even when this social complicity is imaginary: "Our laughter is always the laughter of the group," for laughter also constitutes a form of social interaction.[50]

If humor's aesthetic qualities open it to the political, in the sense of disrupting manufactured consensus, its social dimension seems to do so as well: "Laughter must answer to certain requirements of life in common. It must have a *social* signification."[51] Humor, however, proves aporetic to Bergson. This same social aspect seems to also close it from emancipatory possibilities, however, in its conformity.[52] For while a social environment inevitably creates difference, this difference is corrected by laughter in a society that insists on conformity. Social maladaptation and "*a growing callousness to social life*" are sources for laughter.[53] And yet, not all laughter against the socially maladapted needs to be accompanied by an absence of feeling, nor does it necessarily foreclose the emancipatory possibilities by adhering to the logic of aggression and transgression. Just as important as the satirical, intimidating or humiliating laughter that interested Bergson is the laughter that accompanies the sublime dismantling of rigid and logocentric rational thought that we find in abundance in

Middle Eastern aesthetics and philosophy. Mysticism is but one of the most celebrated of these counter-perspectives to comprehend and represent the world. We might assert that the dominant challenge offered to rational thought in the Middle Eastern context is essentially an aesthetic one, a humorous one. One need only to recall the winding roads in the Iranian director Abbas Kiarostami's diegetic universe, and the search for a single tree on mountainsides dotted with many such trees, to comprehend the implicit uselessness of mapmaking, a most rational undertaking, when confronted by the demands of a perspective that insists on singularity. Metaphors might help us more than maps. Focusing on the aesthetic effects of humor in such a context, for instance, forces us to explore laughter's relation to the sublime. It also forces us to ask: Is there a difference between loud laughter and quiet laughter? Is there humor without laughter at all? Does what we find funny say anything about who we are?

And yet the conventional modalities of humor, like irony or parody or satire, are fundamentally divided; their "ambivalence stems from the dual drives of conservative and revolutionary forces that are inherent in its nature as authorized transgression."[54] Hutcheon indicates that irony is both playful and "belittling," "critically constructive as well as destructive."[55] Parody, for instance, can be an "important ideological positioning," but it is "ideologically suspect," "because parody always implicitly reinforces even as it ironically debunks." Parody is an art that engages history for Hutcheon, which gives it tremendous power, and we see artists who intervene in the present Middle Eastern context employing it to reflect on issues of freedom, identity, and difference.[56]

In fact, parody is put to effective use in one of the earliest humor texts from the Middle East, the *Kitab al-Bukhala* by al-Jahiz, and the manner in which al-Jahiz uses parody of form to satirize a group attests to the possibility of an emancipatory function for such texts. At least since the ninth century AD, satire has been a flourishing art form in Arabic literature, and comedy has enjoyed a healthy niche in the Arab world since the twelfth century, *One Thousand and One Nights* being one of its more celebrated examples. Humor, often of the satirical kind with its corrective intent, or scatological and sexually obscene humor, has also been a mainstay of *adab* literature and culture as evidenced in the popular and humorous didactic texts of al-Jahiz and that of his successor al-Khatib in the eleventh century. Dealing primarily with avarice, or *bukhl,* both al-Jahiz's *Kitab al-Bukhala* and his intellectual successor al-Khatib al-Baghdadi's eleventh-century retreatment of the same subject under the same title provide us with graphic, sometimes excoriatingly funny portrayals of certain individuals, groups, beliefs, and practices in medieval Islamic society.[57] A quick example from al-Jahiz will suffice to show that satirical humor in the *adab* literature already possessed an anarchic and tendentious streak to it in parodying taboo texts and making fun of what, in general, would be considered desirable character traits. In al-Jahiz's satirical text, a desirable character trait (being economical with money) turns into stinginess (*bukhl*) and eventually into greed, which is a vice at the other end of the moral spectrum. Al-Jahiz's satire is, moreover, subversive, as he parodies the *Hadith* itself in order to satirize this perverse transformation,[58] no small achievement, as Bakhtin has indicated the significance of parody as a possible intermediate step to the development of fiction.[59] Al-Jahiz's satire does not get banned because of its ostensible parodic structure, in its reliance on certain scriptural hypotexts, which rescues it from charges of fictitious concoctions; instead, it allows the satire to exist in the realm of the real, the comical, the playful, and the probable, without outright violence done to the original hypotexts and their contexts.[60] In the "Madhhab of Thrift," al-Jahiz recounts the stories of five sheikhs who meet regularly in a mosque in Basra to share with each other new ways of saving money.[61] These are terrific stories, with each sheikh trying to raise the ante on thriftiness with more and more fantastic and absurd postulations. This is also a *Madhhab,* a school of sorts, with a pedagogic context to its discourse. One sheikh saved money by diverting water from the ablutions fountain at the mosque to his house by digging a ditch, instead of digging a new well. Nothing in the *sunna* prohibits this, he tells his friends. Another sheikh's wife saved a ball of dough every day since the birth of their daughter and made her an elaborate bridal trousseau of gold, silver, silk, and dyes by selling cakes made from the dough saved over the years. In order not to be outdone, another sheikh tells the story of a man who proved the truth of the axiom "The beginning of everything is small!" by saving each day some chickpeas and sesame seeds and eventually saving enough to buy a big country estate. These stories, however, pale in comparison to the one told by the sheikh who contracted a terrible cough but didn't want to spend too much money on the cure. The sheikh buys some cheap dates and makes a broth to drink out of them, which instantly cures his cough but also miraculously suppresses his appetite. The sheikh then calls his wife and tells her to make some of the same date broth for everyone in the family. Everyone's appetite is suppressed. In this way, he saves money that would have been spent on food for the family. They later dry the dates and resell them back to the seller for the same price. Breaking even has never sounded so good, according to this anecdote.[62]

This particular humorous technique is a marvelous example of not merely a structural reversal and eventual dissolution of the binaries of good-bad, moral-immoral, and so on, but it is also an aesthetic subversion that is at once based on prior texts (parody) and on a group of people (satire). The comical effect is created by the gradual rise in the volume of the absurdities we encounter, as well as its humorous premise that these are all good and workable instructions to save money, lessons taught in the manner of the scriptures. Humor suffuses both the form and the content of this absurd comic text, the absurdity being the result of a comic human manipulation. We find a brilliant application of this particular type of aesthetic and ethical subversion that is at once both parody and satire in Elia Suleiman's *Divine Intervention,* in the metamorphoses of the billboard and target-practice ninja into a real Palestinian ninja who bravely collects all the bullets fired at her and returns them to the Israeli soldiers who fired them.

Laughter, thus, inevitably implies a relation to power: "Laughter cannot be absolutely just. . . . Nor kind-hearted either. Its function is to intimidate by humiliating."[63] Interestingly, Bergson seems to suggest that laughter has healing power: if it causes pain to those targeted by laughter, "society takes its revenge on those freedoms which are accompanied by laughter."[64] Bergson seems to place society on the side of life, of what is fluid, changing; for society requires attentiveness to others, to the outside, and it requires adaptability and a capacity to change. Any distraction may be a symptom of eccentricity and of rigidity, whether of the mind or of the body, which then society attempts to correct in a gesture of laughter. It is precisely the resemblance to "thingness" to a "foreign body," to a certain "absent-mindedness on the part of life," that elicits laughter.[65] As Bergson reminds us, it is the social rather than the immoral that elicits laughter, and the lack of sociability and sensibility that are the two fundamental conditions for the comical.[66] While laughter has always touched on politics and society, it has also been connected to the aesthetic and to fantasy, which can be considered a "non-comic dimension" of the comic.[67]

The pleasure of laughter is never pure, Bergson argues, in keeping with the Platonic tenor, for it does not simply constitute a disinterested aesthetic pleasure. Rather, he ends his work by suggesting that the gaiety of laughter is always tainted with certain bitterness. According to Andrew Horton, less attention was paid to comedy because it is "enjoyable" and brings "pleasure." Viewed as an "inferior genre" ever since Aristotle designated it as "'an artistic imitation of men of an inferior moral bent,' it has escaped the close schematization that the epic and tragedy have undergone in Western literary theory."[68] Horton suggests that the playful and creative aspects of humor imply "a combination of control and freedom, an awareness of stated or implied rules/codes, and the imagination/fantasy to manipulate them. They also point to *pleasure*."[69] The grounding of this pleasure is precisely in suspending the rules of society as in times of carnival.[70] The carnivalesque laughter has a political dimension for its "liberating effects" on the people: "How 'universal, democratic, and free' such carnivalesque laughter was for 'the people.'"[71]

The general depreciation of the comic has been noted by other scholars as "not particularly significant to our daily lives or to the path of the development of history."[72] In addition to establishing an illusory sense of superiority over others, it has also been a political concern since Plato, because in his view it could "affect the status of the republic,"[73] whereas Aristotle saw its benefits in small measures, being more interested in its mimetic properties, which for him did not involve any relation to the social or the political. Like Plato, Thomas Hobbes recognized its political implications and wrote that laughter was specifically a power struggle manifested significantly in class differences. In *Leviathan,* Hobbes envisions humanity in a constant power struggle, where "victory goes to the one who laughs."[74] Humor is essentially democratic, since it is accessible to all in society; but according to Igor Krichtafovitch, it tends to proliferate in the lower classes.[75]

While humor can be harmless escapism, a way of conquering fear, a means of self-assertion, it can be irrational and a "destructive weapon" but also transformative, since it is intimately linked to power.[76] Ultimately, it may or may not be bound by truth, while negotiating a complex and ultimately triumphant relationship with the real and the rational.[77] Hence its force and its limitations, as the following contributions reveal.

We begin the discussion with an article that explores cinema's aesthetic power to represent the violence dealt by history. Najat Rahman's "Humor, Loss, and the Possibility for Politics in Recent Palestinian Cinema" studies the modalities of humor and the effects of representation on the possibilities for politics in three Palestinian films produced under Israeli occupation: *Laila's Birthday* (Rashid Mashrawi, 2008), *Divine Intervention* (Elia Suleiman, 2002), and *Paradise Now* (Hany Abu-Assad, 2005). While she notes that these films often and strikingly employ humor in its various forms (parody, irony, the absurd, dark humor), she argues that they do so specifically through "radical contingency." The possibility of contingency in the films becomes the source of humor and its unraveling. This contingency also leads to the breakdown of representation and allows for an innovative aesthetic as well as for politics; for politics, as Rancière has suggested, is predicated on a "radical contingency." In consciously reflecting on the act of representation, on its aesthetic and political dimensions, the films represent what seems to defy representation where humor plays a key role, pointing the way to the possibilities and limits of cinematic representation in overcoming "deadening political realities" and in offering an "emancipatory aesthetic." Humor, which emanates precisely from a certain death that historical violence delivers and the deadening daily routines that ensue from it, from the deadening mechanism that generates it and from its breakdown, evokes nonetheless a promise of a new communal life, even as it signals limited freedom.

INTRODUCTION

We continue the exploration of the explicit link between cinema and history with Robert Lang's "Strategies of Subversion in Ben Ali's Tunisia: Allegory and Satire in Moncef Dhouib's *The TV Is Coming.*" Lang explores how Tunisia is confronting certain political, economic, and cultural challenges in the global era, as reflected in the entertaining events that unravel the municipal cultural committee of El Malga in southern Tunisia when it hears that a German television company is planning to make a documentary film in their village. In order to impress their European visitors, and, as one of the characters says, to give them "an idea of what we have accomplished in the very short time since Independence," they busy themselves with the preparation of an itinerary of events, including a pageant representing 3,000 years of Tunisian history, and a short film of their own. In its guise as a satirical comedy, *The TV Is Coming* offers an allegory of resistance to President Ben Ali's authoritarian regime and functions as a work of meta-historiography, a movie about how national-cultural history is written.

Cinema's alleged ties with allegorizing the national space to render both hegemonic and alternate visions of contested histories, as well as the reciprocal relationship between the nation and the diaspora, are explored in Cyrus Ali Zargar's "Satiric Traversals in the Comedy of Mehrān Modiri: Space, Irony, and National Allegory on Iranian Television." Zargar discusses the controversial and immensely popular television serials by the director and actor Mehrān Modiri, whose comedic television productions enjoy widespread popularity in Iran, as well as in the international expatriate Iranian community. Using Michel Foucault's notion of heterotopias and Fredric Jameson's discussion of national allegory, Zargar investigates ways in which Modiri's sitcoms use contrasting spaces to shine a satirical light on matters of national identity. Thus, a leading male character, whether a fool or an intellectual, will usually find himself forced into a setting that highlights his displacement. To that effect, seven of the eight serials Modiri has directed since 2002 involve places that are somehow non-urban, non-central, or, more specifically, non-Tehran, places that serve as foils to Modiri's most prominent theme: Tehran as a consciously modernizing city. In a series of productions, Tehran becomes a space representing the entirety of Iranian mores, troubles, accomplishments, and aspirations.

In "Ethnic Humor, Stereotypes, and Cultural Power in Israeli Cinema," Elise Burton examines modalities of humor in critiques of social and cultural discrimination in Israeli films, where humor emanates from a multicultural society and from the perspective of the marginalized. Burton argues that ethnic humor, which figures prominently in Israeli cinema, performs cinematic functions as well as reflects the dynamics of Israeli cultural politics. Analyzing segments and scenes from different Israeli films from 1976 to 2007, she considers film as a mechanism for social critique of cultural discrimination. In her view, ethnic humor is indicative of the persistence of social and political divisions among Israeli Jews and between Jews and non-Jews. Such humor, she argues, "troubles the very meaning of ethnicity within Israeli Jewish society" and calls into question such hierarchical divisions within society that are based on its hegemonic political power. While this cinematic humor reflects sociopolitical reality and hierarchical divisions, it also constructs them. Burton charts the historical shifts from bourekas and "neo-bourekas" genres to "post-Zionist cinema." She sees resistance by Mizrahis to an Ashkenazi cultural power that forms the norms and values of Israeli society. A critique of Israeli racism and xenophobia can also be detected. She further notes a new cinematic development in ethnic humor that is more direct and "confrontational in its open mockery"; however, she sees in this nonetheless "a desire to cope with the paradoxes of Israeli cultural inequality through laughter as opposed to outright hostility or violence."

We continue exploring the humor modality's ability to parse historical and social inequalities with Najat Rahman's study of three comedy films by the Egyptian auteur Youssef Chahine, whose films explore the gamut of film humor from musical comedies to the melancholic humor of his later films. In "The Laughter of Youssef Chahine," Rahman examines three films of the late and iconic Egyptian filmmaker: *Alexandria, Why?* (*Iskindiria... Leh?*, 1978); *Cairo Station* (*Bab al Hadid*, 1958); and *Cairo as Told by Chahine* (*Al Qahira Minawara bi Ahlaha*, 1991). Rahman argues that in his films a light humor meets a solemn history. His films, with autobiographical inspirations and interrogations, contend with history in a most intimate way. The coming of age of the filmmaker is a coming of age of Egyptian cinema and of

INTRODUCTION

Egypt itself as a nation. The address in *Alexandra, Why?*, for instance, is inextricable from the question of cinema's relation to place and to history, where exuberant laughter of daily living must face the farce of history. The movement of laughter in his film noir *Cairo Station*, from sorrow to pleasure, from hilarity to the horrific, is so subtle as to be barely distinguishable. Humor serves as social critique, so that it fluctuates in its mode and function from aggressive humor at fundamentalists and the exploitative classes, while it is empathetic with the socially marginalized. In *Cairo as Told by Chahine*, humor is a quality he attributes to the people of Cairo. In this tribute to their vitality, endurance, inventiveness, and resourcefulness, humor is a way of wrestling dignity in the face of deprivations, difficulties, and denials, even as we witness the monstrosities of urban developments in the city.

Comedy offers the potential for a more inclusive social setting. It is with this in mind that Somy Kim, in "Comedic Mediations: War and Genre in *Ekrājihā*," explores the allegorized national story of Iran as told through narratives of the Iran-Iraq War. The essay investigates the popularity of *Ekrājihā*, which remains Iran's highest grossing film to date and a successful representative of the "film farsi" genre, so well received that it led to a pair of sequels. Directed by Masud Dehnamaki, who is virtually unknown to the international community, the film is a story of drug addicts and social misfits who attempt to fight at the front during the Iran-Iraq War. Kim critiques the ability of genre comedies to engage with established norms, with particular reference to the first *Ekrājihā*'s attempt to valorize martyrdom and piety in postwar Iran. The essay further examines how departures from these norms in *Ekhrājihā 2* and *3* highlight the potential for sociopolitical critique in these wildly popular films.

Perhaps there is no greater challenge to cinema's complex relationship to representation than the call to represent diegetic death, which constitutes the most complete absence from a historical-materialist, representational perspective. Gayatri Devi explores the liberatory and emancipatory aesthetic of death and humor in her essay "Humor and the Cinematic Sublime in Kiarostami's *The Wind Will Carry Us*." Devi offers a reading of Kiarostami's films as positioned somewhere on the edge of our ideas about "reality" itself, what is knowable, and thus imitable, and what is not. While alert viewers and critics have variously commented on aspects of Kiarostami's films that seem deliberately to test our notions of translating "reality" on screen, such as his fascination with repetition itself as a trope in almost all his films, mainstream critical writing on the filmmaker tends to read and contextualize these films as commentaries on modernity and its structural binaries: rural/urban, dispossessed/affluent, gender/class, center/periphery, and so on. Basing her reading of Kiarostami's films on the aesthetic theory of the sublime defined by its first theorist Longinus as an elevated aesthetic category, Devi argues for a similar non-tendentious and non-aggressive emancipatory ethos to Kiarostami's films, which may all be read on some counts as partaking in this quality of sublime humor. Devi's analysis focuses on how Kiarostami's films partake of the mode of humor and comedy to explore and reveal spiritual dimensions considered to be outmoded and a regressive direction for cinema itself. The author argues that Kiarostami's films present a new way to politicize cinema's subject through the use of humor. Focusing primarily on *The Wind Will Carry Us*, the essay examines how Kiarostami stages the experience of the figure of the sublime simultaneously as a sensory disruption and as a rational reconfiguration that looks toward an exaltation of our perception of the infinite, the unknowable, and the limitless, and in the process invests the characters with a new awareness of themselves as social and political beings. The bringing forth of the new being is a quietly humorous project.

Transnational discourses on Middle Eastern matters, particularly the Hollywood locus of "global" cinema, is discussed in Perin Gurel's essay, "America the Oppressively Funny: Humor and Anti-Americanisms in Modern Turkish Cinema," which traces the development of "America" and "the American" as comic tropes in Turkish films from the Cold War to the present. The chapter presents a preliminary critical trajectory that includes the left-wing dark comedy films of the 1970s, the apolitical neoliberal parodies of the 1990s, and the complex cinemascapes of the early twenty-first century, exemplified by three top-grossing comedies featuring each era's most famous comedian: *Köşeyi Dönen Adam* (The Man Who Turned the Corner, 1978), *Amerikali* (The American, 1993), and *Yahşi Bati* (*The Mild West*, 2010), featuring Kemal Sunal, Şener Şen, and Cem Yılmaz, respectively. Adapting a critical transnationalism, the essay pays attention to local agency and transculturation as well as structural inequality, such as the near domination of Turkish film distribution networks by U.S.-led multinationals following the post-1980s privatization of Turkish economy. U.S.-based signs, symbols, and tropes reach Turkey and are then reassembled to meet Turkish needs in an imperfect and uneven reversal of "cultural imperialism." Comedy films about America and Americans seem aware of the power of the cinematic image, often self-consciously utilizing TV clips, film sets, costumes, and parodic references to Hollywood. As these popular movies show, however, the wish to "laugh back" at U.S. hegemony remains imbued with anxieties about media, while Turkish language and culture remain the provincial that is set against Hollywood's "global vernacular."

Our final essay reverts back to the fundamental question of the ever-changing and blurred boundaries of the "Middle East" in our contemporary world. Is the Middle East a geopolitical region with member nations? Is the Middle East a point of confluence of historical, political, and cultural forces tightly and rigidly strung across time and space? Does the Middle East have a center? Or is it to be known by its margins? The symbolic and unbounded discursive space opened up by the term "the Middle East" is nowhere more evident than in the discussion of an Indian film set in Pakistan that critiques the post–September 11 American "war on terror." Mara Matta's essay, "Laughter across Borders: The Case of the Bollywood Film *Tere Bin Laden*," examines a Bollywood film released in 2010 and written and directed by the Indian filmmaker Abhishek Sharma. Where does "South Asia" end and the "Middle East" begin? The film partakes in three distinct controversial discourses: the location and role of the nations of the Indian subcontinent in the American "war on terror," the historical and contemporary hostile relationship between India and Pakistan, and the triangulated network of loyalty and hostility that binds India, Pakistan, and the United States in the "war on terror." Matta argues that the carnivalesque humor that characterizes the film shows how rigid politics fails to see the benefit of humor and does not employ it yet is threatened by it. The controversial film *Tere Bin Laden,* which violates social and political boundaries in satirizing "the paranoia unleashed by the war on terror," was officially censored in Pakistan, a U.S. ally on the "war on terror." Matta argues that comical or satirical representations of serious reality may be "more challenging than a dramatic narration of facts." Through the liberating power of laughter, the film opens up a possibility for expressing dissent, "for ventilating their disappointment at being forced to live in fear of those same people who should guarantee them protection and security." Interestingly, the film, Matta notes, lacks a clear separation between those who are doing the laughing and those who are its targets. While debunking the opposition between Americans who laugh at Pakistanis and vice versa, the film also sets up an opposition between the powerful state and its powerless citizens who live in a perpetual state of crisis. The government's refusal to allow this laughter is indicative of the power of such laughter.

NOTES

1. Lina Khatib, *Filming the Modern Middle East: Politics in the Cinemas of Hollywood and the Arab World* (London: I. B. Tauris, 2009), 19.
2. For a full discussion of the repeated Hollywood tropes for the Middle East, see ibid., 15–61.
3. Aparna Pande, *Is Pakistan Part of South Asia? Yes!,* www.huffingtonpost.com/aparna-pande/is-pakistan-part-of-south_b_803654.html, accessed November 27, 2013.
4. Viola Shafik, *Arab Cinema: History and Cultural Identity* (Cairo: American University in Cairo Press, 2007), 5.
5. Ibid.
6. See Fredric Jameson, *The Political Unconscious: Narrative as a Socially Symbolic Act* (Ithaca, N.Y.: Cornell University Press, 1982).
7. Henri Bergson, *Laughter: An Essay on the Meaning of the Comic,* trans. Clousdesley Brereton and Fred Rotwell (New York: Macmillan Press, 1912). According to Igor Krichtafovitch, the "laughter of the mind" has to do with a joining of reflection and emotion and is to be distinguished from the "laughter of the body," that of "happiness, bodily joy, 'physical' or 'vital' enthusiasm." See Igor Krichtafovitch, *Humor Theory: Formula of Laughter* (Denver: Outskirts Press, 2006), 12.
8. Bergson, *Laughter,* 85.
9. Andrew Horton, *Comedy/Cinema/Theory* (Berkeley: University of California Press, 1991), 4.

INTRODUCTION

10. Andrew Horton and Joanna E. Rapf, *A Companion to Film Comedy* (Malden, Mass.: Wiley-Blackwell, 2012). Also in Horton, *Comedy/Cinema/Theory*, 3.
11. See, for instance, Krichtafovitch, *Humor Theory*.
12. This includes works such as Jean-Jacques Schmidt's *Le livre de l'humour arabe* (Arles: Actes Sud, 2005).
13. One notes specifically a proliferation of dissertations in English that have begun to construct a field around humor in relation to world literature, such as that of Rania Chelala, "Border Crossing Laughter: Humor in the Short Fiction of Mark Twain, Mikhail Naimy, Edgar Allan Poe, and Emile Habiby" (Ph.D. diss., University of North Carolina, Chapel Hill, 2010), and Mona Fayad, "The Impact of the Absurd on Modern Arabic Literature: A Study of the Influence of Camus, Ionesco and Beckett" (Ph.D. diss., University of Illinois, Urbana-Champaign, 1986).
14. Other theoretical texts of interest include Peter Berger, *Redeeming Laughter: The Comic Dimension of Human Experience* (New York: Walter de Gruyter, 1997); Simon Critchley, *On Humour* (London: Routledge, 2002); Reinhold Grimm and Jost Hermand, eds., *Laughter Unlimited: Essays on Humor, Satire, and the Comic* (Madison: University of Wisconsin Press, 1991); John Marmysz, *Laughing at Nothing: Humor as a Response to Nihilism* (Albany: State University of New York Press, 2003); and Jerry Palmer, *Taking Humour Seriously* (New York: Routledge, 1993).
15. Mikhail Bakhtin, *Rabelais and His World*, trans. Helene Iswolsky (Bloomington: Indiana University Press, 1984), 66.
16. John Morreal, ed., *The Philosophy of Laughter and Humor* (Albany: State University of New York Press, 1986), 2.
17. Søren Kierkegaard, *Concluding Unscientific Postscript* (Princeton, N.J.: Princeton University Press, 1941), 459.
18. George Santayana, *The Sense of Beauty: Being the Outlines of Aesthetic Theory* (New York: Scribner's, 1902), 249.
19. Ibid., 251.
20. Ibid.
21. Ibid., 253.
22. T. S. Dorch, ed., *Classical Literary Criticism* (Harmondsworth: Penguin, 1965), 149–50.
23. Ibid.
24. Immanuel Kant, *Critique of Judgment*, trans. J. H. Bernard (New York: Hafner Press; London: Collier Macmillan, 1951), 178.
25. Ibid., 181.
26. Sigmund Freud, *Collected Papers of Sigmund Freud*, vol. 5, ed. James Strachey (New York: Basic Books, 1959), 217.
27. Ibid.

28. Northrop Frye, *Anatomy of Criticism* (Princeton, N.J.: Princeton University Press, 1957), 163.
29. Ibid.
30. Ibid.
31. Ibid.
32. Ibid., 167.
33. Ibid., 166.
34. Ibid., 168.
35. Ibid.
36. Morreal, *The Philosophy of Laughter and Humor*, 14.
37. Alexandre Kojeve, *Introduction to the Reading of Hegel: Lectures on the Phenomenology of the Spirit*, trans. James J. Nichols Jr. (Ithaca, N.Y.: Cornell University Press, 1969), 50.
38. Mikhail Bakhtin, *The Dialogic Imagination: Four Essays*, trans. Caryl Emerson and Michael Holquist (Austin: University of Texas Press, 1981), 272–73.
39. Bergson, *Laughter*, 135.
40. Bergson, like many other critics, has argued that freedom is essential for the comic; ibid., 20. Charles Gruner points out that everything can be the "subject of humor": death, destruction, disaster. Often such humor is constituted as "sick." See Charles R. Gruner, *The Game of Humor: A Comprehensive Theory of Why We Laugh* (New Brunswick, N.J.: Transaction Publishers, 2011), 44–45. In this case, humor deemed offensive or obscene is usually censored. Gruner, *The Game of Humor*, 47. Gruner further argues (69): "Self-censoring and fear of reprisal from all directions keeps newspapers and electronic media, especially, from repeating much of this. . . . 'Sick jokes offend in two respects: their targets [butts] are aspects of the culture usually considered immune from joking, and the jokes are often disgusting (gross) and/or violent.'" Jokes about "ethnic and racial" groups, Gruner indicates, can be dangerous: "While the 'stereotype' of an ethnic group can be more a 'comic script' and not actually believed by those enjoying jokes about the group's script, with race the stereotype may be much more strongly believed and acted upon in more deliberate, non-joke ways" (84).
41. Bergson, *Laughter*, 79.
42. Linda Hutcheon, *A Theory of Parody: The Teachings of Twentieth-Century Art Forms* (Urbana: University of Illinois Press, 2000), 35.
43. Ibid., 29.
44. Bergson, *Laughter*, 200. Bergson (143) defines gestures as "the attitudes, the movements and even the language by which a mental state expresses itself outwardly without any aim or profit, from no other cause than a kind of inner itching."

INTRODUCTION

45. For Bergson the comic is *human,* both in the sense of not being shared by other species and as a mark of our humanity and its limits. Ibid., 3.
46. Ibid., 10 and 47, emphasis in the original.
47. Ibid., 34.
48. Ibid., 130.
49. Ibid., 4, 5, emphasis in the original.
50. Ibid., 6; Krichtafovitch, *Humor Theory,* 42. Freud has also noted that a social community is constituted around a joke: the teller, the target, and the audience.
51. Bergson, *Laughter,* 8. Others have since addressed humor in different ways. Krichtafovitch, for instance, divides humor theories into three groups: "incongruity theories," where humor emanates from a discrepancy between "the expected, and the achieved result"; "hostility theories," where humor functions to assert superiority or as aggression; and "liberation theories," where humor serves as a release from a real or imagined constraint. Krichtafovitch, *Humor Theory,* 15–16.
52. Bergson, *Laughter,* 198.
53. Ibid., 133–34, emphasis in the original.
54. Hutcheon, *A Theory of Parody,* 26.
55. Ibid., 32.
56. Ibid., xii.
57. H. T. Norris, review of Fedwa Malti Douglas's *Structures of Avarice: The Bukhala in Medieval Arabic Literature, Bulletin of the School of Oriental and African Studies* 51, no. 1 (2006): 131–32.
58. Daniel Beaumont, "Parody and Lying in al-Bukhala," *Studia Islamica* 74 (1994): 28.
59. Bakhtin, cited in ibid., 28.
60. Ibid., 29.
61. Ibid., 30.
62. Ibid., 31.
63. Bergson, *Laughter,* 198. Humor is an efficient expression of aggression. Mark Twain has stated: "The human race has one really effective weapon, and that is laughter." Cited in Krichtafovitch, *Humor Theory,* 79. In *The Game of Humor* (11), Gruner argues, following Freud (1905), that humor as wit can be divided into two categories: "tendency wit and harmless wit." "'Tendency wit' is the common humor directed at a butt, making fun of someone or some institution. 'Harmless wit' was described as humor directed at no one or thing, but which merely relies for its laughter-evoking on its verbal form. The important point here is that Freud was unable to provide a single example of 'harmless wit.'" Essentially to "laugh is to feel superior" (13, 41): this sense of superiority can extend momentarily

to our own past selves or to laughing about death.
64. Cited in Krichtafovitch, *Humor Theory*, 39–40.
65. Bergson, *Laughter*, 87.
66. Ibid., 137 and 141.
67. Horton, *Comedy/Cinema/Theory*, 7.
68. Ibid., 12, 2.
69. Ibid., 224.
70. Ibid., 5.
71. Bakhtin, cited in Horton, ibid., 12–13.
72. Krichtafovitch, *Humor Theory*, 2.
73. Ibid.
74. Ibid., 3.
75. Ibid., 48.
76. Ibid., 2.
77. Krichtafovitch points out how the joker, for instance, is not held accountable for a rational or truthful statement: "The power of the joke is that it does not necessarily have to be well-argued. Its purpose is to psychologically elevate the joker over his rival, and to place the latter in a foolish position." Ibid., 29.

1

HUMOR, LOSS, AND THE POSSIBILITY FOR POLITICS IN RECENT PALESTINIAN CINEMA

NAJAT RAHMAN

In the second scene of Hany Abu-Assad's *Al Janna al 'an* (released in English as *Paradise Now*, 2005), we see Said, one of the two main characters, in a photo shop in Nablus. It is a framing that anticipates and calls attention to the framing of the film and that of Palestinians. Said appears in a close-up profile against a synthetic, kitschy background image of what looks like a New England town with a tree in the blooming colors of autumn surrounding his profile. Said's face looks serious, in contrast to that of the zealous photographer who insists that Said smile for the photo as he adjusts his subject's position against this imposed background. The stubbornness of both Said who refuses to smile and the photographer who otherwise refuses to take the photo elicits a comic tension. A matter-of-fact conversation follows about picking up the photo, a photo that will later serve to identify him after his suicide mission, we later find out. Somehow all is arranged. The photo and the film come to life in a space of dissension.

While recent films directed by Palestinians have often addressed subjects centered on loss, violence, and death, they have often strikingly employed humor in its various forms (parody, irony, the absurd, dark humor) to complicate and lend nuance to their representation, as if to portray first and foremost a fundamentally human experience and to reclaim and salvage selves long lost to given representations and tired meanings. They do so also to mark a certain death that inhabits those lives the films depict, both from the violence that delivers it and from the deadening daily routines of oppression. Humor emanates precisely from this death, from the mechanical that generates it; it seems to call for a work of mourning and gestures toward art as a refuge for politics. Analyzing films from the last ten years, I wish to explore the modalities of humor and the effect of representation on the possibilities for politics in recent Palestinian cinema.[1] I focus on three films produced under Israeli occupation: *Laila's Birthday* (*Eid Milad Laila*, 2008), directed by Rashid Mashrawi; *Divine Intervention* (*Yadun Ilahiyya*, 2002), directed by Elia Suleiman; and *Paradise Now* (*Al janna al 'an*, 2005), directed by Hany Abu-Assad.

In *Laila's Birthday*, Abu Laila, a judge turned cab driver, has strict rules for his passengers but faces a typical day of chaos, contradictions, and lawlessness under occupation when he finally breaks down, assumes his judicial role, and passes judgment. In *Divine Intervention*, an image of a Palestinian fighter used as target practice is transformed into a flying female ninja that wages a mythical battle against the Israel Defense Forces, spanning the history of the struggle in a replay reminiscent of video games and popular global films. In *Paradise Now*, two friends are preparing for a suicide mission. The first one to be videotaped in typical fashion with a prepared speech is frustrated when he discovers that the video recorder has broken down and did not record his solemn speech; on the third retry, he interrupts his delivery and advises his mother instead on the best place to buy water filters.

These films consciously reflect on the act of representation, on its aesthetic and political dimensions. In representing what seems to defy representation, humor plays a key role, pointing the way to the possibilities and limits of cinematic representation. Humor resists any foregone conclusion or easy interpretation. It also renders the situation all the more haunting. Humor sometimes reaches an aporetic function, constructing and deconstructing meaning, all the more to bear witness to the grave historical reality. The following questions concern us here: Can humor, and cinematic art, allow for an overcoming of "deadening political realities" and offer an "emancipatory aesthetic"?[2] If, according to Jacques Rancière in *Dissensus*, very little if any politics exist today, is art (and specifically film) the displaced space for it?[3] To what extent does humor and loss, often present in

Palestinian films, open unto politics? Are these filmmakers reconfiguring what is meant by art as (true) politics? How are the senses of the individuals under occupation affected? How do these films signal this? To what extent do they reproduce, counter, or reconfigure this assault on the senses? These questions are not, of course, limited to Palestinian artists per se. Nevertheless, in these films humor evokes a promise of a new communal life, even as it signals limited freedom.

Films have been providing a certain visibility to Palestinians in the face of their historical invisibility as well as the distorted and imposed representations of their identity. In the preface to *Dreams of a Nation*, Edward Said writes: "Palestinian cinema provides . . . a visible incarnation of Palestinian existence in the years since 1948 . . . by trying to articulate a counter narrative and a counter identity. These films represent a collective identity."[4] It is this contested collective identity rather than a lack of film production that has contributed to the invisibility of Palestinian cinema and to "a lack of a comprehensive film history."[5] Felicia Chan indicates that the controversy around the film "dramatises the tensions in operation as a cultural identity seeks a political one."[6] Palestinian identity is in fact also a political one, given the scattering of a nation ensuing from the *nakba* of 1948 and the *naksa* of 1967. Recent Palestinian films have gained international recognition.[7] As co-productions, except for Hany Abu-Assad's *Omar*, a film released in 2014, often financed by Europeans, the films complicate the notion of national cinema and starkly reveal the tensions between national narratives and transnational forces.

Hamid Naficy maintains that Palestinian cinema is "one of the rare cinemas in the world that is structurally exilic, . . . made either in . . . internal exile in an occupied Palestine or under the erasure . . . of displacement and external exile."[8] This heterogeneous corpus nonetheless shares a quest for "nationhood," according to Chan, who seems to echo Said.[9] Hamid Dabashi writes about the statelessness of these Palestinian films, a "geographical absence" that haunts this film history to become "the creative core of Palestinian cinema, what has made it thematically in/coherent and aesthetically im/possible."[10] This diversity is also reflected in form. While I focus on three features, Palestinian cinematic production has ranged from documentaries to experimental films to art video and video installations.[11]

NAJAT RAHMAN
IS FILM A REFUGE FOR POLITICS?

If politics is "a struggle to have *one's voice heard* and *oneself recognized* as a legitimate partner in debate,"[12] and if speech is the ground for all historical instances of politics, can film then become a space for politics in its absence elsewhere? How does humor in film contribute to this? Palestinian films, which present different voices, counter the erasure that has not only been of identity but of the condition of the political that Palestinian filmic art frames. They counter a double erasure: erasure of the political and erasure as history. As Rancière writes, "The shrinking of political space has conferred a substitutive value on artistic practice. . . . Art is starting to appear as a space of refuge for dissensual practice."[13] In a geography that is also shrinking, where increasingly there is no place for the Palestinian, art becomes that place. This essay follows from Rancière's work, which argues that a shift has taken place that has led to a general depoliticization and a change in artistic practice, where politics may increasingly be found in art. As he insists, however, this is not an argument for art as the place for politics.[14]

Politics conceived as *dissensus* produces internal difference in a society through "the intervention in the visible and the sayable."[15] As such, could we not conceive of humor as precisely that which also intervenes in "the visible and the sayable"? Art and politics, as forms of *dissensus*, can possibly "disrupt forms of domination," in "reorienting general perceptual space and disrupting forms of belonging."[16] Marking this shift to the disappearance of politics, and interrogating aesthetic practices in this context, Rancière signals that these forms, which include film and other visual arts, may create new "political subjectivation." They remain fundamentally aesthetic, however, since such creation cannot be simply willed; the aesthetic process may not yield what is intended.[17] Art, therefore, cannot be simply collapsed into politics, nor can it be completely separated from it. Rancière states: "Aesthetic art promises a political accomplishment that it cannot satisfy. . . . Those who want it to fulfill its political promise are condemned to a certain melancholy."[18] And yet, the way he defines politics shows the affinity between art and politics:

What really deserves the name of politics is the cluster of

perceptions and practices that shape this common world. Politics is first of all a way of framing, among sensory data, a specific sphere of experience. It is *a partition of the sensible, of the visible and the sayable,* which allows (or does not allow) some specific data to appear; which allows or does not allow some specific subjects to designate them and speak about them. It is a specific intertwining of ways of being, ways of doing and ways of speaking.[19]

Rancière interrogates the significance of the relation between art and politics. However, with the aesthetic, "this knot between *poiesis* (a way of doing) and *aisthesis* (a horizon of affect) is undone. . . . The loss brings . . . a promise of a new form of individual and community life."[20] This possibility for new communal life is the opening onto politics. Rancière highlights the democratic nature of art that potentially addresses itself to anyone.[21]

These films propose that art is life. More than that, they propose an art of death, since the art itself evokes the death of politics. The art image of Mona Hatoum's "Negotiating Table" is emblematic in this sense. It reveals a dead corpse shrouded and laid upon a wooden table, murdered, possibly tortured, and absent figures on the opposing empty chairs; in the absence of interlocuters, it announces art as preoccupied with death, in its violent, contemporary forms. Humor, as we see in the next section, also emanates from and signals a certain death.

In this context, what if we were to willingly read Hegel's famous proclamation "Art is a thing of the past," not as an eclipsing of art as it has existed in Europe, so that all art is subject to the history and demarcations of Western aesthetics, but rather as art that enacts a tension with the past? What is taking place today in Palestinian art is the reinscription of a historical loss and an art that makes a claim on the present.

HUMOR: A DIVINE INTERVENTION?

According to Henri Bergson in *Laughter: An Essay on the Meaning of the Comic,* the comic also has to be considered within "the nature of art" and its relation to life, including to politics. For Bergson, the comic cannot be entirely situated in either the realm of art or of life.[22] It is utilitarian insofar as it aims for improvement; and it is aesthetic insofar as the comical emerges from a certain freedom, "when the society and the individual freed from the worry of self-preservation, begin to regard themselves as works of art."[23] Others, such as George Meredith and Percy Bysshe Shelley, also argued that freedom was essential for the comic. And yet what happens when there is no such fundamental social or political freedom?

While laughter signals "a slight revolt on the surface of social life," it nonetheless focuses our attention on mechanical gestures rather than on intentional acts, on missed freedoms.[24] It is precisely the breakdown of these gestures into free acts that the films open up and that we consider here.

Laughter, which is not necessarily subject to will and which is fundamentally human, as Bergson has noted,[25] is more significantly a response to a certain mechanism that we witness or that we elicit. The comical is characterized first and foremost by *"mechanical inelasticity,"* whether "introduced into nature" or into "regulation of society."[26] He writes, "A really living life should never repeat itself. . . . This deflection of life towards the mechanical is here the real cause of laughter."[27] So we laugh when someone living resembles something mechanical or when something mechanical is at the heart of someone living. Ultimately, all humans are prone to rigid habits that turn them against themselves and others.[28]

Laughter, then, which can signal a certain aesthetic, in sharing with it the principles of equality, expressiveness, and indifference, also signals a certain anesthetic in that it appeals to intelligence, not to emotion. Bergson speaks of an *"absence of feeling* which usually accompanies laughter," a laughter that "demands something like a momentary anesthesia of the heart."[29] Indifference and a social environment are prerequisites for it, even when this social complicity is imaginary: "Our laughter is always the laughter of the group."[30]

If humor's aesthetic qualities open it to the political, in the sense of disrupting the consensual, its social dimension seems to do so as well: "Laughter must answer to certain requirements of life in common. It must have a *social* signification."[31] Humor, however, proves aporetic. This same social aspect seems to close it off from it the political, however, in demanding conformity and consensus. For while a social environment inevitably creates difference, this difference is corrected by laughter in a society that insists on conformity. Social maladaptation and *"a growing callousness to social life"* are sources for laughter.[32] Laughter inevitably implies a relation to power: "Laughter cannot be absolutely just. . . . Nor kind-hearted either. Its function is to intimidate by humiliating."[33] At least since Aristophanes, then, laughter has touched on politics and society. Since then, too, comedy has also been connected to aesthetic expression and to fantasy.

RASHID MASHRAWI'S *LAILA'S BIRTHDAY* (2008)

Rashid Mashrawi's film is not simply a "social satire" that aims to expose and to correct; it is also "laughter [that] . . . encounters a void."[34] The film was described as "cinema of the absurd and sociological exposé" (Howard Feinstein, *Screen International*), an "exasperated fidelity to a chronically malfunctioning city" (Ella Taylor, *Village Voice*), and a "dark urban comedy" (Stephen Holden, *New York Times*), one that does not "address politics or document holy war" (DVD case).[35] In each of these descriptions, the film is rendered in a depoliticized urban space and its comic aspects are separated from any politics, as if Ramallah simply suffers from municipal mismanagement rather than from occupation and continued dispossession of a nation, as if the film is simply a study of a social group in a random urban setting. In the face of such erasure of the political, it is as if the film itself can be credible and worth watching only if it showed the Palestinians not as occupied people but as ones trying to survive amongst corruption, not attributed to anyone in particular. Such mystification is also evident in the literal translation of the film, in the subtitles, that turns the political prisoner, who appears in different scenes as a protester, witness, and emblem of a larger conscience, into a "convict." It is important to distinguish clearly between the the political and the social, as Rancière does, "between those who are regarded as capable of taking care of common problems and the future, and those who are regarded as being unable to think beyond private and immediate concerns. The whole democratic process is about the displacement of that boundary."³⁶

The film seems to present Abu Laila as a political subject who attends to common problems and what these problems portend for the future, as well as to the more familial daily matters.

Events of the film take place in one day, implicitly representing a typical day. Asked by his wife at the end of the film how his day was, Abu Laila responds, "As usual." And thus his trials signal an extended existence under a singular occupation that neither resembles classical colonialism nor sovereign statehood. Already his name, Abu Laila, signals a comic tension: rather than his given name of "Jalal," which means "reverence," he chooses Abu Laila, a suggestive parody on the patriarchal practice of taking the name of the first-born son. The feminine name of Laila evokes the nocturnal world of fantasy. In the film, Abu Laila awakes before dawn to a shattering noise, an intrusion from the outside into his home, where evidently he cannot find full refuge. He takes stock of his silent surroundings, opens the balcony, surveys the quiet city, anticipates another day, walks to his daughter's bedroom, returns anxious as he looks at the camera; a mirror image of himself appears before the bustling of the new day begins with preparation for work and school in a familial setting, announcing Laila's birthday celebration in the evening where the father is expected to attend and will oblige.

The day begins with the useless ritualistic morning visit to the Ministry of Justice after dropping off the daughter at school. We learn that the entire ministry has recently been replaced, though the concern remains with the decorative aspects of justice, as evidenced by the preoccupation with the replacement of office curtains. As a judge, a "returnee" seeking to help build a nation, Abu Laila is now a taxi driver. The figure of the returnee reminds us of those who have not returned and highlights how the nation is "partially scattered," and, by extension, that "rights and obligations extend beyond boundaries of nation states."³⁷ He establishes strict laws for his taxi that run counter to the lawlessness, injustice, chaos, and uncertainty that reign in Ramallah, where he lives with his family. These laws, constituting the basis for the film's comical situations, include not going to the checkpoint, not allowing smoking or weapons in his taxi, and not letting amorous teenagers loiter in his car for lack of a private space. The absurdities he encounters include being stopped by a policeman simply because the policeman wants to purchase his taxi for extra income. He renders service within a very limited area bound by checkpoints, revealing the constrained life under occupation.

In our consideration of art and politics and how both redistribute the field of the sensible, the film shows how the senses of individuals under occupation are assaulted and saturated, especially by sounds of shelling, helicopters, gunfire, traffic, cell phones, and so on. Laughter is a release that counters this assault. The assault on the senses heightens some senses but not others, signaling a process of dehumanization, an effort at survival and an eclipsing of the political. The film alludes to this in many different episodes. One such scene of disorientation is when the main character watches the TV news in a café with a group of men. All are listening and begin to speculate about the scene of destruction presented to them, about who the soldiers are and where the event is taking place. Is this the work of the Israeli occupation, the American occupation of Iraq? More than a sign of solidarity and a sense that all occupations are alike, this scene seems to point again to the mystification of political oppression through representation, even to those undergoing occupation. Ironically, a scene of mayhem breaks out amidst the viewers when a shelling occurs in the immediate vicinity, coinciding with their speculations. This shelling breaks down the divide between their reality and the representation on TV that distances them from themselves, framing the limits of representation and the errors of misrecognition. Again, even as they take shelter under a table while they hear more shelling, speculation ensues about whether the shelling is from the Israelis or from factional internal fighting, forcing a sordid and violent collapse between the event and its representation. As Judith Butler points out in *Precarious Life*, "For representation to convey the human, then, representation must not only fail, but it must *show* its failure."[38] All this culminates in a central scene of the film, where the regime of representation and of humor breaks down.

In this scene, located at a gas station where the main character stops, Abu Laila emerges from his absurdly decorated taxi for a wedding. The appearance of the cheerful car contrasts with the grim toll on him. Standing in a distracted fashion as the curious worker who fills his car with gasoline watches, Abu Laila becomes increasingly conscious of how his senses are assaulted by the chaos around him, by the previous shelling and the ordeals of a day under occupation. As the noise of traffic, blaring horns, and helicopters become intolerable, he takes a loudspeaker—significantly, from a police car that is also filling up—to speak out and address his fellow compatriots and the occupiers. He loses control as the tragic seems to coalesce with the comic. He tells two men in two cars who are holding up traffic and creating a traffic jam to move along; he tells the pedestrians to move onto the sidewalks; he tells the young men carrying arms that they are neither soldiers nor policemen and that if they want to carry arms, their place is with the resistance and not amongst women and children. He does not forget the Israeli helicopters and bitterly lauds their military might. Like the regime of representation in which he is implicated, he breaks down in protest to deliver a judgment, to breach an opening onto something new.

The breakdown transforms the mundane space of the gas station into a scene of political protest, of dissensual speech, of judgment. The main character finally passes a judgment and assumes his role as judge. His pronouncement brings temporary order. The quest for freedom is articulated: freedom from flying Israeli helicopters, from chaos, from the dysfunctionality of the everyday in a condition of occupation where authority has signaled simply policing the everyday. The scene counters this daily assault on the senses (among other things) with its own assault: first with speaking out and rupturing the normalcy of the abnormal, then with the return to the domestic, harmonious sphere. It sets up a new sense of the aesthetic as political.

On the one hand, the return to the familial sphere becomes an active way to resist the assault on the senses; on the other hand, instead of pursuing the possibilities of this breakdown, the film privatizes it into a family simply coping with the everyday and trying to survive under singular political circumstances, as if the struggle has been reduced to one simple form: to endure each day. Andrew Horton and Joanna Rapf write in *Companion to Film Comedy* that comedy, which reflects complex sociopolitical problems, "celebrates the human capacity to endure rather than to aspire and suffer."[39] Humor in this film is connected to daily endurance. The scene of the breakdown also suggests that humor lends dignity and complexity to those subjected to a condition that robs them of both. In *Divine Intervention*'s regime of the fantastic or in *Paradise Now*'s regime of contingencies, failures are pursued to their logical end. In all three films, however, the insistence on the absurd—as that which is disharmonious and out of joint with what is proper or with reason—approaches humor to Rancière's conception of *dissensus* as the disruption of consensus.

In this geography, the reduction of politics to policing is evident. Palestinians, a plural proliferation, abiding by a principle of unity in political claims and historical grievances that promise to extend into the future, are caught between the policing of the Israelis and that of their leadership. The scene of the breakdown, however, momentarily transforms this space from one of policing to one of politics, albeit a threatening transformation, as evidenced by the reaction from Abu Laila's fellow men. Rancière states: "The police ... [say] there's nothing to see and so nothing to do but move along. ... Politics, by contrast, consists in transforming this space of 'moving along,' of circulation, into a space for the appearance of a subject: the people, the workers, the citizens. It consists in re-figuring space."[40]

Politics in this film emerges as intimately linked with justice, and with a particular speech act performed as a breakdown of all oppression, provisional as this may be, when those excluded or subordinated speak out.[41] This speech act is significantly humorous, a corrective and an index for a life torn apart. Humor insists on common speech. In order to get anyone's attention Abu Laila has to use a loudspeaker, competing with the helicopter noise, the blaring horns, and the numbing indifference, lest his voice be crowded out. Humor here mitigates the pathos that all too often defines that reality and that becomes the all-too-common representation. As Rancière indicates, politics is not simply about governance or the proclamation of the "Rights of Man":

> Politics begins when those who were destined to remain in the domestic and invisible territory of work and reproduction, and prevented from doing "anything else," take the time that they "have not" in order to affirm that they belong

to a common world. It begins when they make the *invisible visible,* and make what was deemed to be the mere noise of suffering bodies heard as a discourse concerning the "common" of the community. Politics creates a new form, as it were, of *dissensual* "commonsense."[42]

Like aesthetics and politics, humor creates new realities, "invents ways of ... seeing, and saying, engenders new subjects, new forms of collective enunciation."[43] However, the danger of retreating into the private realm is to deny Palestinians the status of political beings, to relegate them to a domestic space as a group.

If there is someone you do not wish to recognize as a political being, you begin by ... not understanding what he says, by not hearing what issues from his mouth as discourse. ... Traditionally, in order to deny the political quality of a category—workers, women and so on—all that was required was to assert that they belonged to the "domestic" space that was separate from public life.[44]

Before the scene of the breakdown, Abu Laila takes home from the hospital a woman who has just lost her husband: it is a scene of silent grief juxtaposed with the later scenes of the wedding celebration, the anticipated celebration of Laila's birthday, and with the many comic scenes. Comedy and tragedy intermingle, as they do in life. The comic then is linked to loss and allows for the maintaining of a certain dignity, precisely the first casualty of occupation, rather than falling into senselessness, or being overwhelmed by the injustice. Associations of loss and mourning are reinforced throughout the day: the birthday cake to Laila is originally a gift from the wife to her dead husband whom she thought was simply recovering in the hospital. The structure of substitution and continuation around loss evokes solidarity and community in the face of dispossession. Such a scene of mourning structurally opens onto the possibility of politics in the breakdown. Humor and mourning are henceforth both responses to loss.

Judith Butler, in "Violence, Mourning, Politics," argues that mourning, which necessitates an acceptance of a transformation, may open onto politics: "It is not that mourning is the goal of politics, but . . . without the capacity to mourn, we lose that keener sense of life we need in order to oppose violence."[45] Butler argues that grief is not simply a private state; rather, it provides a sense of community: "If my fate is not originally or finally separable from yours, then the 'we' is traversed by a relationality that we cannot easily argue against."[46] The experience of loss and mourning is one that could inspire solidarity and justice. Addressing those of us "*beside ourselves,* whether in . . . passion, or emotional grief, or political rage," she addresses those undone by loss: what is lost is not simply a place or an other, but something in that place or that other that cannot be altogether known; something of the self is lost as well, for the self is constituted by its attachment and relation to an other.[47] In the experience of dispossession, a certain relation to the self and to place, to things, a certain tie whose nature remains enigmatic, is lost.[48] As Rancière also argues, loss promises a "new form of individual and community life" through an art that could be available to everyone. And the art that engages loss also holds a promise in that it is democratic. The promise of "political accomplishment" can never altogether be fulfilled, however, and aesthetics remains distinct from politics.[49]

Humor also faces loss in these films. It does so to unsettle oppressive realities. Like Mashrawi's film, Suleiman's *Divine Intervention* creates new ways of seeing a colonial structure in its painfully absurd effects. Humor allows for seizing the tangible in the everyday, in its most profound truth. The human struggle to survive is both elevated and held to unforgiving scrutiny. This poignant chronicle of love and pain, as Suleiman subtitled his film, is a testament to the power of the imaginative in the fantastic that elicits the film's most memorable humor, and challenges us to imagine beyond the violence.

AT THE LIMITS OF REPRESENTATION: ELIA SULEIMAN'S *DIVINE INTERVENTION* (2002)

The effect of humor on representation can be seen in depiction of the fantastic in Suleiman's *Divine Intervention*. By its humorous and fantastic imaginings, the film stages and complicates cinematic representation and the national narrative. The introduction of fantastic elements seems to highlight, through dark humor, irony, and parody, a sociopolitical reality marked by the absurd, where the absurd is an index for power and violence, a manifestation of the state of occupation. Suleiman's film starkly reveals the tensions between national affirmations of identity and globalized representations of them. Inspired by global cultural influences—the film is often evoked in relation to the work of Buster Keaton and Jacques Tati in its negotiation of the serious and of humor, in its reflection on humor and its place—the film represents the political in the mundane and insists on transnational cultural connections in the face of internal rifts in the relations between the self and others.

The film asks the following questions: How does one represent differently? "How does the diasporic inform/disrupt ideas of the national?"[50] One also asks, along with the film scholar Gonul Dönmez-Colin, if memory is enough when making a film about "people and places that are disappearing."[51]

Presented as a chronicle, *Divine Intervention* is a mosaic where events seemingly lack coherence and happen without any context, which creates a poignant effect, both comical and alienating, and which the introduction of the fantastic amplifies. The visual narration, the use of a static camera and wide shots, suggests stifling tedium in Palestinian life, creating the effect of the absurd that the film depicts as everyday sociopolitical reality. Everything is in a liminal state, since the present is one of struggle and continual loss. Such a state is ritualized into everyday social interaction, so that all relations between the self and the other are violently constrained within this state's bounds. The narrator, E.S., portrayed as a filmmaker and a silent witness to his own life, has to meet his lover at the Ram checkpoint, since they live on different sides of it. As such, they both witness and therefore endure daily Israeli harassment of Palestinians. The film begins in his birthplace, Nazareth, and ends in Jerusalem, encapsulating his own life and that of Palestinians from the *nakba* of 1948 to the occupied present.

Suleiman's work significantly appeals to fantastic images, eclectically borrowed from video games and films, seemingly escaping the confines of Palestinian national identity only to reaffirm them. Three scenes constitute the intervention of humor through the fantastic.[52] The first shows E.S. driving to see his ailing father. As he finishes off an apricot, he throws the pit out the window, striking and blowing up a military tank with it. The second shows his female friend crossing the Ram checkpoint on foot against the orders of the Israeli soldiers, which causes the guard tower to fall. The scene I wish to discuss at length, however, is the climax of the previous episodes and also of the film itself. It involves a female ninja figure facing Israeli armed men. The image of the Palestinian who serves as target practice is transformed before the eyes of the attackers into a fighting and flying ninja, "essentially casting the Israelis in the role of Goliath."[53]

Significantly, the incorporation of the fantastic is a humorous staging of representation.[54] If the fantastic is what presumably departs from the real and calls it into question, the real itself has become a theater of the fantastic in the film. In this final scene, the fantastic consists of a representation, an image coming to life and becoming a reality. It is this incongruity of a flying ninja in this typical West Bank landscape juxtaposed with the familiar militarized figures that elicits the laughter and is emblematic of the absurd. The frame of the ninja scene, which begins with an image of a female ninja and returns to that same image after the confrontation, presents the conflict and face-off as one of representation, and hence of political existence: who has the power to represent, who creates images of others, who diffuses these images. In a parody of multiple genres, the escalation of the violence spans the history of the conflict. The ninja, head covered in a kuffiyeh and dressed in black, begins in response by throwing stones, then Molotov cocktails, and then an Islamic crescent at her opponents, who are using heavy military weapons. Everything is mediated by the image. The scene stages dominant representations about Palestinians that justifies more violence against them. When the image of that same Palestinian serves as a target of violence and comes to life as a female ninja figure, it shows the effect of representation on reality. At the same time it presents the struggle of Palestinians against overwhelming force in affirming a national identity. At the end of the scene, the Israeli commander stands alone in a desolate landscape, oblivious to the image of the Palestinian as militant that he installed in the ninja. More than simple testimony to what is absent, the image becomes part of a struggle, challenging representations on the ground, as it were, and participating in forging a different space. The ninja scene becomes the focus for the disparate elements of the film, rupturing the representation and its violence that are imposed on Palestinians.[55] The real and the imaginary connect the mundane and the historical, where film offers a memory that begins from a particular Palestinian standpoint, draws on shared myths, and is addressed to a more global community through film.

The fantastic highlights Suleiman's cinematic language, which "juxtaposes two versions of reality—one present and the other absent, each concealing yet exposing the other."[56] The tendencies of the fantastic seem to also be those of dark humor: Probing "disparate concepts without attempting to reconcile them, favoring the fantastic, . . . (revealing) the 'gap' between appearance on the surface and reality underneath."[57] Dark comedy, which characterizes the work of Elia Suleiman, involves using irony "to attack an apparently absurd universe." It employs violent images, where "there is little sense of hope," as we witness in the ending of this scene and the ending of the film.[58] It is through the fantastic that Suleiman achieves a dark humor, allowing him to focus attention on the process and consequences of representation, on how representation serves as an essential component of the political conflict and as a challenge to his cinematic endeavor.

We see this tendency of dark humor in the use of symbols in this scene, such as the map of Palestine, the colors of the flag, the crescent and star, the halo of bullets. Nutith Gertz and George Khleifi argue that Suleiman's use of symbols is double-edged, introducing the historical symbols of the struggle and placing them in a virtual space. While Suleiman "exposes . . . the fictitious status of these symbols through the use of parody, absurdity, and humor, he also searches for the truth behind them and renews their lost significance."[59] Through these symbols, the intervention of the fantastic presents Palestinian struggle and affirms national identity.

In borrowing from biblical myths and visual popular culture, Suleiman articulates an ironic expression of identity that escapes the narrow confines of nationalism but manages a necessary articulation of self in the face of an aggressive negation and appropriation. Besides being the most spectacular and the most sophisticated scene in the film, the ninja scene testifies to violence under occupation, to its forms and its responses.

The fantastic also becomes a way to face the anguish of loss. Sobhi al-Zobaidi argues that "poetic and imaginary means ... provide Palestinians with the virtual worlds they need in order to negotiate their loss and confinement.... [They are] driven toward virtual worlds in search of continuity."[60] It is this unexpected distance from reality, or the collapse of reality into the fantastic—where an apricot pit, for example, is able to blast a military tank, and where the driver continues nonchalantly—that elicits the laughter. The all-too-real violence of everyday military occupation is reworked and transformed through the imaginary into a virtual response that calls it into question and defies it.

The fantastic—and dark humor—attempts to achieve what is impossible in reality, to bring together what has been torn asunder: "to break down the stifling blocked borders ... to reunite the fractured space and to rejoin the divided identity."[61] In response to Gertz and Khleifi, Zobaidi compellingly notes, however, that it is not simply a question of breaking down roadblocks but also of facing the effacement of Palestinians and their claim to the land: "Palestinian cinema ... goes beyond 'roadblock movies' around which identities clash, power is practiced, and struggles take place. ... It is not the roadblock that presents the crisis, but memory itself."[62] Through humor and fantasy, *Divine Intervention,* which ends on a foreboding note that amplifies the seriousness of the Palestinian predicament under occupation, allows for the possibility of overcoming obstacles in creating another space in cinema.

Suleiman enacts a nuanced and compelling cinematic representation by means of the introduction of humor and the fantastic. In going against prevalent narrations of Palestinian identity, the film reveals the real possibility that politics will rupture consensus in the face of the continued fragmentation of geography, people, and memory. In this act of representation that borders on testimony, Naficy writes, "Suleiman ... gives voice to the film—with all the muteness, inarticulateness, and trauma of coming into language that are the hallmarks of his work."[63] It is in this innovative cinematic endeavor that Suleiman offers fantastic humor to present what eludes re/presentation.

NAJAT RAHMAN

HANY ABU-ASSAD'S *PARADISE NOW* (2005)

Paradise Now, which takes place during the second Intifada in Nablus, from 2000 to 2005,[64] tells the story of two friends, Said and Khaled, who have signed up for a suicide mission together. Living under occupation in Nablus, historically a key site of resistance to the Israeli occupation, and working in a garage to support their families, their present is precarious, their future is uncertain, and their past looms large. Said's father was executed, presumably for being a collaborator, when Said was ten; Khaled perceives his father as having capitulated in his struggle against the Israelis in the first Intifada. The two young men undergo a change and come to radically different decisions regarding the suicide mission. Whereas Said was wavering and Khalid convinced, a reversal takes place with the introduction of a contingency. Together the two positions constitute a chiasmus and a political impasse.

The heart of the film is the possibility of contingency, which becomes both the source of humor and its unraveling: something inexplicably goes wrong. The contingent leads to the breakdown of representation and of the operation itself in the scene of the speeches. Yet it also allows for humor and for representation. This contingency offers an innovative aesthetic and politics. Politics, as Rancière has suggested, is predicated on a "radical contingency."[65]

Early in the film, a scene introduces contingency in representation through the malfunctioning of representation, when the video recording fails, leading to other complications. This humorous and sober scene is a deconstruction of a genre of representation around suicide bombing. The scene opens with a photographer facing us, the viewers, as if he is about to take a photo of us. Behind him are a group of men watching, including Said and Jamal, the facilitator of the mission. We are facing the camera opposite Khaled, who is about to give a speech before he carries out his mission. Then the photographer takes a video camera and begins recording. The camera now frames Khaled. There is a gradual close-up of Khaled as Said looks on gravely. Khaled begins his speech solemnly with familiar recitations from the Qur'an; he addresses his father and mother in formal Arabic, which is itself incongruent and deflates the solemnity. When he has finished, he asks, "So how was it?" This naive concern about his performance, given the reality of death that awaits, is both comical and startling. The photographer indicates nonchalantly that the camera did not record anything. Something went wrong. Repetition ensues, this time with an audience eating sandwiches. It is a repetition that deflates blind discourses of heroic action. Once again, we are being photographed and videotaped, and then Khaled's performance comes to a stop as before. The camera is not working again. In the third try, we now see the back of Khaled and the front of the video photographer. We are still in the film, framed on the side of Khaled. Khaled suddenly stops once he launches into his prepared speech and offers his mother some advice about the best place to buy water filters, as mentioned above. It is as if this faltering performance will unhinge many things, among them the resolve of Khaled.

The breakdown of representation is highlighted in the film, indicating representation's power and shortcomings as well as the need for alternative visions. Late in the film, Said tells his story in an effort to convince the organizer to let him carry out his mission. He represents himself against what he perceives and what he proclaims as the occupier occupying all roles, leaving none for the occupied.

Said's recorded performance is much more solemn, as if to signal how humor also risks falling into the senseless, risks robbing the dignity of living beings. Said's words launch the visual preparations of the body with the participation of the sounds of Quranic recitations. The camera moves in a continuous circle, which seems to be in harmony with the space in which Said and Khaled find themselves. As it circles, a shift signals the advancing of the purification ritual to prepare the bodies for burial (usually performed after the bodies are dead). The camera creates a visual rhythm to the sounds of the Quranic recitation that come to a close with an image reminiscent of the Last Supper in Buñuel's *Viridiana*. We see a large wooden table with Said and Khaled at the center and the group of men next to them sitting for lunch. The idea of the martyr (and witness) in this scene transcends their religious identities. The emphasis seems to be on fluid, harmonious, creative art even as the film portrays a scene of preparation for death. The scene is highly aesthetic with its visual tableaux, rhythmic Arabic of the Quran, circular and continuous camera movement, juxtaposition of Said's solemn words, and images of the purification rites for the dead. The film inscribes the violence but looks toward an elsewhere. A recurrent motif in the film is that "life is death under occupation": "Under occupation we are already dead"; "In this life, we are dead anyway," reiterate Said and Khaled.

Said describes occupation as "life imprisonment." Among its crimes, he states, is that "it breaks any resistance, it ruins families, it destroys morals and people." It is in this sense that collaboration is the principal drama in the family life of Said and the others. The popular consumption of videos showing the executions of collaborators, as we see in one scene, is indicative of this. In addition to showing the abject violence of occupation, and of some of the responses to it, this representation shows how the struggle is political first and foremost. No one can maintain a neutral position, not even the viewer who is framed at several instances within the bounds of the film and who is confronted by the gazes of the characters in the last scene. The viewer is not allowed the luxury of the aesthetic distance. In emphasizing the ravages on the family, the film differs from the resilient vision in *Laila's Birthday*, where the family is the bedrock that allows the individual to endure.

What is striking about a film dealing with such a thorny political issue is its subtle aesthetic, especially its visual elements. One can see this in the way it portrays two different worlds: the old city of Nablus, with its Ottoman stone houses and vestiges ravaged from the violence of occupation, juxtaposed with images of modern and prosperous Tel Aviv, less than an hour away, depicting a semblance of normal life. This separation of political narrative and aesthetic is deceptive. A complex relation exists between them, as evident in many scenes.

In an early scene in a film that is not only a buddy story but has elements of a romantic comedy, *Paradise Now* presents what seems like a sardonic reflection on cinema and the Palestinians. While Suha asks Said about his hobbies one night at her house, she wonders if he likes to go to the cinema. Said explains that there is no cinema in Nablus, that they burned down Cinema Rivoli ten years ago in protest against Israel not allowing Palestinian workers into Israel. Suha asks: "Why cinema?" Said responds: "Why us?"—a question that has plagued Palestinians politically but has not found a hearing.

As she continues her questions about his preferences in cinema, she asks, "What genre?" He responds, "The kind that frustrates." She: "Like what?" He: "Like life." While art always takes on a life of its own, not being solely bound to external constraints, excising life from Palestinian art is not innocent. A discussion follows around struggle and the many ways of resistance. For Suha resistance should always be "non-violent"; for Said, the forms of violence that are imposed determine the nature of the struggle. There are different positions in the film regarding how to struggle. Khaled tells Suha that she is changing a political struggle into an ethical one: "You want to change the struggle into morals; Israel doesn't have morals." He seems to concede her point of view later in the film when he becomes skeptical about the suicide mission. A distinction between the political and the ethical, however, need not lead to a political struggle that negates ethics.

Austere in its aesthetic, with elegant shots, the film produces an effect that is nonetheless of a political nature rather than simply of the beautiful, the technically innovative or the pleasurable. It is an art of experience as well as an art of expression. Like the other films I have discussed, it sets up a new sense of the aesthetic beyond pleasure and beauty: a scene of politics, reframing the aesthetic as political. In fact, the film announces this: Said worries that the effect of his story may be "entertaining people whose lives are a little better"; indeed, he muses, "The world watches indifferently."

In the final scene, each principal character looks at the camera, at us, before we see a close-up of Said's eyes looking at us. Then white. It is a scene that captures dissension, an aesthetic that breaks the regime of representation and reconfigures the field of the sensible: it looks back, implicates us, and refuses to entertain or to continue the violence.

The three films, similar to other recent films not discussed in this essay, use humor as a critical lens through which to assess daily life under occupation and as an index for a political impasse. More than that, humor, in its ability to "partition the sensible . . . the visible and the sayable," in the words of Rancière, can be aligned not only with aesthetics, as Bergson has argued, but with politics, as Rancière demonstrates.

Such humor proliferates and has received a warm welcome from its audiences, following the literary tradition of Palestinian authors such as Emile Habiby. There is no indication that such filmic engagement with humor is fading out, given the recent short films of Abu-Assad and Suleiman's latest work, *Al Zaman al-Baqi* (The Time That Remains, 2009). One notes a proliferation of programs on Palestinian television incorporating humor as well.

While Palestinian film may not be the most viable arena for politics, it has significantly allowed for politics in its absence elsewhere. Film has emerged as a space of dissent, one with multiple voices and visions. Through the filmmakers' innovative (if provisional) dismantling of a familiar regime of representation, the films discussed in this essay push through humor and beyond humor to reconfigure the assault on senses and lives delivered by occupation and by discourses that maintain it, to an aesthetic that neither harmonizes the violence into a simple effect of the beautiful nor falters on its innovative possibilities. Humor opens into a space of critique and of affirmation of the self's aspirations for freedom. The films provide an uncompromising terrain for politics.

NOTES

1. This essay originally appeared in Andrew Horton and Joanna Rapf, eds., *A Companion to Film Comedy* (New York: Wiley, 2012), and is reproduced with permission of John Wiley and Sons. I wish to thank Andrew Horton for his thoughtful comments and for his inspiration which led me to work on humor in Middle Eastern cultural production. I also would like to thank Livia Monnet for the engaging and insightful discussions around issues of aesthetics and politics.
2. Hamid Dabashi, ed., *Dreams of a Nation* (New York: Verso, 2006), 144.
3. I follow Hamid Dabashi and others in considering Palestinian cinema to be one made by Palestinian filmmakers. Ibid., 144. Jacques Rancière, *Dissensus: On Politics and Aesthetics,* ed. and trans. Steven Corcoran (London: Continuum, 2010). Ranicère conceives of politics as *dissensus,* or the manifestation of "two worlds in one" (37), for we are in the order of consensus, according to him, which establishes hierarchies and separation between the social and the political, art and culture, and proper and improper activity or speech.
4. Edward Said, "Preface," in Dabashi, *Dreams of a Nation,* 3.
5. Félicia Chan, "What Dreams May Come: (Palestinian) Cinema/Nation/

History," *Variant* 30 (2007): 8–9.
6. Ibid., 9.
7. This recognition is most notable in the Cannes Jury Prize for *Divine Intervention* in 2002 and in the Golden Globe Award for Best Foreign Language Film and an Oscar nomination for *Paradise Now* in 2005.
8. Hamid Naficy, "Palestinian Exilic Cinema and Film Letters," in Dabashi, *Dreams of a Nation,* 91. See also Hamid Naficy, *An Accented Cinema: Exilic and Diasporic Filmmaking* (Princeton, N.J.: Princeton University Press, 2001), and *Home, Exile, Homeland: Film, Media and the Politics of Place* (New York: Routledge, 1998).
9. Chan, "What Dreams May Come: (Palestinian) Cinema/Nation/History," 9.
10. Dabashi, *Dreams of a Nation,* 10.
11. Naficy, "Palestinian Exilic Cinema and Film Letters," 91.
12. Steven Corcoran, "Editor's Introduction," in Rancière, *Dissensus,* 9, emphasis added.
13. Rancière, *Dissensus,* 145.
14. Corcoran, "Editor's Introduction," 20.
15. Rancière, *Dissensus,* 37.
16. Corcoran, "Editor's Introduction," 15, 2.
17. Rancière, *Dissensus,* 151.
18. Ibid., 133.
19. Ibid., 152, emphasis added.
20. Corcoran, "Editor's Introduction," 16.
21. Ibid., 16.
22. Henri Bergson, *Laughter: An Essay on the Meaning of the Comic,* trans. Clousdesley Brereton and Fred Rotwell (New York: Macmillan, 1912), 135.
23. Ibid., 20.
24. Ibid., 200. Bergson defines gestures as "the attitudes, the movements and even the language by which a mental state expresses itself outwardly without any aim or profit, from no other cause than a kind of inner itching." Ibid., 143.
25. For Bergson the comic is *human,* both in the sense of not being shared by other species and as a mark of our humanity and its limits. Ibid., 3.
26. Ibid., 10 and 47, emphasis in the original.
27. Ibid., 34.
28. Ibid., 130.
29. Ibid., 4, 5, emphasis in the original.
30. Ibid., 6.
31. Ibid., 8, emphasis added.
32. Ibid., 133–34, emphasis in the original.

33. Ibid., 198.
34. Ibid., 85.
35. See Howard Feinstein, "Laila's Birthday," *Screen International*, September 7, 2008; Ella Taylor, "Laila's Birthday Is Mashrawi's Day in the Life of Ramallah," *Village Voice*, May 27, 2009; Stephen Holden, "Navigating Ramallah, an Eye Out for the Absurd," *New York Times*, May 27, 2009.
36. Rancière, *Dissensus*, 58.
37. Judith Butler, "What Shall We Do without Exile," 6th Annual Edward Said Memorial Lecture, American University in Cairo, 2010, www.youtube.com/watch?v=MLgIXtaF6OA, accessed November 30, 2010.
38. Ibid., emphasis added.
39. Horton and Rapf, *A Companion to Film Comedy*, 10.
40. Rancière, *Dissensus*, 37.
41. Corcoran, "Editor's Introduction," 6.
42. Rancière, *Dissensus*, 139, emphasis added.
43. Corcoran, "Editor's Introduction," 7.
44. Rancière, *Dissensus*, 38.
45. Judith Butler, *Precarious Life: The Powers of Mourning and Violence* (New York: Verso, 2006), 21, xviii.
46. Ibid., 22–23.
47. Ibid., 24, emphasis in the original.
48. Ibid., 22.
49. Rancière, *Dissensus*, 133.
50. Butler, "What Shall We Do without Exile."
51. Gönül Dönmez-Colin, *The Cinema of North Africa and the Middle East* (London: Wallflower Press, 2007), 177.
52. On Suleiman's use of fantasy, see Lina Khatib, *Filming the Modern Middle East: Politics in the Cinemas of Hollywood and the Arab World* (London, I. B. Tauris, 2006), 128. Khatib compellingly argues (28) that humor becomes a method of resistance in Suleiman's films.
53. Richard Porton, "Notes from the Palestinian Diaspora: An Interview with Elia Suleiman," *Cineaste* 28, no. 3 (2003): 124–27.
54. Various reviewers of the film saw the incorporation of the fantastic as one of wish fulfillment, not for change but for vengeance. One critic asks if this is "acquiescence or violent desire for revenge": "Is Suleiman sidestepping serious questions about the tactics of the Palestinian intifada . . . by portraying anti-Israeli violence as harmless fantasy?" See Elbert Ventura, "Ghost World," *Pop Matters*, February 20, 2003, popmatters.com/film/reviews/d/divine-intervention.shtml, accessed February 1, 2008.
55. The question of representation has preoccupied the work of Suleiman from the beginning.

56. Nurith Gertz and George Khleifi, *Palestinian Cinema: Landscape, Trauma, and Memory* (Bloomington: Indiana University Press, 2008), 181.
57. Horton and Rapf, *A Companion to Film Comedy*, 10.
58. Ibid., 10.
59. Gertz and Khleifi, *Palestinian Cinema*, 180–81.
60. Sobhi Zobaidi, "Tora Bora Cinema," *Jump Cut: A Review of Contemporary Media* 50, www.ejumpcut.org/archive/jc50.2008/PalestineFilm/index.html, accessed May 15, 2008.
61. Gertz and Khleifi, *Palestinian Cinema*, 178.
62. Zobaidi, "Tora Bora cinema."
63. Naficy, *An Accented Cinema*, 18.
64. Like the other two films, and many other Palestinian films, this is a co-production (Palestine/France/Germany/the Netherlands/Israel). Conditions around filming were difficult and included the kidnapping of a crew member by a Palestinian faction, shelling by Israelis near the filming location, and German members of the crew who left. The location of filming was eventually moved from Nablus to Nazareth.
65. Corcoran, "Editor's Introduction," 21.

2

STRATEGIES OF SUBVERSION IN BEN ALI'S TUNISIA

Allegory and Satire in Moncef Dhouib's *The TV Is Coming*

ROBERT LANG

The premise of Moncef Dhouib's film *The TV Is Coming* is self-reflexive, much like that of a Hollywood backstage musical. When the municipal cultural committee of El Malga in southern Tunisia hears that a German television company is planning to make a documentary film in their dusty, rural village, they busy themselves with the preparation of an itinerary of events, including a pageant representing three thousand years of Tunisian history.[1] They also make a short film of their own to impress their European visitors and, as one of the characters says, to give them "an idea of what we have accomplished in the very short time since independence."[2] In its guise as a satirical comedy—one of the very few in the New Tunisian Cinema[3]—*The TV Is Coming* offers an allegory of resistance to President Zine El Abidine Ben Ali's authoritarian regime, and functions as a work of meta-historiography, a movie about how national-cultural history is written, and about how Tunisia is confronting certain political, economic, and cultural challenges in the global era.

The film functions quite explicitly as an allegory—the village of El Malga, for example, is fictitious (the real El Malga is a tourist theme park in Djerba)—permitting an examination of certain features of Tunisian society not normally acknowledged in public discourse, such as the problem of the extreme authoritarianism of Ben Ali's regime, and the complete absence in Tunisia of freedom of political expression. The allegorical form, which plays here in registers of ambiguity, ambivalence, and contradiction, allows *The TV Is Coming* both to uphold the myth of Tunisia as a historically progressive state and to undercut this narrative at the same time.

In an article titled "Images of Openness, Spaces of Control," Waleed Hazbun describes state-managed forms of cultural production similar to El Malga (the tourist theme park in Djerba) as representing "a dovetailing of tourism development and image making with national identity formation and myth making."[4] The El Malga of the film, not unlike its namesake in Djerba ("a space exposed to the gaze of international tourists and sustained by the flows of hard currency they bring" [28]), offers a performance of (itself as) an authentic Tunisian village, untouched by tourism, with the film satirizing the way in which this space, "like the pseudo-public space of a theme park or shopping mall . . . is a space of control, one that is politically managed rather than defined by the actions and interests of autonomous agents within a system of democratic participation" (28). The film's satire, in part, is directed at the way in which, as Hazbun summarizes it: "Media representations of Tunisia's external openness belie the domestic regime of control" (28). Tourism is used "as a means of promoting global economic integration through the construction of enclaves where state authorities maintain the ability to manage the transnational flows of people, capital, and images" (28). What *The TV Is Coming* suggests, most subversively, is that this effort of comprehensive state control is not confined to theme parks like El Malga on the island of Djerba, but extends to Tunisian society as a whole.

With a "historical" pageant at its core, and the expectation of the residents of El Malga that the German television company will document their efforts at self-representation, *The TV Is Coming* highlights its allegorical intentions; and, like the inventory within the film made by the accountant Lamine (Jamel Sassi) of the props used during the tree-planting ceremony and during the opening of the village's new community center, it offers an inventory of what French historian Pierre Nora describes as *lieux de mémoire*.[5] The filmmaker Dhouib and his characters perform a kind of historiography by attempting to construct a usable past in order to forge for themselves and for the much-anticipated German television company—and of course for us, the viewers of the film—a representation of Tunisia that, to echo Nora, will be suited to the civic as well as intellectual needs of their time. As a satire, *The TV Is Coming* dwells as much on the present as on the past; and as an allegory, speaking frequently to its viewers in code (in order to avoid the heavy hand of government censorship or reprisal), the film functions, of course, as a form of political resistance.

THE COMMUNITY CENTER AND HISTORY'S UNIVERSAL VOCATION

The film begins with a scene in which the six members of El Malga's cultural committee are assembled in their community center. They are seated around a table that has been placed on the stage in a room that serves the village as a theater (the film thereby declaring its allegorical intentions at the outset, and suggesting that democracy in Tunisia, as represented by the committee, is but a charade). They are discussing what should be included in the program of activities to accompany their next planned event, Arbor Day (*La Fête de l'arbre*). While their *chaouch* Ayed (Tawfik El Bahri) incongruously prepares a pot of mint tea over a smoking terracotta brazier on the stage beside the committee, the voice of the chairman can be heard bringing the meeting to order.[6] The camera focused on Ayed pans right and comes to rest on the group.

In keeping with Tunisia's reputation as the country with the most liberated women in the Arab world, Hadhria (Fatma Ben Saïdane), the committee's lone female, is its feistiest and apparently most progressive member. There is Salem (Ali Abdelwahab), the deputy chairman, who will always agree with the chairman. Sghaîer (Chawki Bouglaïa), the youngest member of the committee, representing Tunisia's youth, is allowed to hold the most left-wing views, as long as those views don't actually threaten the status quo. Brahim (Aïssa Harrath), who is blind, represents the voice of Tunisia's moderate and de-politicized Islam. There's Lamine, the treasurer. And most important of all, there is Mr. Fitouri (Ammar Bouthelja), the chairman and local boss, with links to Ben Ali's hegemonic RCD Party in Tunis.[7] Buffoon though Mr. Fitouri may appear to be, he always dominates the proceedings, and, as he is sometimes pleased to remind his fellow members, he is the final authority in all matters even remotely relating to the business of the committee. Mabrouka, the secretary, silently records the minutes of the meeting.

Fitouri's authoritarian impulses represent the bedrock issue to which, in the final analysis, all of the film's satire redounds, just as Tunisia's democracy deficit is the puzzle at the contradictory heart of its bid for recognition as a "modern" society. During the meeting, when Sghaîer stands up and in a state of high excitement, says: "Comrades! I think the right attitude would be to open up to our young talents, in order to put an end to the plot being sown against our Arab and Muslim culture by America and Zionism!" Fitouri becomes comically exasperated. "Shut this disaster up!" he says. "He's talking like the opposition!" Hadhria responds: "Let him talk. So what if he's from the opposition? The opposition is legal now."

"Since when is the opposition legal?" Fitouri sputters. "Why am I the last to know?"

This, in effect, is a satirical reproach by the film to Tunisia's leadership. It is a way of saying to Ben Ali: *Have you not heard? Why are you the last to know? Dictatorships are out of style! For modern, civilized countries, authoritarian governments are a thing of the past!* Every viewer of the film knows that "the opposition" may have been officially "legal" in Ben Ali's Tunisia, but of course such opposition as officially existed was repressed into complete ineffectuality.[8] Salem's response, when he realizes that Sghaîer can be defined as being "from the opposition," is to remind his fellow committee members of their duty as members of the RCD: "If he is [from the opposition], we should denounce him!" But when he is told that "the opposition is legal now," he promptly concludes: "In that case, there's no point in denouncing him." This is both absurd and funny, for it reveals the complete absence, even in a democratic setting, of the right to challenge Tunisia's ruling party, and exposes Ben Ali's multi-party democracy as a sham. (Salem says this without any hint of irony, for his response is the reflex of someone who has lived his entire life without freedom of political expression.)

Later in the film, after they have been (mis)informed that the German TV company will soon arrive to make a film about El Malga, we see Stoufa, a performer in the pageant who has been assigned the role of the Tunisian poet Aboulkacem Chebbi (1909-1934), walking around declaiming Chebbi's poetry. *"Destiny answers the people's call for life, darkness will be dispelled, and chains will break,"* he recites again and again, with as much feeling as he can muster.[9] Hichem (Hichem Rostom), the Egyptian theatrical director whom the El Malgans have taken on to design their pageant, makes his way through the crowd of costumed villagers and confronts the young man:

Hichem: Who are you?

Stoufa: Aboulkacem Chebbi.

Hichem: Who authorized you to speak?

Stoufa: Why? Do I have to pay to speak?

Hichem: It's a silent role, without dialogue.

Stoufa: A poet cannot have a silent role.

Hichem: Keep quiet!

Stoufa: Ah, so, you are telling me to keep quiet? I refuse to keep quiet! Colonization didn't make Aboulkacem Chebbi chicken out, and you are not the one who is going to reduce him to silence! [*He walks off, recommencing his recitation of the same two lines of poetry: "Destiny answers the people's call for life, darkness will be dispelled, and chains will break . . ."*]

In this brief exchange, not only does the film plead for the special role of the artist in the struggle against oppression, it critiques the hypocrisy of the managers of Tunisia's image (the guardians of patriotism—the whole apparatus, both official and unofficial, dedicated to forging a "positive" image of Tunisia, without much concern for historical truth or realities on the ground), and registers the disappointment felt by those who believe the promise of decolonization has been betrayed by Tunisia's post-independence leaders.[10] Stoufa is correct: a poet who has been rendered silent, who is nothing but an image on a postage stamp or a thirty-dinar bill, or a costumed figure in a parade, is no longer a poet, but a commodity, a symbol whose meaning can be hijacked for ideological purposes or used to sanction behavior that contradicts what the poet himself believed in and stood for.[11] In the present context, of course, the poets who refuse to be silenced are the filmmakers themselves—Moncef Dhouib, the actors, everyone involved in the making of *The TV Is Coming*.

"THE MARCH OF PROGRESS"

On the day of the visit of the high functionary who will plant a symbolic tree in El Malga and preside over the opening of their new community center, Fitouri's team arranges a gastronomic pause between the planting of the tree on the one side of the village and the cutting of the ribbon on the other. The visiting official, upon being led to the long table laden with food and drink in the style of a farmer's stand in competition at an agricultural fair, demands of his hosts: "What's this?" to which Fitouri proudly replies: "A pause before the inauguration." The official nods slowly and says, as if explaining government policy: "The March of Progress doesn't like pauses." Fitouri throws his hands up in a gesture of impotence: "But it's the custom!" The official understands that he must nip this obstacle to Progress in the bud: "I know, I know, I'm talking about the future! If you ask me, butter, farm eggs, and all that crap, I don't like it! And I'm not the type who takes bribes."

Getting the message, Fitouri quickly adjusts to this unexpected change in the itinerary—"Ah, yes, of course!"—but the official continues: "I will take this occasion to tell all those who are present that starting today you can consider corruption to be eradicated." Fitouri looks uncertain, as if he has perhaps misheard: "You mean, for now?" The official's reply is unequivocal: "Forever!"

As the band resumes playing, Mr. Ferjani (one of the visiting official's party) staggers and clutches at his breast. Hadhria rushes over to find out what is wrong. And as Mr. Ferjani is led to a stool in the shade, the security officer accompanying him explains: "He has a heart condition, and when that other one announced that there is to be an end to corruption . . ." The camera cuts to the radio journalist, who continues mellifluously into his microphone: "Ladies. Gentlemen. At this moment, cries of joy are reaching me, music from the band, and the sounds of ululation."

The humor of the scene derives primarily from the film's acknowledgment of the brazen hypocrisy of characters like Mr. Ferjani (and his boss, the visiting official), who represent what Béatrice Hibou describes as the "personalized management of power" in Ben Ali's Tunisia. They promote an ideology of national economic progress, but are in government service for personal gain. Those who benefit from the monopolies and exactions that characterize Tunisia's political economy are "close to the President," she writes. "They are private actors and not political pretenders; their only objective is to accumulate wealth."[12]

Fitouri believes that if he does a good job of hosting the German television company, he will receive a promotion. His belief in "progress" is not progressive, but merely instrumental. His idea that El Malga should have a "Cleanliness Week," for example, is not a bad one; but when he comes across Hadhria supervising her drum majorettes picking up the garbage littering the streets, he is incredulous: "You're doing this now, without the television here?" Hadhria explains that cleanliness is a sign of civic spirit, which has to be inculcated in children from a very young age. "Exactly!" he replies. "That's why you have to wait until the television gets here, to be a witness to our civic spirit." When she asks, "OK, so what now?" Fitouri tells her to put all the garbage back where it was, and to wait until the television company arrives!

The theme of education, as a cornerstone of Tunisia's prosperity and as a hallmark of its investment in modernity, is strong in the national imaginary, and, not surprisingly, it occurs throughout *The TV Is Coming*. Unlike Tunisia's first president, who invested almost twenty percent of the national budget in education, Fitouri does not take the long view. He only pretends to grasp the relationship between an investment in education and the hoped-for prosperity that would be its consequence; as an investment in the future, education is too abstract, too amorphous, and too risky. (He would not personally live to see the benefit, which is why he has difficulty imagining it; and it is perhaps relevant in this context that he is not shown in the film to be a father of children, someone with a stake in the long-term future.) In capitalist terms, the investment is too expensive and the return not quick enough. Paradoxically, his attitude recalls Ben Ali's belief that economic prosperity is more important than civil society, democracy, or even human rights (Ben Ali's argument being, in effect, that Tunisia could not yet "afford" democracy). Fitouri is a short-term thinker. No sooner has he announced that El Malga will sponsor a "Cleanliness Week" than he begins to fret that, "with our limited means, [the pageant] will scarcely be able to cover seven hundred years." Hadhria, however, insists: "It's three thousand years, not a day less!" Like a poor businessman who does not know how to borrow against the future, he replies: "Seven hundred years is enough. Give me the money, and I'll do six thousand years with it!"

Progress has its price, which not everyone is willing to pay.

SHOWING "OUR CULTURE, OUR HISTORY, AND OUR VALUES"

When Fitouri receives the phone call informing him of the television company's imminent arrival, he announces to his fellow committee members: "If I'm being telephoned from on high, it's because there's a political message underneath, which only I can decode." His first instinct, we have said, is to seize the opportunity for personal gain. As a politician in a one-party state, Fitouri knows that the promotion of a positive image of the nation is—and must be seen to be—inseparable from an endorsement of the ruling party. As in most societies, patriotism is an effective tool of social control; and whether or not the citizens of El Malga understand that they are being manipulated by their government, we see that they are willing and able to subordinate their differences to the higher, patriotic purpose of burnishing a positive image of their country.

Fitouri decides that El Malga should have a statue in the village square, as they have in Europe. He commissions Brahim's son, Kafza (H'mida Laâbidi), to make the statue. Kafza, who has actually visited Europe and is an artist, understands that a public monument of the kind Fitouri wants should be allegorical. Accordingly, he seeks the input of the cultural committee, whose discussion about what the statue should represent—they want it to represent everything positive the nation stands for (allegorized as "the Tunisian Woman")—itself nearly becomes an allegory of what a majority of Tunisians were convinced would be the result if they had real, multi-party democracy. The popular belief, encouraged by Ben Ali's regime, was that Tunisia would become like its neighbor Algeria, a dysfunctional democracy with crippling parliamentary conflicts and protracted violence among several of the society's constituent groups. Out of fear, most Tunisians supported their "strongman" form of government and rarely complained about the absence of a real opposition party, preferring instead the oxymoronic fiction that their leader was democratically elected—usually winning, according to the published figures, around 99.5 percent of the vote—and that he was maintained in office by the free will of the overwhelming majority of the people.

Without Fitouri's "leadership" guiding them, for better or worse, toward agreement about how they should represent themselves (he is absent during the discussion about the statue), the committee's democratic process of arriving at a decision does not, in fact, fall apart.[13] On the contrary, it proceeds admirably. The outcome, although imperfect, will not resemble the contemporary Algerian body politic. The significant, if ambivalent, point of the scene is that the committee is able to arrive at a decision that is acceptable to the majority. The realized sculpture, of a giant, bare-breasted woman with an amphora under her arm, will resemble the centerpiece of a grand and implausible, eighteenth-century European fountain; but despite everything, the village is ready for the German television company when it arrives—ready even with a stream of water gushing from the plaster maiden's amphora—all of which, if not effectively symbolizing the authenticity and modernity of "the Tunisian Woman," nevertheless stands as proof of a project conceived, developed, and accomplished in a timely manner.

As an example of democratic teamwork, the committee's achievements are impressive. Examples of Fitouri's authoritarianism, however, also abound in the film. The actor Bouthelja's charm and his expert comic timing perhaps allow the viewer to forget sometimes that Fitouri represents the violence of the police state. "Unlike 'police states' in the region," Hazbun notes, "the Tunisian regime continued to articulate a discourse of pluralism, democracy, and openness to buttress its cosmopolitan tourist image throughout its period of political deliberalization" (29). State control over society was expanded under Ben Ali, whom it is said quadrupled the number of police (including secret police) in his first ten years in office. *The TV Is Coming* makes reference to this practice of police states, and to what Hibou describes as the "totalitarian conception of social relations and relations of power" in Tunisia.[14] Throughout the film, we see Fitouri's spy Bahoussi (Abdelkader D'khil) at work. Although not quite the village idiot, Bahoussi is depicted as a childlike fool who takes it upon himself to keep Fitouri informed with gossip and the happenings in the village that he thinks "Uncle" Fitouri will find useful.[15] He also spies on Fitouri himself, which is how he knows that Fitouri will probably be upset to discover that "the Egyptian" (Hichem) has chosen Fitouri's mistress Selma for the role of Zezia in the pageant.

Eventually, after a couple of false alarms and a seemingly endless wait, the now-weary radio reporter, who was earlier present for the tree-planting and ribbon-cutting ceremonies in the village, begins to wonder if the German television company will ever show up. "We are still awaiting the arrival of the TV," he says into his microphone. "And we will continue to wait. But our waiting will not last forever. Because . . . as a matter of fact . . . we don't need to make our image better in the eyes of the West. We have no need to name all our qualities. And we are warning you not to export your so-called democracy to this noble land."[16] It is one of the film's few direct references to "democracy," and it alludes to the perception, described by Hélé Béji in *Nous, décolonisés,* that the West uses the "democracy deficit" in countries like Tunisia as a club with which to beat them: "The Europeans continue to reserve a right to look down on our democratic shortcomings. Democracy serves now as a legitimate means of spreading civilization, and it demands of these very subjects, who yesterday were judged to be unfit for democracy, something that it did not know how to give them."[17] Indeed, the modern conscience measures a society's moral value by the yardstick of democratic virtue, and countries like Tunisia are found wanting. The radio reporter's remarks reveal an awareness (perhaps widespread in third-world societies) that democracy, while no doubt admirable and desirable, is often promoted by Western countries as a way of exercising neocolonial domination.

This same complaint will be articulated by Hadhria, albeit rather differently, toward the end of the film, when the El Malgans discover that the German television company is not in fact there to film them, but to observe a species of deadly scorpion unique to North Africa. Just as Béji remarks that, ever since democracy "became a quasi-*religious* moral charge in the world, we [the decolonized] have felt guilty about not knowing how to exercise it properly [and] we tie ourselves in knots trying at least to give the appearance of knowing how" (45), Hadhria stands before the German television crew and blasts them with a fierce reproach: "Are you entertained? Are you mocking us? For a month we've been preparing! Men and women have rallied to show you our culture, our history, and our values. And you, you just don't give a damn! We look up to you, and you look down on us. We treat you as human beings, and you see us as animals. You are all excited about scorpions and beetles!" The scene is all at once poignant, painful, and funny, for Hadhria then turns to face her fellow El Malgans: "And I say this in front of all of you: there will be no more drum majorettes—they're finished! I'm going to put a match to their uniforms! Yes, a match!"

The era of the colonized subjects' mimicry of their European colonizers—symbolized by the incongruous spectacle of Hadhria's smartly dressed little group of drum majorettes in their European marching-band outfits, complete with tall, white shakos (or of Hadhria struggling in her high-heeled shoes that are better suited to Paris streets than the rocky, desert terrain around El Malga)—is over. The film announces, as Driss Abbassi observes in *Quand la Tunisie s'invente,* that in effect the word "homeland" [*patrie*] has replaced the word "nation" in Tunisia's political vocabulary: "It speaks a new conception of the national space, conceived as an inheritance; which is to say, a patrimony transmitted by ancestors. In this way, national identity is circumscribed by a territory (Tunisia), where the memory of earlier inhabitants is properly honored."[18] Henceforth, in François Hartog's phrase (echoing Pierre Nora): "The homeland is the *alter ego* of memory" ["*le patrimoine est* l'alter ego *de la mémoire*"].[19]

This is exactly what the film does in the pageant organized by the residents of El Malga—it seeks to honor the memory of Tunisia's earlier inhabitants. But the committee members cannot agree on whom or what, or in what degree, to honor.

Sghaîer repeatedly voices his support for the underdog, and despite Fitouri's attempts to shut him up, he reminds his fellow committee members at every opportunity that "Palestine is Arab!" and that they should be vigilant against the predations of "the imperialist plot." He repeats his earlier exhortation to "support our young people," and to mount a cultural project "capable of defeating Zionism and the reactionary forces that plot against Arab and Muslim culture." These forces, he explains, "want Western culture to rule over the entire world."

If Sghaîer's reminder to his fellow committee members that "Palestine is Arab" is a way of reminding them that Tunisia, too, is Arab, then Brahim's role on the committee, as he sees it, is to remind them that they are Muslims. When Fitouri tells them about the German television company, Brahim's reaction is contradictory. "Don't trust them," he warns; "they don't have our best interests at heart." But he also sees the visit of the television company as an opportunity: "We should show them our traditions, our customs, our values, and our beautiful religion. Who knows! They might otherwise leave out [any mention of] the faith." For him, Islam is not a political vehicle, but the repository of Muslim values. He has always disapproved of his son's marriage to Ingrid (Bernadette Machillot), for example, because it was not arranged in the traditional manner by the respective families of the bride and groom. When Ingrid puts her arm around Kafza and explains, simply: "He is my husband, and I love him," Brahim replies: "Listen, Westerner, you may have overtaken us in technology, but we surpass you in morality! Do I go around saying that I love my wife? Or that she loves me? If and when you embrace Islam, *then* you may marry my son!"

Brahim will be unhappy to discover that the symbolic representatives of his religion are going to bring up the rear in the pageant being organized, but his indignation goes unheeded: "Islamic civilization is our pride!" he declares. "It ought to be put up front!" Hichem reminds Brahim that the pageant is meant to be historical. Fitouri, too, has priorities that are ahistorical: he wants to put the Romans before the Phoenicians (because the Romans have the more beautiful costumes), just as Brahim wants to put the Muslim Arabs at the head of the parade (to show the proper "respect" for Islam). Hichem can only repeat: "We must respect the course of history!" Brahim shakes his head ruefully and mutters to himself: "History is being turned upside-down. Instead of putting the Muslims in front . . . Come [*placing his hand on Bahoussi's shoulder*], take me back to the house."

Among the many amusing scenes revealing the characters' conflicting notions of how their pageant should represent the history of the Tunisian people, the exchange between the pageant's accountant and its director stands out. When Lamine arranges for a manufacturer of tomato-based products to sponsor the "Egyptian" section of the pageant, Hichem becomes upset: "He wants to put [placards advertising] the tomatoes with Ramses! It's indecent!" Lamine asks: "And what does your Ramses have to do with anything? Is he in our history?" Hichem replies: "You, in Tunisia, you have three thousand years of history; while we in Egypt have five thousand! Listen, we are Arabs, brothers—same people, same history—we help each other. We need to do this thing together, OK?"

Hadhria's role in the film is central. She represents the advanced status of women in Tunisia, and much that is socially progressive about her society; and she will have plenty to say about the role of women in the three thousand years of Tunisia's history. But she is also an allegorical figure representing the way in which Ben Ali's RCD party, following Bourguiba's Neo-Destour Party, co-opted the UNFT (*L'Union Nationale des Femmes Tunisiennes*). She is properly introduced to the viewer at the beginning of the film when she addresses her fellow committee members in a lively spirit of patriotic complicity: "Listen, my brothers: In the name of the Tunisian woman—take this down, Mabrouka [*she turns to the secretary, who is recording the minutes of the meeting*]—in the name of Tunisian women, and of the women's organization that I represent—you're getting this down?—I propose that we do not miss this opportunity to inform the West about the important achievements of the giant steps made by women on the road toward liberty and emancipation, not counting the gigantic achievements that have accumulated and which redound to the credit of woman. [*She turns to Mabrouka again.*] You got that?"

Her portrait is filmed with affection and with the same pride that Hadhria herself has in "what [Tunisians] have accomplished in the very short time since independence." The film pretends to be ironic about some of its material, such as the radio reporter's announcement on the day of the pageant to his "dear listeners [that] we have been here since early this morning awaiting the arrival of our TV friends, who are going to acquaint themselves with the depth of our civilization, the authenticity of our culture, the rootedness of our traditions." But in fact the film is completely sincere; and Fatma Ben Saïdane's superbly understated, comic performance as Hadhria helps to ground it in this sincerity of purpose, so that when the reporter adds, "As a sign of friendship and fraternity, we are welcoming them today with flowers," his expression of goodwill is nevertheless believable— despite what we have already seen of the recycled bunch of dusty, artificial flowers presented to the government official on Arbor Day (and again, a few minutes later, when he opens the new community center).

In one of the earliest scenes in the film, during the festivities to celebrate the opening of the new cultural center, we see Hadhria in the front row of the audience attending the dancer Hnia's performance. Watching the dancer triggers a desire in Hadhria to dance as well, and she rushes off to one of the deserted rooms in the community center, ties a scarf around her hips, and dances for a few, frenzied minutes, then returns to her seat, smiling to herself. The scene, we could say, is an allegory of the energies of women that have been liberated in Tunisia by the Personal Status Code of 1956. But the scene is satirical, too, for Hadhria herself is not exactly the liberated woman she wishes she were; nor does she fully embody the image of the woman Tunisia extols as one of its most progressive accomplishments in an Arab world more typically marked by female subordination to neopatriarchal rule. State feminism cannot be expected to make true feminists of all Tunisian women; but this is not the real point of Hadhria's character, who, it must be remembered, is an RCD Party member. She is an unwitting stooge for a party that pretends to be progressive but is not. Her character draws attention to the hypocrisy of Ben Ali's regime, which never shied away from taking credit for the advances and accomplishments of women in Tunisia, especially if the occasion could be used to advance the regime's political agenda and reinforce its stranglehold on the Tunisian political system.

Ben Ali's shameless attempts to imply that Tunisian women had the reformist fervor of his regime to thank for their "gains," and that their emancipation only became real in the years after his ouster of Bourguiba in 1987, make the viewer wonder about the value of women's rights in a country where their human rights are dispensed with at the slightest perceived threat to the regime.[20] As the film's chief representative of "Benalism,"[21] Fitouri gives the viewer some idea of what may have lain behind Ben Ali's claim to support what the 2008 United Nations Human Development Report on Tunisia calls "building the capabilities of women." When Fitouri protests to Hichem about his casting of Selma in the role of Zezia, Hichem shrugs: "Propose some women. You talk about women's emancipation. Where are they, these women?" Fitouri replies: "We'll do it without women."

Hadhria's response, predictably, is immediate: "What do you mean, 'without women'? [*She turns to Hichem.*] I'll provide the women. What do you need?" Hichem says: "We need three women—Elissa, the founder of Carthage; Zezia, the Hilalian [*Fitouri is nodding and grunting his approval at the mention of each name*]; and Kahina, the Berber." Hadhria makes a note of the names. All three women, however—Elissa (or Dido, as she is more commonly known in the West), Kahina, and Zezia—are inscribed in the film within a general context of Arab machismo. Dhouib makes fun of one macho character who auditions for a role in the pageant and is told by Hichem: "You'll shave off your mustache and be a Roman soldier." The man protests that he will be a Roman *with* a mustache. "You heard!" Hichem snaps back. "Shave off the mustache." The man explains that he cannot shave off his mustache, because he is a married man. "My friend," Hichem tells him, "the Romans didn't have mustaches." To which the man replies: "It's not my fault the Romans weren't manly!" Hadhria tells him firmly that there will be no further discussion on the subject, and calls on the next person in line to step forward. Later, the man will ask his barber: "Tell me—Mribeh's son, the one who is playing Ibn Khaldun, is he more manly than I am?" The barber says to him: "If you had a beard, they'd have given you Harun al-Rashid."[22] The man expostulates: "A beard! For the one [character] you need a beard to get the job; and for the other, you have to shave off your mustache! Fine [*he gets up from the barber's chair*], I refuse to work!"[23]

As for Fitouri, the film's chief representative of masculine bluster, there is a scene that parodies the ancient dynamic between men and women that Zezia in the film represents. Cutting a ridiculous figure in his pajamas, as he sits on his bed beside his wife, Fitouri says: "Listen, dear spouse. Highly placed officials have charged me with a very important mission. If I succeed, I shall be promoted, and I'll become an important person." His wife's response—"And as they say: 'Behind every great man is a great woman, but well hidden'"—is all the funnier because Fitouri, accustomed to hearing only what he wants to hear, pays no attention to it. (The viewer, of course, might also think of the woman behind Tunisia's president: Ben Ali's second wife, Leïla Trabelsi Ben Ali, who was rather the opposite of hidden.) He tells her not to wait up for him during the coming days, for his time will be taken up with important meetings and lengthy, round-table discussions that will extend late into the evening. But what the viewer knows (the scene immediately prior to this suggests it) is that he intends to use the preparations for the television company's visit as an opportunity to spend more time with his mistress, Selma.

TELEVISION HAS ARRIVED

When the television company finally arrives, the half-dozen or so Germans turn out to be not a television crew at all, but, as has been noted, a group of scientists and documentary filmmakers engaged in research to find an antidote for the sting of a species of poisonous scorpion. They enter El Malga by the back road, where they are apprehended and held at Brahim's oil mill, until Fitouri can be brought to the scene to decide on their fate. One of the hostages asks for a telephone, so that he might call the German Embassy in Tunis. When Fitouri learns the truth about their identity, he orders them freed at once, but turns to Ingrid, his interpreter for the occasion, and asks: "You're saying they're from Germany?" (The camera tracks from one hostage to the next, corresponding to his gaze: the group includes a black man, a blonde woman, and a man with Asian features, among others.) Fitouri is puzzled. How can they all be Germans? "They're the real thing,"[24] Ingrid confirms.

Fitouri asks Ingrid if, since her "cousins" have finally arrived and have their cameras with them, she might persuade them to film "some souvenirs" of El Malga (he gestures toward the expectant pageant performers). When the Germans discover that they are out of film, Fitouri says: "Just pretend to film—nobody will know the difference." When the entire cast of the pageant is assembled in front of Brahim's oil mill, however, Sghaîer manages to make himself "heard," after all. Dressed as a Roman soldier, he pushes his way to the front, and at the moment he believes the cameras have started rolling, he unfurls a prepared banner that reads: "Palestine is Arab."

The fact that the film's credit sequence at the end contains a scene nearly identical to the one that begins the film—of the committee discussing what they should do in their next program of "cultural" events—is a wry comment not only on the gap between the official narrative regarding Tunisian national identity and the realities that complicate and contradict it, but on Tunisia's stagnant political culture as well. The never-ending struggle in the debate about national identity is framed as one between tradition and modernity (where modernity, as Marx understood it, means constant change). When Salem, for example, argues for couscous as "the best thing in our cultural program," Hadhria proposes a change of menu. "Let's vary it," she says. Fitouri suggests they have a "couscous with tripe," and Hadhria agrees, adding that she thinks the committee should also give its support to some kind of "artistic creation." Fitouri's predictable reply is that they tried that once before, and it produced no tangible return on the investment. All the committee members start talking at once. We see Fitouri, his voice louder than the others', pointing at Sghaîer and telling Mabrouka: "Get all of that down, except the suggestion of the opposing voice."

The relationship between the emergence of a Tunisian national cinema in the spoken vernacular and the creation of an imagined, uniquely Tunisian identity is illustrated by *The TV Is Coming* on both an allegorical level and quite literally. The presence in the film of Hichem the Egyptian, and the El Malgans' choice of a pageant that is staged in order to be televised—and all of it a film, directed by Moncef

Dhouib—attests to the existence of those mass "publics" identified by Benedict Anderson in *Imagined Communities* as the bases for national consciousness, publics that in Tunisia's case were created not so much by the printed word as by the image and the spoken word in the vernacular. Despite the fact that there is a sense in which we can still say that the majority of mankind is monoglot, the evolution of global media capitalism and the emergence of an identifiably national cinema have allowed Tunisia to assert a more confident national identity that is polyglot.

This argument, of course, is not only and literally about languages (Arabic, French, English, and so on), but about Tunisia's evolving economic, political, and social fluency, its degree of cosmopolitan "globalization." The film shows, and is itself evidence of, Tunisia's fluency in the contemporary languages of our globalized world. Thanks to an education system that does in fact give Tunisians access to and potential mastery of several European languages, and through satellite television, the Internet, and other communications technologies, Tunisians have been able to construct a usable past and identify and elaborate a specifically Tunisian/local culture, while becoming thoroughly familiar with, and lively participants in, global culture.

Unlike *Halfaouine*, Férid Boughedir's very popular comedy, which broke all box office records in Tunisia when it came out in 1990, *The TV is Coming* is intentionally and self-consciously—and more dangerously—a satire. *Halfaouine*, which could have been called *Laughter in the Dark* (after the title the playwright in the film gives his new play), seeks to offer humor and eroticism as the best responses to political repression, while attempting also through allegory to examine the nature and the causes of the darkness that it sees slowly enveloping Tunisian society. But viewing *Halfaouine* now, more than twenty years after it was made, one is forced to acknowledge that its answer to the police state amounts to no more than a minor form of rebellion (in the narrative: a way of avoiding the father's anger, when it is provoked). Laughter and erotic adventure are merely survival techniques. As a real defense against tyranny, they were truly ineffectual.

The TV Is Coming, however, unambiguously indicts the Ben Ali regime. Made only four years before the events that prompted Ben Ali to flee the country, the film in effect throws down the gauntlet. There is no mistaking the film's satirical intent: it all but points a finger directly at Ben Ali's corrupt and repressive leadership and exposes the hypocrisy of the image projected abroad of Tunisia as a progressive, "open," and tolerant society, which was so much at odds with the lived reality of the Tunisians in Ben Ali's police state. The problem in Tunisia, by this time, was not that the cinema was unduly constricted by censorship, but that Ben Ali's regime was no longer responsive to criticism by the country's artists working through allegory and satire. Despite having a reflexive tendency toward censorship (especially at the level of script approval, when a filmmaker was seeking the small government subsidy that would allow a film to be officially called "Tunisian"), Ben Ali's regime, toward the end, revealed that it was beyond caring—or perhaps even recognizing—what its critics had to say through allegory and satire.

And the rest, as they say, is history.

NOTES

1. For the sake of convenience, throughout this essay I refer to the group of research scientists—who, properly speaking, constitute neither a company nor a TV crew—as the "German television company."
2. The radio reporter will become the narrator of the short film the residents of El Malga decide to make (we infer that it will be what the French call a "*making of*," a documentary about the preparations for the pageant—for we do not see the completed film, nor any of the footage shot by Ingrid, the German wife of the artist, Kafza). Shooting begins with the reporter looking into the camera and saying: "Free men of the world, peoples of the civilized West: We know that you are living in the era of speed, and that you don't have the time to explore all our accomplishments. This is why we have taken the initiative of preparing a little film, as a sign of fraternity between our peoples: to give you an idea of what we have accomplished in the very short time since independence."
3. The New Tunisian Cinema is the cinema of a generation of filmmakers working during the Ben Ali era, where "era" is understood to refer to the authoritarian regime of Habib Bourguiba's last days and the two decades of Ben Ali's dictatorship that followed. While this designation is approximate, there is general agreement that the New Tunisian Cinema begins with Nouri Bouzid's *Rih Essed/Man of Ashes* (1986). Some scholars, like Jeffrey Ruoff, refer to the "Tunisian New Wave,"

which he describes as "a period, from approximately 1986–1996, when Tunisian cinema was simultaneously popular at home and abroad, attaining critical success at international film festivals" (Jeffrey Ruoff, "The Gulf War, the Iraq War, and Nouri Bouzid's Cinema of Defeat: *It's Scheherazade We're Killing* [1993] and *Making Of* [2006]," *South Central Review* 28, no. 1 [Spring 2011]: 33n8). Rather than rely on this notion of a "new wave," which ends when the public feels the novelty of the "new" cinema has worn off, I make the claim that the "New Tunisian Cinema" emerged as "new" because it was different from what came before it; and until another, recognizably new approach or style began to emerge in response to new or changed conditions, it remained the "new" cinema. The New Tunisian Cinema, therefore, comes to an end around the time of Dhouib's *The TV Is Coming* and Bouzid's *Making Of, le dernier film* (2006), when the filmmakers of this cohort begin decisively to change what I call, in the title this essay, their strategies of subversion.
4. Waleed Hazbun, "Images of Openness, Spaces of Control: The Politics of Tourism Development in Tunisia," *Arab Studies Journal* 15, no. 2/16, no. 1 (fall 2007/spring 2008): 10–35. Subsequent page numbers are cited in the text.
5. Pierre Nora, ed., *Les Lieux de mémoire* (Paris: Éditions Gallimard, 1984, 1987, 1992). In this work of historiography about France (in English, published as *Realms of Memory: The Construction of the French Past*, Vol. 1, *Conflicts and Divisions*, trans. Arthur Goldhammer, ed. Lawrence D. Kritzman [New York: Columbia University Press, 1996]), Nora explains that he and his team of contributors sought to "institute a symbolic history better suited than traditional history to the civic as well as intellectual needs of our time" (xviii). "The point of departure, the original idea," he writes, "was to study national feeling ... by analyzing the places in which the collective heritage of France was crystallized, the principal *lieux,* in all the senses of the word, in which collective memory was rooted, in order to create a vast topology of French symbolism" (xv).
6. Ayed is their handyman. He is a municipal employee and does odd jobs for the committee—everything from being the driver of the municipal minivan to making tea for the committee during meetings.
7. Ben Ali was chairman of the RCD (*Rassemblement Constitutionnel Démocratique / Democratic Constitutional Rally*), which in some ways resembled a mafia organization. Cf. Béatrice Hibou, *The Force of Obedience: The Political Economy of Repression in Tunisia,* trans. Andrew Brown (Cambridge: Polity Press, 2011), for the most detailed and sophisticated analysis of what the RCD was and how it functioned.
8. It hardly makes sense in a one-party state to talk about legal opposi-

tion to the ruling party. Like most dictatorships, Tunisia under Ben Ali was not officially a one-party state, but for all intents and purposes it was, and opposition parties had a phantom reality; they existed in a twilight zone between irrelevance and the preservation of the idea of democracy.

9. "Destiny answers the people's call for life, darkness will be dispelled, and chains will break" is my own preferred translation (by David Bond, of the Institut des belles-lettres arabes in Tunis) of the last two lines of the Tunisian national anthem, "Humat Al-Hima" (Defenders of the Homeland; revised in 1987), written by Mustafa Sadiq Al-Rafi'i, incorporating lyrics by Aboulkacem Chebbi. A widely repeated version of these lines from the chorus, in unidiomatic English, is "If one day, a people desires to live, then fate will answer their call, and their night will then begin to fade, and their chains break and fall." (Cf. Anthony Shadid, "Yearning for Respect, Arabs Find a Voice," *New York Times,* January 29, 2011.)

10. The scene also alludes to the widespread perception that Egypt is no longer the leader of the Arab world, and to the growing conviction among Tunisians that a country like theirs, small as it might be, has no reason to feel culturally inferior to historically more influential players on the global stage like Egypt.

11. Cf. Larry Rohter's remark in his review of Che Guevara's memoir, *The Motorcycle Diaries:* "Che Guevara is widely remembered today as a revolutionary figure; to some a heroic, Christ-like martyr, to others the embodiment of a failed ideology. To still others, he is just a commercialized emblem on a T-shirt" ("Che Today? More Easy Rider Than Revolutionary," *New York Times* May 6, 2004). And before the 2011 uprising in Tunisia, when the last two lines of the Tunisian national anthem would be repeated throughout the world as a mantra for what became known as the "Arab Spring," Aboulkacem Chebbi's name might have resonated with an added intertext for Tunisian viewers recalling that policemen during the Ben Ali era, when asking for a bribe, would sometimes ask for an "Aboulkacem Chebbi" (a thirty-dinar bank note, one side of which was printed with a portrait of the poet).

12. Béatrice Hibou, "Domination and Control in Tunisia: Economic Levers for the Exercise of Political Power," *Review of African Political Economy* 108 (2006): 198.

13. In their book *Le syndrome autoritaire: Politique en Tunisie de Bourguiba à Ben Ali* (Mayenne: Presses de Sciences Po, 2003), Michel Camau and Vincent Geisser describe how, during the struggle for independence, Bourguiba succeeded in raising the morale of the colonized Tunisians and restoring their dignity, but made them understand that

they would only succeed in overthrowing their colonizers if they submitted to the authority of an elite (*el nukhba*) under his firm leadership. This elite took it as an article of faith that the people needed not democracy but a strong leader: "Left to themselves, the people would display their divisions and weaknesses; under the guardianship of an elite, they would [be able to] show themselves united and powerful" (120). Ben Ali's authoritarianism, so much more comprehensive than Bourguiba's, had its roots in Bourguiba's example, which did not take long to degenerate into a familiar pattern of repression, according to which criticism of the president's leadership became synonymous with "plotting against the security of the state" (149).

14. Hibou, *The Force of Obedience*, 118.
15. Lamine will also play the role of an informer when, in secret, he dictates a letter to Mabrouka that begins: "Monsieur le Ministre: It is my duty to inform you of what is going on here."
16. Later, during the sudden storm that wrecks their pageant and their hopes of being filmed by the German television company, the giant statue representing the "authentic" and "modern" Tunisian woman topples forward. With her one arm held high in a salute, and because of the way in which Dhouib films her fall, she reminds the viewer at this moment of the historic toppling of the statue of Saddam Hussein in Baghdad's Firdos Square on April 9, 2003. The radio reporter's warning to the West, thus, "not to export your so-called democracy to this noble land," is very likely an allusion to the American invasion of Iraq in 2003, and a general warning to all foreigners with neocolonial designs on Tunisia.
17. Hélé Béji in *Nous, décolonisés: Essai* (Paris: Arléa, 2008), 45. Subsequent page numbers are cited in the text.
18. Driss Abbassi, *Quand la Tunisie s'invente: Entre Orient et Occident, des imaginaires politiques* (Paris: Éditions Autrement, 2009), 9n7.
19. François Hartog, *Régimes d'historicité. Présentisme et expériences du temps* (Paris: Seuil, 2003), 163-64. Cited in Abbassi, *Quand la Tunisie s'invente*, 9.
20. Like Ben Ali's strategy of proclaiming Tunisia the most modern country in the Arab world (and holding up Tunisia's advanced Personal Status Code as "proof" of this) while ruthlessly suppressing all oppositional voices, Israel has long deployed the ideological strategy of touting itself as "the only democracy in the Middle East," while denying millions of Palestinians both within Israel and in the occupied territories their basic human rights.
21. "Benalism" (or *Benalisme/bénalisme*) is a pejorative term used by many of Ben Ali's detractors not only to describe his systemically

baleful style of governance but also to allude to its oppressive longevity. (For some, the word also alludes to Hannah Arendt's phrase "the banality of evil," which she incorporated into the subtitle of her 1963 work, *Eichmann in Jerusalem: A Report on the Banality of Evil.*) Cf., on *Le Nouvel Observateur*'s online network, "Réflexions sur les 21 ans de Benalisme," nouvelobs.com, 3 November 2008.
22. Harun al-Rashid (763-809), son of Caliph al-Mahdi, was the fifth and most famous Abbasid caliph. In 782, before becoming Caliph in 786, he was appointed governor of Tunisia, Egypt, Syria, Armenia, and Azerbaijan. Due to the way in which he and his magnificent court are fictitiously depicted in the tales of *The Thousand and One Nights,* Harun al-Rashid turned into a legendary figure that quite obscured his true historic personality. This is perhaps why Dhouib alludes to him here—to make a satirical point about how fact and fiction too often become intertwined when national histories (like the El Malgans' parade) are being written.
23. Dhouib is alluding to the fact that throughout the Ben Ali era, Tunisian men understood that if they wore a beard, their chances of successfully navigating the bureaucracy (to obtain an identity card, passport, or other document from the state) would be considerably diminished, as the wearing of a beard could be taken by the RCD as a political provocation—a sign of resistance to the regime, or even outright support for the Islamists' cause.
24. What Ingrid says, in Arabic, is "bel haq," which means "That's true." The French subtitle reads: "Pur souche," which literally means "pure stock." Dhouib is not only making fun of Fitouri's prejudices and assumptions (he probably thinks that, like Ingrid, all Germans have blond hair and blue eyes), but is also critiquing every nationalism grounded in ethnic or religious exclusivity (Saudi Arabia, or Hitler's Germany . . . or that most peculiar case of all, Israel), and with justifiable pride, he is endorsing Tunisia's commitment to a plural national identity.

3

SATIRIC TRAVERSALS IN THE COMEDY OF MEHRĀN MODIRI

Space, Irony, and National Allegory on Iranian Television

CYRUS ALI ZARGAR

Director and actor Mehrān Modiri's comedic television productions enjoy widespread popularity in Iran as well as in the international Iranian community. Using Michel Foucault's notion of heterotopias and Fredric Jameson's discussion of national allegory, this essay investigates ways in which Modiri's sitcoms use contrasting spaces to shine a satirical light on matters of national identity. In a series of productions, Tehran becomes a space representing the entirety of Iranian mores, troubles, accomplishments, and aspirations.

I find myself torn when wanting to describe the comedy of Mehrān Modiri. On the one hand, the few American and British sources that have discussed him depict him largely as a formidable political player using television as his outlet. *Newsweek* named him the twentieth most influential person in Iran in 2009.[1] The BBC Monitoring Service, mentioning political allegories in the show and the reaction of a hardline newspaper, deems the popularity of his most famous sitcom, *Shabhā-ye Barareh* (Barareh Nights), an important if puzzling issue.[2] And *Foreign Policy* writer Azadeh Moaveni discerns anti-foreign propaganda in one of Modiri's productions.[3] Having watched more of Modiri's output than anyone else I know, I find it difficult to disagree.

On the other hand, I worry that, in its focus on Iranian television and culture as primarily political entities, the context of such discussions misses the real Mehrān Modiri. As things stand, American and British interests in Iranian television—the media outlets above emphatically included—lie less in entertainment, laughter, timeliness, wit, beauty, or any of the other trademark products of a beloved humorist. State-run Iranian television exists to be understood mostly insofar as it is the tool of the state, so a producer such as Modiri can only be either deliciously subversive or underhandedly propagandistic. The few mentions made of him fit either description, since, after all, they occur in short articles meant for news or policy media.[4]

Undoubtedly, Modiri's popular serials warrant more analysis than that, since they are cultural artifacts still in production, commenting on a living Iran. Hence my discussion of Modiri's productions will focus on patterns in his depictions of Iranian life, past and present, focusing especially on matters of space. Seven of the eight serials Modiri has directed since 2002 involve places that are somehow non-urban, non-central, or, more specifically, non-Tehran, places that serve as foils to Modiri's most prominent theme: Tehran as a consciously modernizing city. Political allegories do indeed play an important part in his productions, and these are discussed here as well. However, they cannot always be considered essential motivators in his productions. Ethical critique dominates his serials thematically far more than political commentary. Moreover, to say that Modiri himself is primarily motivated by political objectives seems to assume too much. Most probably what drives American television producers, namely, the desire to entertain in order to make money, also seems to drive Modiri, who is "state broadcasting's highest-grossing producer," one who has moved beyond television and started a trend of selling his sitcoms privately, on discs, through vendors.[5] If Modiri's productions serve as part of an Iranian culture industry, especially insofar as they support the status quo, that too is nothing surprising. Anatoly Lunacharsky once described satire as "a moral victory, lacking a material victory."[6] In this case, millions of viewers laughing at once would share in a moral victory devoid of a material victory; the ills of their society and their nation would receive a laugh (distancing them from those ills) and a release, far removed from any moods of indignant activity.

The satire of television sitcoms, both in Iran and in America, usually works this way; as Lunacharsky points out, the changes effected by satire are often too subtle to be noticed.[7] More valuable here is the notion that such sitcoms can tell us something about how Modiri and his viewership see Iran, its past, present, and future.

Most of Modiri's productions focus on spaces within Iran, spaces that still, nevertheless, comment on Iran. Modiri's most celebrated productions rely on two contrasting spaces, which Modiri and his writers (especially Paymān Qāsemkhāni) then use to depict an ironic traversal: a figure leaves one space, enters the other, and endures the comical estrangement of an outsider, episode after episode. These depictions verify the assertion of Edward Soja that humans are historical, social, and spatial beings.[8] We often speak of time and societies, and we often imagine a place—such as Iran—to be a passive geographic receptacle for that society in that time. Yet space, in the way it appears and becomes imagined, is not static; it retains infinite possibility. Space is not mere background or location, but one of the dimensions of human existence, perception, and culture. Space, moreover, shows itself fully when some incongruous marker emerges—an alien, a stranger, something out of place. Using the stranger as an incongruous marker in his serials allows Modiri to depict Iran as a place of multiple spaces, multiple cultures, and multiple voices, but the critical eye of satire also means that nothing ever changes and certainly never improves. Shifts within time and space provide the overarching narrative of many of Modiri's productions: They allow not one but many "Irans" to appear in a series.[9] Mehrān Modiri's serials regularly tackle matters of national narrative; they are candidly representative; and they add to the element of space the scrutinizing element of time. Time, past versus present, forces contrast and hence forces judgment. It allows Modiri to use one space in multiple ways, very often creating a geographical allegory. This raises another important issue, one I hope to discuss in this essay's conclusion, namely the matter of Fredric Jameson's claim that all "third-world literature" (including film) should be read as national allegory, along with the counter-argument of Aijaz Ahmad that Jameson's categories fall short.[10] Geographical allegory in Modiri's sitcoms seems to result from his high degree of attention to Iranian national identity, a degree of attention not found in most other Iranian television sitcoms. To these matters I return below.

As mentioned, my discussion of Mehrān Modiri touches on critical studies of space, but only in order to focus on satirical themes. The analytical tools within this essay largely originate in a lecture given by Michel Foucault in 1967 on "heterotopias," a lecture that later garnered attention and interest among philosophers and geographers working on urban space. Foucault's thesis—that there exist places of otherness of certain varieties—seems to have been matched in importance by his call to the study of space in an academy preoccupied with history, that is, time. This makes my discussion rather difficult because time (in the form of history) plays such an important role in the comedy of Mehrān Modiri. One might wonder how, in a sitcom about a historian traveling through time, for example, I might justify the focus on space. I am arguing, though, that space—especially Tehran—is central; time allows Modiri to change one particular space. Time provides the element of contrast as well as the element of distance. Tehran might become draped in nostalgia and backwardness to the point that it is unrecognizable, but Tehran, the city, is still center-stage. Moreover, while I often set up a dichotomy (old versus new; city versus country), and while I do so based on real observations made in Modiri's serials, I hope to show that a certain complexity and multiplicity arises in Modiri's juxtaposing two places, or one place in two times. It is for this reason that geographer Edward Soja's studies on space, extending the work of sociologist Henri Lefebvre, are so useful. Soja discusses ways in which spaces can have infinite possibilities, bringing together "real and imagined," "consciousness and the unconscious," and—most relevant here—"everyday life and unending history."[11] He calls this power of space "Thirdspace," as opposed to Firstspace (perceived, measurable space) and Secondspace (conceived or interpreted space), reimagining Lefebvre's thesis that space is a social product and modifying Lefebvre's original trialectic.[12] As a geographer, Soja concerns himself largely with real cities. Still, he sees and often indicates the relevance of his theory to those working outside of geography, including those working on literature and, one can assume, film and television.[13] My concern here is to think spatially, to explore the implications of fictional representations of lived spaces, in order to examine Modiri's humorous sitcoms as responses to conceptions of Iranian identity. Foucault's lecture and Soja's writings on space have affected my thoughts, certainly, but the focus here is more on introducing and examining Modiri's productions than on the finer points of spatial theory.

WHO IS MEHRĀN MODIRI?

Mehrān Modiri is one of the most influential figures in Iranian popular culture today. Anyone with a television knows him: he has been an increasingly popular television director and actor since 1993. Moreover, almost anyone speaking in today's Persian idioms has probably used a phrase invented in one of his shows. The word *pācheh-khār*, meaning "sycophant," can now be heard throughout Iran and was invented in one of Modiri's serials.[14] One blog reports that after the Nowruz holiday, Iranian members of parliament returned mimicking phrases from Modiri's *Mard-e Hezār Chehreh* (Man of a Thousand Faces).[15] Whether true or not, the story is certainly believable: every person seems to find himself, herself, or others quoting Modiri's comedic productions, often unwittingly. His pioneering efforts in producing Iranian television comedies with interesting plots and effective jokes has changed the face of Iranian television; today, in part thanks to Modiri, comedic television programs in Iran are extremely popular,[16] and their ability to influence perceptions is taken seriously.[17] In fact, in interviews, actors and directors refer to him as a pioneer in satire (*ṭanz*), and he is generally acknowledged as the master of Iranian comedic directing.[18] His praise can be heard in underground Iranian rap, or on Persian-language websites celebrating his recent honorary doctorate bestowed upon him by an American university.[19] The sense of Modiri's status as a giant of Iranian pop culture is palpable, even if his name is also subject to the dismissive rebuffs customary to those working in comedy.

CONTRASTING SPACES IN *SATELLITE*

Modiri directed and appeared in a nearly one-hour comedy segment that was never officially released and is referred to both as *Māhvāreh* (Satellite) and more popularly as *Bomb-e Khandeh* (Laugh Bomb). In a letter published on the online news site *Tābnāk*, Modiri comments that the episode was merely a prototype, never completed, and meant to be part of a series of discs that was canceled because of his work on *Mard-e Hezār Chehreh* (Man of a Thousand Faces).[20] He comments that discs of the episode have been distributed illegally, made to appear as if he has given his consent, and that "this matter is being pursued most seriously." Modiri must be aware, however, that dissemination of the episode has exceeded the medium of disc; the episode can be downloaded easily and even seen on Youtube, though the latter option might be difficult for many inside Iran because the site is censored. Clearly, also, the episode as it stands would never have been granted approval by Iran's Ministry of Culture and Islamic Guidance, as it depicts suggestive dancing scenes. So it seems that the episode was never meant for official distribution. It is by far the most politically candid of Modiri's productions; those broadcast on television rely mostly on situational comedy, commenting on contemporary political issues through allusions and allegory.

In his letter, Modiri expresses astonishment at the rate at which discs of the episode have spread. Yet this should not surprise anyone: the raw and sometimes shocking humor of the episode displays Mehrān Modiri and his group at their comedic best. Modiri portrays Iranian American satellite personalities as out of touch, ostentatious, hypocritical, and vile, but he does so by creating unforgettably humorous caricatures of those satellite personalities. For those unfamiliar with Los Angeles–based Persian-speaking satellite channels, I should here mention that Iranian state censorship of television means that there are a limited but growing number of official, state-sponsored stations currently in Iran.[21] Expatriates, mostly in the Los Angeles area, have for roughly the past twenty-five years run their own satellite stations, which Iranians inside Iran can watch illegally.[22] The approximately thirty-seven stations (at present) broadcast into Iran provide an alternative source of culture and especially news, particularly during those times when Iranians sense that state-sponsored sources cannot be trusted.[23] The stations also serve the expatriate Iranian community inside America, having a psychological or almost cathartic function for that community that has been treated in depth by Hamid Naficy.[24] The stations often discuss politics, promoting an anti-regime stance, and mingle that with variety shows, talk shows, music, advertisements, and even rebroadcasts of sitcoms and films produced inside Iran. While Modiri's video mocks almost all types of channels offered by LA-based satellite, the most controversy has been caused by Modiri's parody of satellite talk shows concerned with Iranian politics and culture.

In Modiri's depiction of these stations, a man, his wife, and his children wait excitedly as their new satellite is installed. The man wonders in amazement at the nine hundred channels at his disposal and must be told by the installer that not all will be worthwhile, a reality that he will soon witness himself. Modiri then presents this Iranian family in the comforts of their well-decorated living room watching uncomfortably as people "inside" the television expose their family to vile language and behavior. The expatriate Iranians running satellite channels are not simply immoral; they are brazenly, sometimes even hostilely so. Thus, for example, one skit mocks eccentric figures with aspirations for power, satellite hosts who often combine romanticized evocations of Iran's ancient, pre-Islamic past with calls for radical and even martial changes to its present. Here the aging man, dressed as a general and surnamed Tondar, proclaims that he is a potential prime minister of Iran. A guest calls in, worried about Tondar's well-being: "Please protect yourself against the evil eye. My mother recommends, if possible, that you definitely burn a gram of opium, a few hairs from a dissolute woman, droppings from an illegitimate child, rue incense, and onion peels tonight to protect yourself."

Tondar's response unwittingly reveals his immorality: "But my dear . . . at this time of night where can I get a hold of rue incense and onion peels?" In other words, finding opium, dissolute women, and illegitimate children would not be a problem. In another skit, a woman giving love advice tells a female caller that she understands less than a cow, should never have gotten married at nineteen, and should immediately proceed to file for divorce and for her bride-token. While watching satellite television, the parents always seem embarrassed, the children confused. Modiri intersperses skits and even parts of skits with shots of the parents eyeing their children, worried about possible corrupting influences. The television embodies a lack of traditional Iranian values in its depiction of dancing, filthy language, homoeroticism, and drug use. In presenting Los Angeles satellite figures as morally degenerate, aligned with a foreign and even inverted value system, Modiri refashions the diasporic *world-out-there* portrayed on satellite television. No longer is satellite television a voice of delight coming from an unattainable Persian-speaking paradise (unattainable since leaving Iran for America or Europe is for so many Iranians a near-impossible ambition). Iranian life outside of Iran can be a nefarious and hostile force.

The message of Modiri's video is clear: LA-based satellite hosts clearly lack any shred of ethical decency or sincerity, in contrast to their naive if well-meaning native Iranian viewership. In depicting this contrast, Modiri reverses the nation-diaspora power relationship. For over two decades, LA-based satellite stations have interpreted Iranian life for those in the diaspora, also inviting those in the nation of Iran to share in a general consensus that what was valuable about Iran has left its borders. Here Modiri reinterprets Iranian life for those within Iran, inviting his viewers to share in his vision of Iran: a nation sought by all, those within it and those without, a nation under attack by those whose values are very *un*-Iranian. In Modiri's video, the nation watches the diaspora, not with longing admiration but with disgust.[25] Comedy, moreover, gives Modiri's version of the satellite world an air of satiric accuracy; his characters are exaggerations (and thus—the logic of comedy says—not fabrications) of that which everyone has seen on satellite television. In terms of credibility, his depictions also enjoy the status of being uncensored: the disc makes use of the same power of unofficial media that drives illegal satellite television, since it is a "leaked" video. Thus, Modiri's clip has accomplished a reversal of credibility: LA-based satellite is supposed to be unofficial, the uncensored voice of truth, the diaspora's alternative to state-run television for those inside Iran. Modiri has created another unofficial voice, an unreleased disc, one that highlights the self-serving political objectives of satellite television, thus rendering it an aspirant to power just as perfidious if not far more so than the state.

The video does more than simply foreground ethical or moral

contradictions; it does so using space. In Modiri's setup, there is the room, which is inside Iran and which is wholesome. Then there is the world inside the television, which is in Los Angeles and which is depraved. Central to his depiction is the sanctity of the home—in this case, an apartment in Tehran—as a space violated by foreign influences. The home is a controlled space. It is real and unitary. On the other hand, the space inside the television is virtual, shifting, multiple (with nine hundred channels and endless programs within each channel), and imperious; the sights and sounds within it are imperious in the sense that television is a one-way medium of communication and promotes its ideas forcefully with no ability to hear. Satellite television promises multiplicity in its channels and personalities, but actually dictates one unified message of hedonism. The sheer power of the satellite appears in its effect on space: Its sound fills the room; it forces its audience, a family that before was spread out casually throughout the house, to sit before it in strained attention; and it causes apprehension. This power is best suggested in the episode's ending: The family has fled the couch and is nowhere to be found, nowhere to be found within their own home, but the television still blares, still continues to exert itself over their domestic space.

Connections to matters of space are not simply in the episode's television-versus-home dynamic. Rather, the tension between the nationalistic claims of the satellite figures and their absurd behavior highlights tensions in claims about space, namely, the identity of Iran itself, epitomized in its capital Tehran. Indeed, the first appearance onscreen of the satellite world, ridiculous, humorous, and self-celebratory, has a man in a tuxedo refer longingly to "that old Tehran—that beautiful, old Tehran," by which he means pre-revolution Iran. The satellite personalities long not for Tehran as it is but for the Tehran they remember, one in which freely occurred the immoral behavior they now enact in America. In fact, Modiri implies that the "Tehran" for which they long is actually "Los Angeles." A female singer, who has just described her escape from Iran (an escape which seems to have involved sexual relations with anyone who would help her), proudly asserts her love for her Iranian identity. She proclaims that, at one point, she boarded a plane, "counting the seconds" until her return "home." When the interviewer assumes that she flew to

Tehran, she responds, "No! I flew *here*"[26]—in other words, Los Angeles.

The fight over Tehran's identity is in no way one-sided. One of Modiri's own two appearances in the episode, in which he depicts notable satellite station host Shahram Homayoun, provoked the ire of Homayoun himself, who has used his own LA-based satellite station, Channel One, to reply to Modiri's caricature. Modiri's caricature of Homayoun has all the marks of the former's comic abilities: distinctive tics, sporadic obscenities, a focus on ethical flaws, and a sense of timeliness. His caricature of Homayoun—whom he has named Bahrām Aryāni—curses at his viewers while at the same time asking them to contribute the paltry sum of $200,000 to his station. He sells bags of Iranian dirt and balloons of Iranian air for $1,000, and blasts other LA-based satellite stations in a series of slurs. All the while, the host unwittingly reveals his desire to be "nothing more than the head of radio and television in Iran," as well as his clandestine relationships with young female viewers.

Homayoun's response turns the argument back on Modiri; if Homayoun has selfish motivations, Modiri's motivations are political, coordinated, and dangerous. Modiri, according to Homayoun, is a policy theorist for the Islamic Republic, working for Iran's intelligence agency.[27] While Modiri might present himself as a mere comedian and director, his shows are part of a larger conspiracy to present satellite stations negatively and to vitiate the intellectual and cultural capacities of Iranians. As Homayoun makes these claims on his station, pictures from Modiri's past, one of which is from his days of military service as a young man, but most of which are shots of him in costume, portray Modiri as a stereotypical Iranian religious fanatic: the suit with no tie, the army fatigues and headband, the slight beard.[28] Homayoun's analysis of Modiri's famous sitcoms focuses on the fact that they distract Iranians from the real problems of their country, especially since not only the shows but the language from those shows are on everyone's lips.

At its core, Homayoun and Modiri dispute the sincerity of their respective media outlets, namely, LA-based satellite programming versus Iranian state television. Homayoun clearly describes Modiri's episode as an attack covertly orchestrated by the Islamic republic against famous satellite personalities working for the freedom of Iranians. Homayoun devotes hours of discussion, on separate occasions, to analyzing Modiri's clip; he criticizes the foul-mouthed caricatures created by Modiri as false, but also deplores the lack of civility. Homayoun is especially offended that Modiri's parody of him tries to sell his own mother on the show, because such an affront to motherhood highlights the decline in ethical values one finds in Iran under the current regime. Homayoun justifies, moreover, selling items on television (as mocked by Modiri) by emphasizing the financial independence and hence financial need of his station, one that undertakes such important work that even the U.S. government has offered aid (aid that, on account of viewer support, Homayoun can refuse).[29]

On the other hand, Modiri's clip speaks for itself: by the end of Modiri's episode, the head of the household (the father) should realize that the five state-run Iranian channels he has were actually more in his and his family's interest than the nine hundred offered by LA-based satellite. More than a mere conflict about media, however, Homayoun and Modiri's contending depictions concern Iran itself. Homayoun's Iran is a country with a rich historical past, whose noble people have become the victims of a dictatorial, fanatical regime; those inside Iran need the help of those outside Iran, those in the diaspora, to realize this and take action. Modiri's Iran is also a victim, but a victim of external forces, such that those inside Iran should realize the danger posed by those outside Iran. The claims of satellite figures to be credible outlets for Iranian culture and politics appear absurd, mostly because of major character flaws: Los Angeles satellite personalities have lost their Iranian identity, adopting instead affected, Western ways, and they are flamboyant about their lack of morality. Satellite figures, according to Modiri, see Iran exclusively as a field of potential influence, both political and moral, and their vision for Iran relies on a dead Iran, one of an idealized past. By portraying satellite personalities as avaricious, hungry for both power and money, Modiri's clip—which has since been imitated by other directors for state television—does indeed accomplish that which Homayoun claims. If Modiri's depiction can influence opinion, then Homayoun's call for regime change in Iran and for the country's immediate and complete isolation will seem to stem from selfish motives and not from a profound concern for the well-being of that country's inhabitants.[30] Homayoun himself, in discussing the clip at such length, seems to be aware that Modiri's serials define things for their viewership—they define Iran, Tehran, and LA-based satellite stations. While Modiri does so in *Satellite* by contrasting a Tehrani living room with a circus of idiots in Los Angeles, most of Modiri's productions focus on spaces within Iran.

CONTRASTING SPACES IN *BARAREH NIGHTS*

My second example comes from Modiri's most famous production, *Barareh Nights* (*Shabhā-ye Barareh*). Barareh is a fictional Iranian village notable only for its garbanzo beans. The village had appeared before in another Tehran-based Modiri production—*Pāvarchin*—and it seems to have been popular enough to warrant a prequel that would give prominence to the village, its comical, fictitious, and often absurd dialect, the irrational and hardheaded feuds of its dwellers, as well as their circumscribed view of Barareh as the center of the world. The serial takes place in the Pahlavi age, sometime in the 1930s, when a journalist in Tehran named Kiyānush publishes an opinion piece critical of Reza Shah's regime and is arrested. He escapes and flees through the woods, but is bitten by a snake and rescued by a villager from Barareh. As a wanted man, Kiyānush effectively becomes a fugitive trapped inside this village. He marries into the family of the villager who saved him, a man named Shīr-Farhād, played by Modiri himself. Kiyānush is educated and cultured; his refinement can be seen in everything from his thin, well-groomed mustache, his suit and spectacles, to his polite manner of speech in a formal-sounding Tehrani dialect. Conversely, his new wife wears the clothes of a villager and has a jagged disposition; her voice is gruff, her temper easily provoked, and she sometimes wields a sword. She regularly makes threats of violence against her husband, whom she and her family see as effeminate in name and manner.[31]

Not just Saḥarnāz—the protagonist's wife—but everyone in Barareh stands in contrast to their Tehrani guest-in-exile. They have random street fights, in which everyone present participates, whether or not the reason for fighting is known. They cultivate their land by sitting on it, harvesting positive energy. They have elaborate and strange rituals, especially revolving around marriage where the male suitor must be beaten and the bride must be stolen. Their beliefs lack any sense of historical accuracy: they believe that Genghis Khan was defeated by the inhabitants of Barareh, that Alexander the Great fell in love with Roksānā, a Barareh woman, and stayed in that village, and that the cemetery of Barareh is brimming with the remains of famous personages, including Victor Hugo. Their language is beyond illiterate: The third-person plural form of all verbs is the ridiculous-sounding word "vuygulanjz." Yet in all cases, especially when Kiyānush tries to correct or reform them, the inhabitants of Barareh see the intellectual from Tehran as backward and an imbecile. Their response to most of Kiyānush's rational observations and advice is usually the phrase "In hichi navafahmah," meaning, "He doesn't understand a thing." While many episodes show Kiyānush's persevering attempts to change things, to teach the villagers—in one example—to stand in line, inevitably Kiyānush will yield to their stupidity and express frustration. That frustration is often captured by a long meta-dramatic stare into the camera, a trademark feature of Modiri's productions. Education, intelligence, culture, and goodwill prove to be no match for the sheer stupidity of the villagers.

As a space, Barareh is nowhere. Kiyānush cannot leave and only attains contact with the outside world when someone comes to or passes through the village. The inhabitants of the village are not only unaware of the outside world; they are willingly unaware, as seen in their resistance to Kiyānush. The village, however, pulls Kiyānush and the viewers of this show into itself, creating a world with charms of its own. Barareh is verdant and in that sense quite beautiful. The dusty, old-fashioned walkways of the village—its architecture overall—evokes nostalgia, as captured by the theme music that opens each episode, a well-known folk song, "Bezār Berim Dasht" (Let Us Go to the Field). The theme is played in the style of earlier twentieth-century Iranian ballads, thus including a classical Iranian orchestra, while accompanied by a title sequence that is visually sentimental, namely, pictures in black and white surrounded by beautiful calligraphy. Like other theme songs in Modiri's shows, it is sung by the director himself, and the message is one of escape: "Let us go to the mountain. Which mountain? That very mountain that has all the deer." The clothing of the people of Barareh evokes Iran's simpler, almost idyllic rural past. Insofar as it is nowhere but represents a certain sort of everywhere, and insofar as it is a place of exile from an outside norm, in some ways like a psychiatric hospital, Barareh reminds me of what Michel Foucault famously called a "heterotopia."[32]

Barareh functions for Kiyanush as a "heterotopia of deviation," a place set aside for those who stand outside of accepted behavior; Kiyanush is, after all, in exile there, and the village serves as his self-imposed substitute for the prison from which he has escaped. While Kiyanush and the villagers are there for differing reasons, they all have no place in normative Iranian society, that is, Tehran. Like Foucault's description of heterotopias, not everyone can enter and not everyone can leave. More especially in its ability to bring multiple external places together inside of one place, here a village, Barareh is an imagined heterotopia. The village has everything a larger city would have, even if much of it is not functional; it has a doctor, whose folk medicine borders on malice; it has a poet, whose poetry in the local dialect only aims to impress its unsophisticated financial benefactors; it has an incompetent governing body, as well as an incompetent army. It is its own inverted world. Moreover, Barareh is "a space of illusion that exposes every real space, all the sites inside of which human life is partitioned, as still more illusory."[33] The shockingly ridiculous rituals and manner of life there have their counterparts in contemporary Tehran and thus expose Tehran's ridiculousness. Borrowing Foucault's image, one could describe Barareh as a mirror for contemporary Iran itself. Its rejection of this journalist and intellectual mirrors a complaint often heard in Iran, namely, that intellectual accomplishments lack real social value when compared with money and connections. Its rough handling of grooms mirrors a common complaint in Iran, that it is simply too difficult for young men to pass the many financial and social hurdles that exist for getting married. The focus on Barareh as the center of the world mirrors Iran's insular concern with all things Iranian. The mixture of fascination and dismissal vis-à-vis an outsider mirrors the experiences of many foreign or foreign-born visitors of Iran.

The show's use of time clearly ties into its metaphorical use of space. Foucault related heterotopias to spans of time that stand outside of normal time—what he called "heterochronies"—places like libraries or museums where time stands still, for example. He even uses specifically the example of Polynesian villages, in which visitors can discover a time before time, a time of nudity. Here, too, Barareh allows Modiri to capture themes important to an Iranian viewership but disconnected from any particular time, placed in an imaginary past and in a place out of touch even with its own present. Barareh is not only behind in relation to contemporary Tehran; it is behind in relation to Tehran in the past. Or, rather, instead of "behind," it creates its own inverted standards and culture.

Yet Barareh appears through the lens of satire and hence is humorous. Since it is humorous, it is in the end lovable despite its ethical shortcomings. Modiri's satire is of the variety that renders the absurd into the endearingly human; one might think of the character Archie Bunker from the 1970s sitcom *All in the Family*, whose bigoted views on women and minorities raised controversial issues, but whose lovable personality simultaneously apologized on behalf of the large number of Americans who might agree with him. This is common to the sort of mainstream nationalistic satire one would expect on national television—the jabs must be softened to reach a wide audience. In terms of lovability, remember that Kiyānush not only falls in love with and marries a woman from Barareh, but as the episodes progress (and there are ninety-two in all), Kiyānush often shows an understanding of these people, especially when another foreigner enters the scene. In certain episodes, Kiyānush even succumbs to the unethical ways of the villagers and becomes entangled in their self-obsessed machinations. This is the ambiguous role of such satire—critique coupled with complacency, embodied in an act that is critical and complacent all at once, that is, laughter. Thus, while laughter in Modiri's comedies is based on a judgment (I, the viewer, am better ethically than those depicted, so I laugh at them), upon viewing them one is never moved to judge oneself—there is no self-reflexivity. In this sense, the one laughing remains complacent. To some degree, Homayoun's warning to his viewers (the warning about degenerating Iranian culture) shows his sensitivity to this function of satire.

The contrasting spaces of *Barareh Nights* also serve to highlight Tehran as a space, even if it only appears by proxy for most of the series. Tehran is a place of education, journalism, power, and culture when juxtaposed with Barareh. Travelers coming from Tehran bring products unrecognizable to the villagers, and all the advancements Kiyānush tries to introduce to the village (including a newspaper) are those he has known in Tehran. Modiri often explores the meaning of Tehran in his serials. Sometimes, such as in the serial *Mard-e Hezār Chehreh* (Man of a Thousand Faces), Modiri and his usual partner (until recently, head writer Paymān Qāsemkhāni) cast a critical light on the city. A simple and honest clerical worker from Shiraz moves to Tehran, slowly becomes a first-rate criminal, and encounters the pretentiousness and ineptitude of that city. (Of course, it should be mentioned that he also encounters its wealth and technological advancements.) More often, however, Modiri's serials focus on Tehran as a contemporary, flourishing city contrasted with a backward counterpart. In *Barareh Nights*, the village provided such contrast. In other serials, especially in a more recent serial—*Qahveh-ye Talkh* (Bitter Coffee)—a leap back in time allows the director to contrast Tehran with its former self.

CONTRASTING SPACES IN *BITTER COFFEE*

Bitter Coffee tells the story of a down-and-out historian. No one cares about his expertise in Iranian history, not even when it might be helpful; the historian—Nimā Zand-e Karimi—tries to offer his help to a radio station and its trivia show, but is told that sports matter more to people than history. His discipline also fails him financially, and he decides to move back to his hometown in the country, when he receives an anonymous phone call inviting him to the Sa'dābād Palace in Tehran's Shemirān area, a palace once occupied by the Pahlavis and the Qajars before them. There the historian drinks some coffee and is transported to the court of a Persian shah in the early nineteenth century, a fictional shah who has happened to escape the annals of history. After the historian correctly predicts (or rather remembers) an earthquake and saves the king's life, the king—Jahāngir Shāh—spares him and makes him his head advisor. The historian's attempts to advise and change the course of Iranian history turn out to be exercises in absurd futility, paralleling the situation of Kiyānush in the village of Barareh; fittingly, both roles are played by the same actor. Such scenes are certainly humorous but have a sense of poignancy for Iranians familiar with their own national narrative, one in which Iran comes up short vis-à-vis foreign powers. The historian, for example, cannot restrain the shah from selling or even giving away national treasures, including oil wells to the British, who kindly offer to remove what they describe as a filthy and greasy substance from the shah's hands.

Bitter Coffee is an exploration of one space—a palace in Tehran—using leaps in time. The space in question appears relative; its appearance and order depends on the historically situated knowledge of those who occupy it. When a historian from the future returns to improve Iran's history, he does not fit, and he cannot be heard. The message is one of comic despair; the humor in episodes focused on the historian's oddness emphasizes the ridiculousness of those in Iran who cling to outdated ways, those who refuse to acknowledge progress and new information. So important is the theme of Iran's missed opportunities that Modiri's serial even leaves the boundaries of satire to communicate it: When Jahāngir and his court successfully foil the historian's attempts to change the course of Iranian history for the better by contacting Fatḥ-ʿAli Shāh (r. 1797–1834), Modiri superimposes hauntingly melancholic music over their imbecilic celebrations, veering momentarily from the satiric mood. Refusal to change and improve almost always appears, however, as a comedic matter. Thus, when in later episodes the court of Jahāngir drinks the bitter coffee and leaps forward to the present, court notables appear even more ludicrous than before and must be confined to the historian's apartment. Characters in the show have circumvented the usual rules of time but remain bound to one space, Tehran. Their inability to accomplish anything during any period of time fits into the mode of satire—nothing improves, and so everything stays ridiculous and hence comical. It also fits the serial's allegorical message that Iran, while rich in culture and worthy of improvement, must recognize the limits imposed upon it by its own history. While there is no hope for changing Iran's (and more specifically Tehran's) past, Modiri's serial does depict the city as having a hopeful future. The future—seen in the enormous changes, technological and cultural, occurring in Tehran—can make one space (Tehran) become foreign to its own inhabitants, who have traveled from a time of backwardness to a time of coming prosperity.

Life in Tehran certainly proves difficult for our historian, mostly on account of his career path, but even this points to Tehran's being a forward-looking city uninterested in its own history. The apartment buildings, libraries, and other structures usually appear contemporary, clean, and pleasing to the eyes. Trips back to the future usually highlight great technological advancements available to someone in Tehran: a new metro, computers (laptops and tablets), automobiles, elevators, and MP3 players. Tehran appears especially new and modern when the focus is on a restaurant of the grand Milād Tower (the sixth tallest tower in the world).[34] Modiri presents Tehran as a city that is beautiful and livable despite its historical failures. In fact, even the past testifies to Tehran's inherent beauty and nobility, notwithstanding that circumstances never allowed it to see its full potential. The city appears classical and rich when Modiri decorates it with lavish nineteenth-century sets and nostalgic, courtly modes of attire. Tehran is dressed in seemingly endless layers of history. Beautiful but abused, Tehran can glance at itself in a mirror of virtual history placed before a mirror of virtual present. Mirror images echo within one another, giving a sense that Tehran is infinite: Tehran is the world. This production is not Modiri's only historical-satirical ode to Tehran, since he created a similar situation in the far superior series *Bāgh-e Moẓaffar* (Moẓaffar's Garden). As a more recent production, however, *Bitter Coffee* shows that Modiri's satire is still primarily concerned with defining Tehran. In doing so, in focusing on this one metropolis, as he, Shahram Homayoun, and every other Iranian knows, Modiri's satire acquires the ability to define Iran. After all, Tehran has become a space representing the entirety of Iranian failures, accomplishments, and aspirations, a mirror, in other words, in which Iran views itself.

CONCLUSION: THE HUNGER FOR ALLEGORY IN "THIRD WORLD LITERATURE"

This discussion of representational spaces in the comedy of Mehrān

Modiri has hinted at another problem in English-language discussions of Iranian satire, including perhaps this one. Those of us outside Iran tend to be most excited about the political dimensions of that country's literature, film, and television, perhaps because to us Iran is a political entity before all else. Mehrān Modiri's productions certainly do touch on events of the day in Iran, often criticizing shortcomings within Iranian society and even government. As I have indicated, the focus of Modiri's serials is often less on institutions or political structures; it is almost always on human foibles and ethical shortcomings. As such, in a way, Modiri's serials are incredibly political, more than any overtly political satire can be; they focus on universal ethical truths to define Iran and its identity. To some extent, moreover, they are apologetic: Iranian culture, past and present, is flawed but always redeemable, because characters are lovable and the serials' sets often focus on the beauties of Iranian culture, its gardens, interior design, and even architecture. Yet, once we admit that all art is ideological, we must also admit that there is something that separates art from pure propaganda, a pleasurable quality that Fredric Jameson, among other Western critics, saw as mostly alien to third-world or postcolonial literature.[35] To see these serials as merely ideological is to strip something pleasurable, pleasurable in its ability to make the viewer laugh, down to a tool designed for an immediate political purpose. If the American viewer's primary concern is to determine the degree to which these serials (or a film or book) are complicit or critical of the current regime, then our consideration reduces the complex experience of satire. Iranian narratives then become simple narratives, part of a black-and-white, two-sided power struggle. This assumes that the "third-world" viewer, too, is simple, wholly political, passively subjected to viewing as opposed to imaginatively engaged in the viewing and laughing process. While it is true that Modiri's serials invite the viewer to see his or her living room as normal and indeed normative, and in doing so accomplish much politically, they also comment on the human psyche, on ethical conflicts, on familial relationships, on marriage, and even on the very ironies of the human body (insofar as they have slapstick humor). They certainly are more explicitly "political" than the average American sitcom, but not always, and the utter lack of political relevance in the American sitcom is itself—one might argue—a sharper political tool than anything Modiri could fashion.

Often what we outside of Iran expect is more than a mere recognition of Iranian national identity; we expect the artist to move Iran's viewers in a certain direction. This is certainly true of the few American and British sources that have discussed him; they assume that Modiri's serials, either in effect or in intent, nudge (or should nudge) Iranian audiences in a direction for or against the Islamic regime. The same can be said for Shahram Homayoun's televised attack on Modiri, which seems to have occurred numerous times on his satellite talk show. Homayoun's assessment of Modiri's satire as "dangerous" only makes sense if complacency, especially a failure to stimulate discontent inside Iran, is dangerous. If such is Homayoun's intent, and it might be, then his observation might be extended to a rather astute one about the function of satire and even art in general, because then *any* artistic work produced inside a country without a politically subversive message further establishes that country as a place of cultural richness and multiple voices. Thus any artistic production that does not noticeably criticize Iran's political structure would be dangerous. Homayoun's concern, of course, is not about satire in general, not about sitcoms broadcast in Los Angeles that fail to arouse contempt for America's political and social ills, but rather for those inside Iran alone. This is mirrored, for example, by Moaveni's comment in *Foreign Policy* that Modiri's satire "pokes fun" at the Iranian government's failings while returning its audience to "a comfortably status quo stance at the end."[36] Something about that status quo seems so wrong, in the case of Iran, that Modiri's ability to give his audience a fulfilling ending becomes almost villainous. A popular Iranian sitcom that dabbles in national allegory must either be pro-regime or anti-regime; it must be something close to propaganda. Yet those who view and enjoy Modiri's serials do not share one political vision; the serials are popular within Iran as well as in the diaspora; they are popular in a general sense, by those weary of the regime as well as those supportive of it. His serials use national allegories to entertain, and, in entertaining, strike the careful balance between critique and lightheartedness demanded by a large viewing demographic.

This brings me back to Fredric Jameson's hypothesis that all "third-world literature," if there is such a thing, should be read as national allegory. Jameson sees a divide between West and non-West, which is also a de facto divide between canonical and non-canonical; those who are non-West and non-canonical (those in the "third world") are so aware of their national situation that all forms of literature, even the most seemingly personal, speak to that situation through allegory. Aijaz Ahmad's response is multifaceted. Ahmad contends that the very category of "third world" ignores the fact that people across the world (such as minorities inside America) often have more in common than can be indicated by nationality. Instead, Ahmad offers a Marxist view that the world is united in its being subjected to a capitalist mode of production and in its resistance to that mode in varying degrees.[37] Moreover, many forms of literature in places that Jameson would recognize as third world in no way reflect themes of national identity (Ahmad's examples are from Urdu poetry). The problem, according to Ahmad, is that the matter of translation makes only certain literary productions available to American and European scholars, so it might seem as though we can speak of all third-world literature being a certain way. In other words, if I may extend the argument, scholars in America and Europe receive via translation literary productions that suit their expectations; they expect products that speak to the national situation; they expect products that speak out against Western hegemony and colonialism or at least respond to such matters; they expect products that are what we might call "third-world-ish."

Jameson's theory and Ahmad's response might shed light on why Modiri and so many other Iranian film directors draw our attention and why they draw our attention in a certain way.[38] Modiri's productions show an awareness of being the Other, of being depicted on American satellite stations, of being behind in terms of social progress from the colonialist age onward. National identity is tied to Iran's major metropolis, its capital Tehran, and thus to industrialization, with an eye toward post-industrialization. In other words, if Modiri's body of work fits Jameson's hypothesis, it is because it *is* third-world (or third-world-ish) literature; it sees itself as part of a dialogue about nations and development, and it responds to its identity as a creature on the losing end. This is not to say that there must really be such a thing as third-world literature, especially since such categories have become even more nebulous since 1986 when Jameson wrote his article. It does, however, mean that Jameson's observation was founded on the sort of literature that shared with Modiri's sitcoms an awareness of Otherness. Jameson was concerned about canonization and about the place of world literature in American classrooms. Modiri's sitcoms might not make it into classrooms, but, if taking part in the dialogue of Otherness qualifies art as worthy of American and European interest—and I think it does—then his sitcoms have an advantage over those that say little about Iranian national identity.

Space in Modiri's serials, in the end, does relate directly to national identity, especially two facets of that identity—progress and backwardness. Tehran becomes an overarching metaphor for Iran in its totality, its past, present, and future. In that sense, Modiri's productions echo the sentiment that a geographical region can speak for a people's identity; his creation of spaces that explore that identity make for geographical allegories that resonate thunderously with Iranian viewers. While one might argue that this does not tell us much about the film, literature, and television of a difficult-to-define and probably non-existent place known as the "third world," it certainly tells us much about how Modiri's audience sees itself.

NOTES

1. "Iran's Top 20," *Newsweek,* June 1, 2009, 36–37.
2. "An Iranian Sitcom Barareh: Why Was It So Popular?" *BBC Monitoring Middle East,* April 10, 2006.
3. Azadeh Moaveni, "900 Channels of the Great Satan," *Foreign Policy* 188 (September/October 2011): 1–4.
4. It should be said, though, that American media can at times be unashamedly out of touch with Iranian culture outside of the Los Angeles area. Take, for example, an article by Michael Lewis, in which he comments that "satire in Iran seems as unlikely as bobsledding in Jamaica," thinking that he has happened upon the only satirist in all of Persian-speaking television, a satellite-based skit actor named Ali Fakhredin, while having lunch in Los Angeles. See "The Satellite Subversives," *New York Times,* February 24, 2002.
5. Moaveni, "900 Channels of the Great Satan."
6. Anatoly Lunacharsky, *On Literature and Art* (Moscow: Progress Publishers, 1965), 310.
7. Ibid., 307–9.

8. Edward W. Soja, *Thirdspace: Journeys to Los Angeles and Other Real-and-Imagined Places* (Cambridge, Mass.: Blackwell, 1996), 73. I thank my colleague Eric C. Stewart for many enlightening discussions on this topic.
9. The comparison to American television sitcoms I have made above should not be taken too far. After all, the American and British media outlets mentioned are certainly right to see political allegory in Modiri's productions and even in the contrasting spaces and times depicted therein, while political allegory is less common in popular American television sitcoms. Consider for a moment, to highlight differences, the "narrative" of the television sitcom *Everybody Loves Raymond*, similar but so different. Its overarching narrative is, similarly, largely within its geography: A sports columnist (Raymond), his wife, and children live in Long Island adjacent to his overprotective mother, his boorish father, and his jealous brother. Their Italian-American working-class roots, Raymond's wife's bourgeois background, and the textbook personality disorders within the family all come into conflict because of this simple geographical setup: they live next door to one another. The geography is explored episode after episode, much as it is in Modiri's productions. Yet one would not venture to call it geographical allegory, simply because the episodes only rarely if ever indicate that the national American narrative is at stake. The neighbor-setup does not seem to represent the United States.
10. Fredric Jameson, "Third-World Literature in the Era of Multinational Capitalism," *Social Text* 15 (1986): 65–88. Aijaz Ahmad, "Jameson's Rhetoric of Otherness and the 'National Allegory,'" *Social Text* 17 (1987): 3–25.
11. Soja, *Thirdspace*, 57. The relationship between real city and fictional-real city should be clear: Tehran on television is an imagined version of Tehran as it is experienced on the ground, for those who live there; that Tehran, the experienced or "lived" Tehran, is different but reliant on the physical location demarcated as Tehran.
12. Henri Lefebvre, *The Production of Space*, trans. Donald Nicholson-Smith (Oxford: Blackwell, 1991), 39; Soja, *Thirdspace*, 73–82.
13. Soja points out that interest in space has expanded beyond the purview of geographers and reached into a "growing transdisciplinary community of scholars who see the spatial dimension of our lives as of equal critical importance to life's embracing historicality and sociality." See Edward Soja, "Keeping Space Open," the author's own review of *Thirdspace: Journeys to Los Angeles and Other Real-and-Imagined Places* in *Annals of the Association of American Geographers* 89, no. 2 (1999): 348–53, here 353.
14. See www.loghatnaameh.org, accessed September 2012. The word is defined in this online Persian dictionary as a word of "Barareh-i" origins; Barareh is an imaginary village created in Modiri's serials.

15. See sadrizadeh.blogfa.com/post-14192.aspx, accessed September 2012.
16. "Iranians Watch Four Hours of TV a Day, and Like Comedy," *BBC Monitoring World Media,* March 4, 2008. The BBC relies on a survey run by the Research Center of IRIB.
17. Such was the case when a satiric program (not by Modiri) ridiculing Afghan names and accents roused controversy and complaints among prominent Afghans in Iran and Afghanistan. See "Paper Slams Iranian Comedy Series for Ridiculing Afghans," *BBC Monitoring South Asia,* October 31, 2007.
18. Javād Rażaviyān, a nationally known comedic actor and now director, one who has appeared in many of Modiri's serials, even refers to Modiri as "the captain of all film and television satire," despite Modiri's having publicly called him an "ingrate." See the interview show "Goft o Gu-ye Tanhā'i," first broadcast in 2012 by IRIB, Channel Four. Also, in a survey taken by *iFilm,* a state-run channel, Modiri was voted the best comedic director in Iran. See the online newspaper '*Aṣr-e Irān,* www.asriran.com/fa/news/207936, accessed September 2012.
19. This award was given to him by American Liberty University on account of his "artistic and humanist endeavors." See, for example, the online Iranian newspaper *Mehr,* www.mehrnews.com/fa/newsdetail.aspx?NewsID=1364288, accessed September 2012.
20. "Nāmeh-ye Mehrān Modiri beh mardom darbāreh-ye CD-e 'Māhvāreh,'" *Tābnāk* (28 Dey, 1389). The letter is reproduced along with Modiri's signature and dated "Dey of 1389," corresponding to December–January of 2010–2011. www.tabnak.ir/fa/news/143147, accessed September 2012.
21. At the present moment there are eighteen nationwide and twenty-nine provincial channels.
22. Satellite dishes were banned by Iran in 1995, probably due to increased popularity. Moreover, the national constitution (section 175) prohibits private broadcasting networks and limits expression on IRIB (Islamic Republic of Iran Broadcasting) to that which corresponds to Islamic law and national interests. See Pierre Pahlavi, "Understanding Iran's Media Diplomacy," *Israel Journal of Foreign Affairs* 7, no. 2 (2012): 21–33, here 24 and 22.
23. Ibid., 22.
24. Hamid Naficy, *The Making of Exile Cultures: Iranian Television in Los Angeles* (Minneapolis: University of Minnesota Press, 1993).
25. I must here recognize Gayatri Devi's insightful comments for encouraging much of the discussion in this paragraph.
26. I have here quoted Azadeh Moaveni's translation. See Moaveni, "900 Channels of the Great Satan," 3.
27. The Islamic Republic of Iran does indeed see Shahram Homayoun as

a threat, as evidenced by the Iranian government's request for a "red notice" to be issued for the arrest of Homayoun in December 2009 for inciting terrorism. See Libby Lewis, "Are Some Countries Abusing Interpol?" *CNN Online,* July 18, 2011, www.cnn.com/2011/WORLD/europe/07/18/interpol.red.notices/index.html, accessed April 6, 2014.
28. See www.youtube.com/watch?v=C_u-NiFbq5Y, accessed September 2012.
29. See an interview uploaded in separate segments on Youtube, www.youtube.com/watch?v=Vm7obzOVAOg and www.youtube.com/watch?v=vn6Qbke3nJU, accessed December 2012.
30. See Neil MacFarquhar, "Exiles in 'Tehrangeles' Are Split on Iran," *New York Times,* May 9, 2006.
31. "Shabhā-ye Barareh," episode no. 8, broadcast in 2005 by IRIB, Channel 3, directed by Mehrān Modiri.
32. Michel Foucault, "Of Other Spaces," trans. Jay Miskowiec, *Diacritics* 16, no. 1 (1986): 22–27.
33. Ibid., 27.
34. Even the name of the serial—mentioning "coffee"—refers to a drink that has come to represent all that is chic in Tehran (as opposed to the old standard, namely, black tea).
35. This discussion draws from Indira Karamcheti, "Minor Pleasures," *Postcolonial Discourse and Changing Cultural Contexts: Theory and Criticism,* ed. Gita Rajan and Radhika Mohanram (Westport, Conn.: Greenwood Press, 1995), 59–68. See Jameson, "Third-World Literature," 66.
36. Moaveni, "900 Channels of the Great Satan," 4.
37. Ahmad, "Jameson's Rhetoric of Otherness and the 'National Allegory,'" 9–10.
38. Consider, for example, exuberant American and European reactions to Aṣghar Farhādi's Academy Award-winning film *A Separation (Jodā'i-e Nāder az Simin),* from 2011. A brilliant accomplishment in its own right, the film concerns life in Iran, the problems involved therein, and the desire to escape to America, while more subtly indicating issues of national identity through metaphor (the senile father representing Iran itself). Numerous American newspaper reviews of the film discuss matters of state censorship and sometimes offer—in turn—national-allegorical interpretations of the film. See, for example, John Powers's "'A Separation' of Hearts, Minds and Ideas in Iran," *National Public Radio,* "Fresh Air," January 17, 2012, www.npr.org/2012/01/17/145164129/a-separation-of-hearts-minds-and-ideas-in-iran, accessed April 2014. The film is a major artistic achievement, deserving of all the attention given to it and more, yet, without acknowledging the sense of otherness so explicitly, one wonders if it would have succeeded in capturing so much American and European attention.

4

ETHNIC HUMOR, STEREOTYPES, AND CULTURAL POWER IN ISRAELI CINEMA

ELISE BURTON

Ethnic humor is a major feature of Israeli cinema, having a central prominence not only in comedic films but also often providing comic relief in films with little other humorous content. It occurs in numerous forms, ranging from subtle dialogic remarks, insults, and jokes made toward stock ethnic characters to entire scenes and plotlines that center on caricatured portrayals of ethnic identity; not uncommonly, several of these manifestations of ethnic humor appear in the same film. Such expressions of ethnic humor in Israeli cinema not only perform cinematic functions, such as the self-identification of the audience with the social interactions portrayed on film, but also reflect the fluctuating dynamics of Israeli cultural politics. By noting the changing prevalence of certain expressions of ethnicity on the Israeli screen in response to social and political demographic trends, we can observe how humor, in its various forms, has served as a mechanism for social critique over time. In this chapter, I offer analyses of brief segments and scenes from eight different Israeli films released between 1976 and 2007, covering multiple genres and dealing with multiple facets of ethnic and racial identity.[1]

These ethnic identities are ordered along hierarchies, which are, of course, determined by political hegemonies, but I focus here on how these hierarchies manifest themselves in social interactions in terms of "cultural power." Cultural power is a commodity that renders visible one's access to political power and thus one's relative position in any given social grouping; it encompasses all of those outward expressions through which an individual's ethnicity is read and performed, ranging from physical appearance, speech (both its accent and semantic content), mannerisms and social behavior, taste in food, dress, music, and so on. In any nation-state, then, the cultural power ascribed to any given ethnic group is a function of that group's place along a vertical spectrum; the politically hegemonic ethnicity inevitably defines the "national culture" on its own terms (which inevitably change with time), and the farther one's cultural performance deviates from the hegemonic "national," the lower (or higher) one's sociopolitical capital can be in any given social context. This is not an original concept; in its emphasis on constant fluctuation and relative rather than absolute inequality, it is indebted to Foucault's work on power. Rather than make a theoretical intervention, I intend to apply this abstraction of cultural power to concrete analysis of the cinematic performance of ethnicity in the context of Israeli society. In particular, I am interested in how humor can intervene in and even temporarily overturn the social power dynamics of the cultural discrimination which is symptomatic of ethnic politics in Israel, where the project of Zionist nation-building has configured an ethnic and cultural identity in deliberate contrast to the diasporic historical experiences of most of its citizens, albeit in an unequal manner.

The European roots of the Israeli state, through both its founding Zionist ideologies and its Ashkenazi sociopolitical elite, produced a cultural hegemony that long delegitimized any positive acknowledgment of its "non-Western" Others, whether internal (non-Ashkenazi, and especially Mizrahi, Jews)[2] or external (non-Jewish Palestinians). Even during the first twenty years of Israeli statehood (1948–1968), when an unambiguous majority of the Jews immigrating to Israel were arriving from the Arab states of the Middle East and North Africa, the state's established political, economic, and cultural elites stubbornly promoted aesthetic values adhering to European conventions of classical and folk music and art. While all new immigrants were pressured to abandon their diasporic tastes and habits, Mizrahi Jews in particular found their culture portrayed at the national level as exotic at best and primitive and barbaric at worst, with most opportunities for cultural expression limited to their own ethnic enclaves. With this in mind, let us briefly review the historical context of film production in the Israeli state.

Cinematic production was a primary venue through which young Israel represented itself as Herzl's "rampart of Europe against Asia," and Ilan Pappé argues that until the 1970s, Israeli commercial film, more than almost "any other cultural agency or institution within the country," followed the agenda of Zionist nationalism.[3] In the immediate post-independence Israeli context, Arabs were cinematically depicted as "pathetic stereotypical figures who always yielded to the superior Euro-Jewish Israeli hero,"[4] while the experiences of Mizrahi Jews in Israel were largely omitted from the screen entirely. The first filmmaker to break out of the stilted formulas of 1950s Zionist realism, the Iraqi immigrant Nuri Habib, was bold enough to produce not only Israel's first Technicolor film but also its first film about and for Mizrahim, namely Yemenites, *Be-en Moledet* (Without a Homeland, 1956). Despite his enthusiasm and desire to boost the Israeli film industry, Habib faced severe censorship for his later films and went bankrupt, never receiving for any of his films the tax rebates due him by the state under its own legislation to subsidize local cinema production.[5]

By contrast, the well-examined and extensively critiqued "bourekas films" of the 1960s and 1970s, which were mostly directed by already established Ashkenazi filmmakers, utilized Yemenite, Moroccan, and other Sefardi and Mizrahi Jewish ethnic stereotypes to great popular success.[6] Many of the bourekas films were slapstick comedies, with much of the humor stemming from the grotesque ethnic caricatures embodied by leading and supporting characters. If these portrayals were not necessarily sympathetic to Mizrahim, fashioned as they were in terms of reductionist stereotypes, at least they and their grievances were rendered visible to the Israeli and international public, although the cinematic potential for social critique was here softened by the vehicle of comedy. Nevertheless, bourekas provided the founding conventions for the representation of certain ethnic stereotypes, which have been perpetuated into present-day films, such as the middle-aged Mizrahi male, who is often a simple-minded and easily offended deadbeat, or the Russian doctor, who enjoys the authority and respect granted to his/her socioeconomic position yet is completely lacking in every other social grace. An important feature of these early representations of Israeli Jewish ethnic heterogeneity is the emphasis within the plotlines that the Ashkenazi-Mizrahi rift was solely a problem of cultural differences, easily resolvable through interethnic marriage,[7] a goal celebrated through the oft-repeated phrase *"kulanu yehudim"* (we are all Jews); in short, they glossed over the evidence that the superficially obvious cultural rift was increasingly one of socioeconomic class difference. Later, by the 1990s and 2000s, more tragicomic films such as *Tipat Mazal* and *Ha-Kokhavim shel Shlomi* (billed in English as *A Drop of Luck* and *Bonjour Monsieur Shlomi*) offered increasingly sympathetic portraits of Mizrahim, although they nonetheless capitalized on these established stereotypes to infuse humor into the drama as well as to critique more openly the systematic and persistent economic disadvantages attached to the sociocultural discrimination against Mizrahim.

The persistent success and influence of the bourekas' ethnic-humor model was acknowledged through the simultaneous emergence of films focusing on the Russian immigrants who flooded Israel following the collapse of the Soviet Union, which have been analogously dubbed "pierogi films,"[8] indicating their thematic and plot similarities to the bourekas genre. However, the pierogi films and their contemporary Mizrahi-interest counterparts are significantly more complex in their portrayal of ethnic relations, rather than relying on the excessively stereotyped characters of bourekas, which reflects the significant sociopolitical and demographic changes in the Israeli Jewish population. Within the last ten years, casts have become even more conspicuously multicultural and multilingual, striking a balance between the humor value of ethnic stereotyping and its efficacy as a mechanism for social critique. This is especially true in more recent non-comedic films featuring Palestinians and other Arabs, such as the work of Eran Riklis. These more recent films strive to perform ethnicity with greater depth in characterization, attaching stereotyped behaviors to characters who are otherwise shown to be three-dimensional; they also tend to use more diegetic mechanisms of comic relief, such as the use of racist jokes or mutual misunderstandings caused by language barriers between characters.

This cinematic trajectory betrays a sort of obsession with ethnic identity in the Israeli film tradition, an obsession clearly born of the political tensions surrounding cultural expressions that deviate from the hegemonic. Yosefa Loshitzky has astutely observed that Israel is a "meeting point of conflicting and conflating identities," yet all these identities share "a strong sense of being victimized by the Jewish state" and a desire to have their past sufferings officially acknowledged.[9] The acknowledgment, or rather the construction, of ethnic difference through Israeli cinema has been brilliantly analyzed by Ella Shohat's critical survey *Israeli Cinema: East/West and the Politics of Representation,* which remains the seminal text on ethnic representation in Israeli film. However, while her postcolonial approach highlights the state-societal power structure that framed the early emergence of Mizrahi and Palestinian film characters as ethnic caricatures, she does not analyze in depth the possibilities for humor to (re)negotiate the related ethnic-cultural power structures.

I propose to build on Shohat's analyses of Israeli cinema by specifically focusing on the deployment of ethnic humor, combining a Freudian perspective on humor along with the aforementioned Foucauldian lens on situational power. Israeli cinema has a well-developed tradition of portraying existing sociopolitical power dynamics by utilizing ethnic stereotypes to render varying levels of cultural capital, but how these humorous stereotypes can also serve a critical function has not been closely examined. I argue that the dialogic and visual language of ethnic humor has often been used to underscore temporary situational reversals of cultural power dynamics. Furthermore, the trend of deploying ethnic humor and stereotypes in Israeli cinema has developed over time toward increasingly direct and self-conscious critiques of cultural discrimination, in a way that gestures toward the depth and persistence of social and political divides within Israeli society, both between different "ethnicities" of Jews and between Jews and non-Jews.

My sequence analyses are conceptually indebted to Freud's understanding of how humor can be used to verbally express hostility and aggression under social circumstances that prohibit its expression by physical actions. Freud suggests that humor can function as a replacement for overt violence, since "by making our enemy small, inferior, despicable or comic, we achieve in a roundabout way the enjoyment of overcoming him."[10] While this framework has been used to analyze Jewish ethnic jokes as a way to cope with the "oppression" and "victimization" of living as minorities in Western society,[11] it has not been enthusiastically employed within the Israeli/Middle Eastern context, in which Jews can be differentially victimized and can take on the role of the oppressor. Freud's concept of aggressive humor has been employed to understand Middle Eastern humor in a political mode, such as to examine political jokes as a form of popular resistance to oppressive regimes in Egypt,[12] but it is not clear that this has ever been applied to Middle Eastern cinema. In other words, my intervention here is not a theoretical one, but rather one of conceptual application in film analysis. I apply these notions about humor here to understand Israeli ethnic humor[13] as a form of resistance to cultural hegemony: in some cases, Mizrahi resistance to the Ashkenazi-based sociocultural norms and values of Israeli society, and in others, as a sharp critique against the prevailing forms of Israeli racism and xenophobia. For my diegetic analyses, I also incorporate Foucault's notion of the circulation of power through society[14] to examine how the aggression or resistance conveyed by ethnic humor reinforces or disrupts expected power dynamics between individuals with different levels of cultural capital within cinematic scenes.

Ella Shohat's work has already indirectly suggested the applicability of this theoretical power-reversal framework for bourekas films. She characterizes the bourekas genre as "escapist" for the Israeli sociocultural underclass: "In the world of the oppressed, the oppressor is a constant (historical) presence in relation to whom the repressed must either assimilate or rebel. The 'bourekas,' in this sense, are characterized by . . . 'carnivalesque' humor; the people on the margins laugh irreverently at the powerful, at characters who for the Oriental collective consciousness represent the oppressive center."[15]

Shohat's interest in the function of humor as/against power, in other words, is primarily about the engagement of socially marginal audiences with the humorous themes and content of the film. But before delving into an examination of specific films' use of humor, we must remember how the framework of weaponized humor may be approached at multiple levels, of which Shohat's comment reflects only one. First, we may see such humor at work within the diegesis, usually operating explicitly through dialogue in terms of jokes and slurs. Second, humor may operate primarily between the film and its audience, wherein the audience is invited to laugh at situations and mannerisms not necessarily humorous (or visible) to the film's characters, such as stereotyped behaviors and stock characters. Finally, humor may be detectable at a meta-level of cinematic production. At this last level, humor can make otherwise risky topics of social critique politically permissible and/or commercially viable for filmmakers, which is important for understanding the context of the bourekas genre and the current transition away from its favored forms of ethnic representation and use of humor (for example, grotesque caricature and slapstick comedy). In the European context, Jörg Schweinitz has discussed how "progressive directors" have mobilized character stereotypes, in particular, for cinematic social critique: "The aim was to invoke a pattern, exaggerate it, and then take it to the point of absurdity by the staging of obvious difference—thus tangibly revealing the stereotype as a deficient, distorted image.... The intention was to criticize such stereotypes as crystallizations of a false consciousness."[16] I believe this is also an appropriate understanding for Israeli cinema, as we consider the persistent role of stereotype as a form of ethnic humor across time.

I divide my analyses into two major threads. In the first I consider film sequences containing humor that troubles the meaning of ethnicity within Israeli Jewish society and engages the question of Mizrahim as "Arab Jews," focusing on the historical transition between the bourekas and "neo-bourekas" genres. The second group of sequences are selected from films that deal substantially with the themes of Ilan Pappé's "post-Zionist cinema" and highlight moments of Israeli Jewish characters interacting with Others who are, in various ways, located within Israeli territory but outside Israeli society: Egyptian soldiers in the conquered Sinai Peninsula, Syrian Druze in the occupied Golan Heights, and African and Asian migrant workers in Israeli urban centers.[17] These representations of ethnicity intersect, of course, with other very important categories of identity, such as gender and class, but for the sake of coherence I have had to limit my discussions of these related aspects to the analysis of ethnic-based humor; in other words, I have directly addressed only those issues that form part of the joke.

STEREOTYPES AND CULTURAL POWER IN ISRAELI CINEMA

JEWISH ETHNIC HUMOR: BOUREKAS AND BEYOND

Rather than take another pass at well-analyzed films such as *Sallah Shabati* (1964), *Salomoniko* (1973), or *Kazablan* (1974),[18] I apply my analytical framework to another bourekas cult film, *Giv'at Halfon Enah 'Onah* (*Halfon Hill Doesn't Answer*, 1976). In a slapstick movie replete with abundant visual and verbal ethnic humor, we can find a specific interaction in which a Mizrahi character—stereotypically inscribed as both dull-witted and quick-tempered—actually deploys his ethno-cultural knowledge to invert the power dynamics of dangerous circumstances.

The buffoonish Victor Hasson, who has inadvertently wandered off his military reserve base in the Sinai Peninsula across the Egyptian border, is picked up by the neighboring Egyptian army station for interrogation. Assuming he is an Israeli intelligence agent, the Egyptian commanding officer sarcastically offers Victor a drink during his interrogation, but when the attending soldier Attallah mockingly hands Victor a "coffee"—which is really an electric shock device, placed undisguised, wires dangling, into an Arab-style coffeepot—Victor does not react with the sense of humiliation or fear appropriate to his position as a war captive facing potential torture. Instead, he indignantly snatches the device out of the pot, scolding the Egyptians, "What are you, crazy? What, have you become Ashkenazim? Is that the way to make coffee?"[19] He proceeds to instruct the taken-aback Egyptians on proper coffee preparation, completely taking control of the situation. When the Egyptian officer discovers that Victor is an Egyptian Jew from his own hometown of Alexandria, the two bond over their mutual acquaintances and cultural knowledge; the same ethnic background that systematically puts Victor at a disadvantage in Israel therefore rescues him from the danger presented by his national "enemies."

The lack of fear betrayed by Victor in the interrogation (in fact, he seems quite comfortable) is underscored by his hostile comment, meant to shame his former co-nationals, that poor coffee-making is a disgraceful mark of "becoming like Ashkenazim," a loss of the cultural knowledge that Victor himself has resisted despite the pressure of Ashkenazi cultural dominance in Israel. The two then proceed to mock Ashkenazim together (here embodied by the comment, "Who am I, Rothschild?"), while Victor maintains his paternalistic tone throughout the interaction. With a final flourish he ends the conversation with an invitation to visit him in Israel for the holidays and a patronizing reminder not to boil coffee. The stock character of the Mizrahi is therefore portrayed as infantilized and effectively powerless in Israeli society, where Ashkenazim reign with their ersatz coffee; yet upon returning to an Arab cultural milieu, he takes up his proper patriarchal role—in this military situation, Victor's ethnicity is empowering. Not only does he (unwittingly) invert the situational power flow between interrogator and prisoner to remove himself from danger, he also positions himself as more Egyptian than the Egyptians, possessing a higher level of cultural capital—an inversion of the ethnic power scale inhabited by Mizrahim vis-à-vis Ashkenazim in Israel (though not vis-à-vis "Arabs," who remain at the bottom of cultural-power schematics in both the cinematic portrayal of Victor's Egyptian escapade and the reality of Palestinians in Israel).

I turn now to the transformation of the bourekas genre toward portrayals of Mizrahim, which, while strictly conforming to certain stereotypical conventions, are calculated to arouse sympathy through both situational humor and verbal jokes. Analyzing scenes from two films that can be classified as neo-bourekas,[20] directed by Moroccan Jews primarily about Moroccan Jews, I start with Ze'ev Revah's 1990 *A Drop of Luck*. Much of the humor in this tragicomedy is situational, surrounding the caricatured antics of Moroccan immigrant Jojo, a famous wedding singer in his native land who struggles to establish himself and his young daughter in the anti-Mizrahi sociocultural milieu of 1960s Israel. His cultural disempowerment is starkly highlighted in a scene where he is called upon to fill in for a no-show performer in the stuffy Israeli restaurant where he has just been hired to work as a waiter. He immediately bursts into a popular Moroccan wedding song, to the horror of the uppity German clientele and the confusion of the Ashkenazi musicians, who cannot figure out how to accompany him with their European-tuned instruments. The humor embodied by Jojo's naive enthusiasm and obliviousness to the ethnically marked shock of his restaurant audience (one of whom viciously asks the restaurant owner if he has "brought in an Arab") easily evokes the sympathy of the spectator, which is further amplified to a sense of righteous indignation when Jojo switches to a Hebrew song lamenting the hardships of Moroccans in Israel, appropriately hitting the line "*tistalek mipo*" ("get out of here") as he himself is forcefully carried, feet kicking in the air, out of the restaurant. The aggressive aspect of the scene's humor is projected onto the non-diegetic audience, who is expected to sympathetically identify with the endearing Jojo and disapprove of the pathetic cultural chauvinism of the snooty Ashkenazim, and even as we laugh at the slapstick comedy, we are clearly intended to soberly and critically reflect on the history of Mizrahi absorption and the cultural politics wielded against Arab Jews in particular.

Arguably more sophisticated examples are provided by the verbal humor of Shemi Zarhin's 2003 *Ha-Kokhavim shel Shlomi* (*Bonjour Monsieur Shlomi*). The father of Shlomi, the teenage protagonist, fits many of the conventional Mizrahi stereotypes. Robert, a deadbeat who cheated on Shlomi's mother and was thrown out of the house, resides in a hovel and spends most of his time onscreen complaining about his victimization: by his wife, his father (Shlomi's grandfather), his wife's seductive friend, and his Russian doctor. In one scene, Shlomi arrives to deliver lunch to his father, who insists that he is dying of cancer. When Shlomi asks Robert if he has gone to the doctor, he becomes defensive, arguing that his doctor's medical authority is negated by his Russian ethnic background:

Shlomi: Did you go to the doctor?

Robert: He's a Russian immigrant. He doesn't know nothing.

Shlomi: Why, don't they have cancer in Russia?

Robert: Loads of it. They're all dying of cancer. What does that mean, Shlomi? That they know nothing about cancer. He asks me if I'm Moroccan. I say my mother was a Moroccan Jew and my father an Iraqi Jew. "Then stop eating spicy food," he tells me. Can you believe that? [Shlomi smirks.] What are you laughing at? Your patient has cancer and you're laughing?[21]

Through his comically indignant delivery, Robert not only insults Russian medical knowledge (a pointed critique at the general Israeli stereotype of Russian immigrants as well-educated, particularly in science), but also lambasts the doctor's own racism by angrily reporting the doctor's comment that Robert should stop eating spicy food to solve his health problems. When Shlomi snickers, his father chastises him, using the same words he clearly wanted to say to his flippant doctor, but could not in a social situation in which he held a lesser degree of both social and cultural power. Alone with his son, however, he is free to express the tempered hostilities of the situation through ethnically marked sarcasm, projecting cultural inferiority onto his doctor rather than himself.

The longevity of the stereotypical portrayals of Mizrahi masculinity embodied by Victor, Jojo, and Robert, who are derived from earlier bourekas-genre characters beginning with the titular *Sallah Shabati*,[22] and their embeddedness in the Israeli cultural landscape, is underscored by their overt repetition in contemporary films in which they, alongside or instead of Ashkenazim, can represent the Israeli in interactions with non-Jews. For example, the 2004 film *Masa'ot James ba-Erets ha-Kodesh* (released in English as *James' Journey to Jerusalem*), directed by Ra'anan Alexandrowicz, centers around an African man's experiences with Israelis. A major subplot involves Shimi, a middle-aged Mizrahi man, and his difficult relationship with his elderly, wheelchair-bound father, Sallah. (Although their last name never surfaces in the dialogue, we can deduce from Shimi's advertising that their last initial is "Sh," as in the first letter of "Shabati.") Just like the famous caricature portrayed by Haim Topol in 1964, this Sallah is constantly playing backgammon, gambling, cursing in Arabic, and bemoaning the materialistic behavior of Ashkenazim (in this case, his son's wife). Yet in this case, the director has consciously reappropriated the popular stereotypical figure to make a new social critique that reaches beyond the internal ethnic divides of Israeli Jewish society and casts them against a much broader social world, a world that is nonetheless equally ordered along cultural hierarchies of power—and hierarchies equally disrupted by instances of humor, albeit generally of a darker or more ironic variety.

JEWS AND OTHERS: DARK AND DARKER HUMOR

One of the most poignant scenes of Arab-Israeli interaction in cinema history is the delivery of Shylock's monologue from Shakespeare's

The Merchant of Venice in *Avanti Popolo* (1986). Generally categorized as a dark comedy and an absurdist antiwar film, *Avanti Popolo* is set in the immediate aftermath of the 1967 Six Day War, centering on the attempt of two stranded Egyptian soldiers to escape from the Israeli-occupied Sinai Peninsula. Suffering from thirst as they cross the desert, the soldiers, Khaled and Ghassan, drink the only liquid they can find—a dead UN peacekeeper's alcohol—before drunkenly staggering into the path of an Israeli patrol. The amused Israelis sadistically play with the intoxicated Egyptians, shooting at their feet, shoving them, and dragging Khaled away from their water canteen. After two failed attempts to drink, Khaled—a former actor—defiantly rises to his feet from the sand and shouts, in accented English, "I am a Jew!" The Israelis look on with puzzled smiles as Khaled passionately performs the entire monologue, dropping to his knees with the line, "If you prick us, do we not bleed? If you tickle us, do we not laugh? If you poison us, do we not die?" He then looks up expectantly at the Israelis, one of whom asks, "What's he mumbling about?" The other responds, "He's mixed up the roles." Yet, perhaps recognizing the ironic sensibility of Khaled's performance, he orders his comrade to let Khaled drink.

The forms of humor in this scene are numerous and complex; there are overtones of slapstick in Khaled's exaggerated gestures, which prompt the Israeli soldiers' smiles and dismissive reactions. But it is clear that the cosmic joke is really on the Israelis; even the more sympathetic one who recognizes the dramatic reference remarks only that Khaled, as a non-Jewish Egyptian, must be confused, as he is performing a Jewish character's address to Christians in front of Israelis, who are real Jews. Meanwhile, it is clear to the non-diegetic audience that Khaled is projecting Jewishness for himself in a different way—the performance has nothing to do with ethnic, cultural, or religious identity, but everything to do with the situational power dynamics. Khaled, seeking mercy from the well-armed Israeli patrol, is highlighting his position as the proverbial Jew of historical Western Christendom: the despised Other, a vulnerable minority whose humanity is consistently denied and whose rights are given and taken away according to the whims of sympathetic or antipathic interlocutors. By performing the role of Shylock, he is not attempting to pass as a Jew, and he is certainly not confused about anyone's identity.

Rather, Khaled is performing the Jew as a type of status—namely, as a subordinate social status, a status historically defined as devoid of power, which over time became conflated (at least in Europe) with an immutable racial/ethnic identity. This immutable identity has been thoroughly absorbed into the Zionist ethos, with the result that the Israelis on the screen are comically unable to dissociate Jewishness from themselves—they reject Khaled's claim to metaphorical Jewishness with regard to his powerlessness, since as a Muslim Egyptian he is categorically excluded from Jewishness. He is confused; he is not ethnically Jewish as the Israeli soldiers are. The abstract applicability of Shakespeare's monologue to the situation at hand is only reluctantly acknowledged by the Israelis' magnanimity; they forgive the error of his enthusiastic performance by rewarding him with mercy and water.[23]

This critique of the hypocrisy internal to Israelis' ahistorical Jewish identity, which always configures the (Jewish) self as an inherent victim and the (foreign) Other as an inherent victimizer, heedless of the constant shifting of power between individuals within a society and between societies and nations, is central to the aforementioned *James' Journey to Jerusalem*. The eponymous James, a devout South African Christian, is sent on a pilgrimage to Jerusalem by his small village. Yet upon arrival in Israel, due to the comically racist attitudes of Israeli immigration officials (including a long-suffering woman who lamentingly asks why James didn't go looking for work in America, France, or Germany when Israelis themselves can barely make it in "this God-foreseken place"), he is identified as an illegal labor migrant and detained, only to be "rescued" by Shimi, who procures foreigners for domestic cleaning services. The migrant laborers represent a thorough snapshot of the developing world—Romanians, Moldavians, Thais, Filipinos, and a broad assortment of Africans—a whole set of foreign Others against whom the film's Israelis define themselves and by whom they claim victimization. The film's verbal leitmotif, the Yiddish slang term *"frayer"* (a "sucker" who allows others to take advantage of him), is a status obliquely claimed by many of the Jewish characters (as in, "What am I, a *frayer*?") as they justify their manipulative and unethical actions toward each other and the foreign workers.

Yet while the film contains intra-Jewish ethnic tensions, namely the Mizrahi-Ashkenazi filmic allusions and plot themes discussed above, the presence of the foreign laborers allows the Israelis to have an illusion of unified Jewish identity. It is only James's racial Africanness that allows Sallah to choose sides in a game of backgammon with him by declaring ironically, "You're black and I'm white—just like in real life." This is a far cry from the "black" self-consciousness of the original *Sallah Shabati* of 1964, whose titular Mizrahi character shouted at a well-to-do "white" Ashkenazi couple, "It's always like this—black's no good, but if it were white it would be fine.... Only the color matters."[24] Thus, it is only through James's subordination that an older, modern-day Sallah can now access the social and cultural power of white Jewishness, the cultural superiority originally denied Mizrahi Jews in favor of Ashkenazim.[25]

Those whose culture has been most systematically devalued in Israeli society—Arabs—have also enjoyed cinematic moments in which they project a measure of cultural superiority over foreigners through ethnic humor. In Eran Riklis's 2004 *Ha-Kalah ha-Surit* (The Syrian Bride), the complexities of the power held by ethnically diverse individuals, in this film primarily the Druze of the occupied Golan Heights, fluctuates dramatically from scene to scene, encapsulating the huge range of the political dilemmas and social consequences derived from the Israeli-Palestinian conflict. Unlike the Druze who live within Israel proper, hold Israeli citizenship, willingly serve in the Israeli military, and disavow any Arab solidarity, most of the Golan Druze characters in this film are shown to identify with Syria—the title character is having an arranged marriage to a Syrian Druze man who lives in Damascus, and her father is a Syrian nationalist shown marching in a protest to return the Golan Heights to the control of Bashar al-Assad. Thus, although the middle-aged generation of characters interacts regularly with Israelis, are fluent in Hebrew, and harbor ambitions to attend Israeli universities, the older Golan Druze are shown to have solid ties to an Arab ethnic and cultural identity, which provokes generational conflict.

For example, the character Hatem, a Druze man who moved to Russia and married a Russian woman, Evelyna, brings his family back to the Golan to attend his sister's wedding. The Druze community shuns Hatem for marrying outside the faith, and Evelyna bears the brunt of the ostracism, as her foreignness most potently represents the threat of contemporary educational and labor migration to a traditionally insular Druze society. As in the example from *Halfon Hill Doesn't Answer,* food preparation is highlighted as a locus of cultural identity. In one scene, as Evelyna attempts to help chop vegetables for the wedding feast, one of the Druze women remarks caustically, "She's blonde, but she doesn't know how to slice a tomato. . . . She probably serves [her husband] hospital food." Amidst the laughter of all the other women in hearing range, Hatem's mother tries to defend her daughter-in-law's respectability through Evelyna's status as a high-ranking doctor in Russia; however, she implicitly accepts her neighbor's critique as valid, since she kindly yet patronizingly moves to show Evelyna how to properly slice a tomato.

We can read the Druze women's treatment of the Russian wife as an approach to correcting the daunting fluctuations in the community's generational and gendered power structure by reinforcing customary ideas regarding both what constitutes acceptable food and what a wife's appropriate skill set should be. The neighbor's witticisms are just shy of outright insult, and the directness of the hostility is enabled not only by Evelyna's inability to understand Arabic but also by the mother-in-law's shared anxieties with the other (laughing) women regarding the future of the community; accordingly, both older women's exercise of cultural authority over the Russian wife are embedded in their own awareness of losing power amidst the changing social sensibilities of the younger generation.

Evelyna does experience her own moment of situational power later on, when her brother-in-law Amin passes out from dehydration and the whole family crowds around her breathlessly as she rushes to his aid; her authority as "the Russian doctor," however, is exhibited semi-comically, as her treatment is only to call for water as she slaps her relative awake. In this portrayal, we can see certain continuities with *Bonjour Monsieur Shlomi* in the stereotyped figure of "the Russian doctor"; just as Evelyna is found to be deficient in cooking skills, Robert's doctor is clearly lacking in his bedside manner. But their medical knowledge is never directly challenged in the diegesis (Robert does not insult his doctor to his face, and Evelyna's slapping treatment only appears silly to the non-diegetic audience). This is a testament to the cross-genre prevalence of ethnic stereotyping and its comic value in Israeli cinema—Evelyna is neither Jewish nor an immigrant to Israel, and so her version of "the Russian doctor" is not a participant within Jewish ethnic cultural power struggles. Rather, she is a more abstract figure of global foreignness as well as a harbinger of local community breakdown, marked by technical skill and cultural sterility.

As Israeli cinema's casts and scripts become increasingly multilingual, the plot device of characters who do not share a language has driven a certain trend of ethnic "humor" toward increasingly direct ethnic insult. To examine this trend more closely, I turn away from the exhaustively analyzed Israeli cinematic representations of Jewish and Arab ethnicity and back toward the newer and less understood dimension of ethnicity in Israel presented by non-Jewish refugees and labor migrants, who have just begun to emerge on the Israeli screen in the past decade. While *James' Journey to Jerusalem* was perhaps the first to showcase this phenomenon, in that film, differing moral sensibilities rather than language barriers lead the characters to misunderstand each other. This is not the case in the 2007 film *Meduzot (Jellyfish)*, in which one of the main protagonists is a Filipina immigrant named Joy, who labors as a domestic worker to send remittances to her young son in the Philippines. Joy speaks no Hebrew and thus can only communicate with Israelis in English, which becomes problematic when she is hired to care for an elderly woman, Malka, who knows only Hebrew and German. While this feel-good plotline reveals the process by which the two women overcome their language barrier and become friendly by the end of the film, the intermediate scenes delicately engage with the issues surrounding non-Jewish labor immigration through the lens of stereotyped mockery. The Ashkenazi Malka, caricatured as gruff and impatient, constantly insults her employee Joy, who cannot understand the ethnic slurs. For example, in the scene evoking the film's title, Malka says condescendingly to Joy: "What's on the beach besides dog shit and jellyfish? You people eat them, don't you?"[26] Meanwhile, Joy, made powerless by her inability to comprehend, can only stare vacantly. This is only one of many scenes wherein Joy's ethnocultural background, and especially her inability to communicate in Hebrew, mark her as an

Other in Israel worthy only of contempt, even as the Israeli characters are dependent on her supportive labor. Unlike many other examples of overcoming ethnic difference in Israel, the "happy ending" for Joy is not eventual absorption into Israeli society but returning to the Philippines, loaded with gifts for her son.

Joy's situation and that of James in *James' Journey* reflect a new reality of the Israeli economic underclass: most of the lowest-paying jobs in agriculture and domestic care surrounding urban areas are now held by non-Jewish migrant laborers and/or refugees from Southeast Asia and East Africa. The ubiquity of these workers is further reinforced in the film when Malka chastises her daughter Galia for hiring Joy, who "doesn't know a word of Hebrew," and mentions that her friend had a wonderful Filipina assistant. Galia responds by wearily asking her mother, "If I replace her, will you be happy?"[27] This is only one of numerous chillingly depersonalized references to Joy made by the Israeli characters, who tend to identify her not just in terms of ethnicity ("Filipinit") but also of possession. For example, in a previous scene, Joy's first Israeli employer, Menahem, introduces her to his mother in Hebrew:

Menahem: Mom, I want you to meet . . . [to Joy:] What was your name again?

Joy: Joy.

Menahem: Joy.

Mother [to Menahem]: Your woman?

Menahem: Yours. She'll help you.[28]

Joy, discussed as though she were a slave, is powerless to intervene in these dehumanizing Hebrew conversations. Yet to some degree, her very inability to understand Hebrew can also give her situational power, and these temporary reversals of the real power dynamic are attended by a sort of painful humor. For instance, the context for the jellyfish joke emerges when Joy arrives to pick Malka up from the hospital, where the doctor conveys crucial medical information to Joy in English, excluding Malka from understanding her own treatment. He switches to Hebrew only to suggest to Malka, benignly yet patronizingly, to take a walk on the beach. In retaliation to this infantilization, Malka lashes out not at the doctor but at Joy, who stands with the authority of the doctor's pills in her hand, with the bitterly racist jellyfish remark. Later in the film, when Malka attempts to fire Joy, shouting in Hebrew and German, she is completely defeated by Joy's incomprehension and exhausts herself in the process of trying to convince Joy to leave. Here, Joy's lack of Hebrew knowledge is empowering both in the sense of preventing her from losing her job as well as provoking the tragicomic spectacle of the old woman revealing her own physical need for her unwanted nurse.

CONCLUSION

Both *The Syrian Bride* and *Jellyfish,* when contrasted with the films previously discussed, vividly highlight the increased hostility of expression that may arise due to a lack of mutual intelligibility among Israel's multiplicity of victimized identities. The analyses of bourekas and neo-bourekas films suggest that Hebrew as the shared language of Israeli Jews may have tempered the cinematic expression of anger, resentment, and criticism of ethnocultural discrimination through the visual and verbal languages of ethnic humor. The positive slant of this humor is perhaps tied to the old popular sentiment of *"kulanu yehudim"* that pervades much of the bourekas (and to a large degree also the neo-bourekas) genre, promising the reconciliation of the Mizrahi-Ashkenazi social inequities through shared laughter and, in many cases, ethnic intermarriage. Recent films have emerged that deal with intra-Jewish ethnic discrimination head-on, such as the independent low-budget *Vasermil* (2007); in this film, the characters are essentially flat representatives of their ethnic types, yet not in a way that allows for irony or humor—almost the opposite of the bourekas *Halfon Hill Doesn't Answer,* in which the stereotyped characters were so comedic that they could hardly be taken seriously at all. This demonstrates the extent to which sociopolitical change in Israel has allowed for new possibilities of cinematic production; it is now possible for filmmakers to critique the ethnically coded socioeconomic disparities between Jews with deadly seriousness, even if it remains more popular and thus commercially profitable to use comedic stereotypes, as seen in the neo-bourekas *A Drop of Luck* and *Bonjour Monsieur Shlomi*.

To some extent, this trajectory is also evident within the films that look beyond the fissures of Israeli Jewish society at the non-Jewish Others in the Israeli cultural landscape, although even in the past such films tended toward a more acerbic use of ethnic stereotyping. However, the films of this group which I have analyzed here, especially *Jellyfish, James' Journey to Jerusalem,* and *Avanti Popolo,* tend to incorporate more negative stereotypes of Israeli Jews than of the Others with whom they interact (such as the characters of Joy, James, and the Egyptian soldiers Khaled and Ghassan), showing the increasing Israeli openness toward self-criticism in recent decades. Israeli directors seem to appreciate the model described by Schweinitz, wherein the absurdly exaggerated stereotype, or even a stereotypical feature embedded within a rounded character (such as Malka's irritability), delivers a social critique while simultaneously providing a source of narrative humor.

Yet while this selective use of the ethnic stereotype remains prevalent in Israeli film, ethnic humor is clearly beginning to take new directions. The diegetic opportunity presented by multilingualism—that of *not* being understood—allows characters (as it does real people) to express the prejudices born of victimization more aggressively, without couching them in the disarming comic facade that Freud imagined to be necessary for those with precarious situational power. However, while the new cinematic trend may be more confrontational in its open mockery, it still reflects a desire to cope with the paradoxes of Israeli cultural inequality through laughter as opposed to outright hostility or violence, true to the Freudian paradigm. In any case, the omnipresence of ethnic humor in Israeli cinema and its many variations merits thoughtful analysis to perceive its simultaneous reflection and construction of Israeli society. We laugh not simply out of the possibility for self-recognition offered by these ethnic jokes and caricatures, but also because we are both amused and troubled by what they tell us about the politics of cultural hierarchies and our place within them.

NOTES

1. The terms "ethnicity" and "race" are highly vexed in the Jewish-Zionist context, and it would be too lengthy of a digression to fully interrogate if/how these terms can be appropriately applied to/against Jews. For the purposes of this chapter, and with full acknowledgment of the ensuing reductionism, I adopt, if not condone, the Zionist delineation of Jews as a race among other non-Semitic races (Africans, Asians, Europeans), although I am here lumping the representation of such non-Jews in Israel under the more flexible purview of ethnic humor. By ethnicity I am referring to the socially constructed concept of an essentialized, biologically inherited identity which is performed to the outside world through articulations of a specific (Arab, Ashkenazi, Russian) culture. Finally, regardless of the Semitic argument, the ethnic-cultural divide between Israeli Jews and Palestinians has frequently been configured by Israelis as a "racial" one. For more on this issue, see Raz Yosef, "Homoland: Interracial Sex and the Israeli-Palestinian Conflict in Israeli Cinema," *GLQ* 8, no. 4 (2002): 553–79; Carol Bardenstein, "Cross/Cast: Passing in Israeli and Palestinian Cinema," in *Palestine, Israel and the Politics of Popular Culture*, ed. Rebecca L. Stein and Ted Swedenburg (Durham, N.C.: Duke University Press, 2005); and of course Ella Shohat, *Israeli Cinema: East/West and the Politics of Representation*, 2nd ed. (London: I. B. Tauris, 2010).
2. I use the term "Mizrahi" throughout this article in reference to Jewish immigrants to Israel from the Middle East, North Africa, and the predominantly Muslim areas of the Caucasus and Central Asia. Although this term is anachronistic until the late 1970s, I maintain it for consistency.
3. Ilan Pappé, "Post-Zionism and Its Popular Cultures," in Stein and Swedenburg, *Palestine, Israel and the Politics of Popular Culture*, 86.
4. Ibid.
5. Nirit Anderman, "The Book of Rachel," *Haaretz*, April 11, 2010.
6. Shohat, *Israeli Cinema*.
7. See Judd Ne'eman, "The Death Mask of the Moderns: A Genealogy of 'New Sensibility' Cinema in Israel," *Israel Studies* 4, no. 1 (1999): 100–128.
8. Olga Gershenson and Dale Hudson, "New Immigrant, Old Story: Framing Russians on the Israeli Screen," *Journal of Film and Video* 60 (2008): 25–41.
9. Yosefa Loshitzky, *Identity Politics on the Israeli Screen* (Austin: University of Texas Press, 2001), xiv.
10. Sigmund Freud, *Jokes and Their Relation to the Unconscious* (New York: Norton, 1960), 122.

11. See Samuel Juni and Bernard Katz, "Self-Effacing Wit as a Response to Oppression: Dynamics in Ethnic Humor," *Journal of General Psychology* 128 (2001): 119–42, and Joseph Boskin and Joseph Dorinson, "Ethnic Humor: Subversion and Survival," *American Quarterly* 37 (1985): 81–97.
12. Samer Shehata, "The Politics of Laughter: Nasser, Sadat and Mubarek in Egyptian Political Jokes," *Folklore* 103 (1992): 75–91.
13. Interestingly, some psychologists have found a correlation between racial prejudice and preference for aggressive humor; see Gordon Hodson, Cara MacInnis, and Jonathan Rush, "Prejudice-Relevant Correlates of Humor Temperaments and Humor Styles," *Personality and Individual Differences* 49 (2010): 546–49.
14. Here, I am not engaging with Foucault's broader work on power but rather with a specific facet, most clearly articulated in *The History of Sexuality, Volume 1* (New York: Vintage, 1990, 93): "It is the moving substrate of force relations which, by virtue of their inequality, constantly engender states of power, but the latter are always local and unstable.... [Power] is produced from one moment to the next, at every point, or rather in every relation from one point to another."
15. Shohat, *Israeli Cinema*, 119.
16. Jörg Schweinitz, *Film and Stereotype: A Challenge for Cinema and Theory*, trans. Laura Schleussner (New York: Columbia University Press, 2011), 44.
17. Regrettably, the Palestinians—both Israeli citizens and those in the occupied territories—are glaringly absent from the analyses I have included in this chapter, and there is no reason to believe that the analytical framework I use here could not be applied to the representation of Palestinians in Israeli cinema. The absence is primarily due to structural and space constraints within a piece that is an outgrowth of work I have done on the place of Mizrahim in Israeli national culture, and, simply put, the Palestinian case is deserving of far more space and analytical depth than could presently be included. Thankfully, there is quite a good body of literature examining the representation of Palestinians in Israeli cinema, including many of the works cited here. See, among others, the works of Nurith Gertz on Israeli and Palestinian cinema; Shohat, *Israeli Cinema*; Loshitzky, *Identity Politics*; Raz Yosef, *Beyond Flesh: Queer Masculinities and Nationalism in Israeli Cinema* (New Brunswick, N.J.: Rutgers University Press, 2004); Stein and Swedenburg, *Palestine, Israel and the Politics of Popular Culture*; and Miri Talmon and Yaron Peleg, eds., *Israeli Cinema: Identities in Motion* (Austin: University of Texas Press, 2011).
18. Compelling and opposing interpretations of these films are offered by both Shohat's *Israeli Cinema* and Yaron Peleg's "From Black to

White: Changing Images of Mizrahim in Israeli Cinema," *Israel Studies* 13 (2008): 122–45.

19. Fascinatingly, the line "What, have you become Ashkenazim?" is (mis)translated in the official English subtitles as only "What are you?" I can only speculate on the reasoning behind this omission, but it certainly indicates the general lack of foreign awareness of Israel's Ashkenazi-Mizrahi cultural divide (at least among English-speaking audiences), hence the subtitlers' choice to gloss over this Israeli ethnic inside joke in the translation.
20. See Yaron Shemer's "Trajectories of Mizrahi Cinema," in Talmon and Peleg, *Israeli Cinema: Identities in Motion,* for his delineation of neo-bourekas and post-bourekas film representations of Mizrahi identity.
21. Text transcribed from the English subtitles.
22. For detailed analyses of the cinematic representation of Mizrahi masculinity, and gendered ethnicity more broadly, see Yosef, *Beyond Flesh;* Peleg, "From Black to White"; Yaron Peleg, "Ecce Homo: The Transfiguration of Israeli Manhood in Israeli Films" in Talmon and Peleg, *Israeli* Cinema; and Nurith Gertz, "Space and Gender in the New Israeli and Palestinian Cinema," *Prooftexts* 22, no. 1–2 (2002): 157–85.
23. For another reading of this scene, interpreted in light of the Palestinian actors cast to play the Egyptian characters, see Carol Bardenstein, "Cross/Cast: Passing in Israeli and Palestinian Cinema."
24. Transcribed from the Hebrew dialogue: *"Kakhah zeh tamid, 'im shaḥor lo tov aval 'im hayah lavan hayah beseder. . . . Rak ha-tseva kove'a."*
25. For more on the Ashkenazi identification of Mizrahim as "black Jews" in Israeli history, see, for example, Samuel Koenig, "East Meets West in Israel," *Phylon* 17, no. 2 (1956): 167–71, as a historical document; and the work of Sami Shalom Chetrit, such as *Intra-Jewish Conflict in Israel: White Jews, Black Jews* (New York: Routledge, 2010).
26. Transcribed from the English subtitles.
27. Transcribed from the Hebrew dialogue. The English subtitles perhaps represent this dehumanization even more strongly: Malka: "Tovah had a wonderful Philippine woman, experienced . . ." [. . .] Galia: "If I get you a new one, will you be happy?"
28. Transcribed from the English subtitles.

5

THE LAUGHTER OF YOUSSEF CHAHINE

NAJAT RAHMAN

With the passing of Youssef Chahine (1926-2008), one of the most notable and iconic filmmakers in the Arab world, critics have begun to contend with his remarkable cinematic legacy, one with a distinct sensibility for humor.[1] A diverse cinematic career, spanning nearly forty films and sixty years, earned him recognition at home and abroad, most notably a Cannes Lifetime Achievement Award. He is inextricably linked to the aesthetic and humorous ethos of Egyptian cinema, one of the world's oldest and most prolific with regard to comedies. The development of national cinemas in other Arab countries has in many cases been in response to the Egyptian model.[2]

While humor in Middle Eastern films can sometimes be simply entertaining or escapist, in Egyptian cinema, and especially in Chahine's films, humor is most commonly deployed as a social critique. In the context of a critical everyday defined by "political oppression and economic deprivation," Chahine's cinematic humor reflects on social issues, and it is aligned in favor of the poorer classes, showing the resourcefulness and the dignity of the poor in the face of everyday challenges. The humor projected in this cinema, according to Terri Ginsberg and Chris Lippard, is "dark, absurdist, sardonic . . . or conversely, over-the-top kitsch and camp."[3] While humor in Chahine's films can also be subtle, not always translating culturally, films such as *Alexandria, Why?* (*Iskindiria . . . Leh?*, 1978); *Cairo Station* (*Bab al Hadid*, 1958); and *Cairo as Told by Chahine* (*Al Qahira Minawara bi Ahlaha*, 1991), have been able to translate this humor. Such humor emanates from every aspect of Chahine's filmmaking, from the visual narration, the play of sounds, the interplay between pathos and hilarity, the verbal bantering, and the physical language.

In addition to its social indictment, humor in his films expresses and reinforces social connection. It engages the emotions, both solemn and lighthearted. It is also closely connected to ethical and to political concerns. If it is aggressive and seemingly incongruous, it remains meaningful, for it is against the absurd and the farcical in history. A humorous aesthetic counters repressive social and political structures and norms, and so it bears a promise of transformation and of freedom.

CHAHINE'S FILMMAKING

Chahine, who studied film in the United States (at the Pasadena Playhouse in Los Angeles), worked most of his life in Egypt. His films, preoccupied with Egypt's history and future, a preoccupation that can be situated within a broader concern for Middle Eastern societies, had limited international distribution, and were often subject to censorship as well as to threats from fundamentalists.[4] Foremost among his concerns are Egypt's colonial past and its critical present in a neoliberal economy.[5] His films represent the struggles of the poor and of the middle class as well as his own struggles growing up in Alexandria. Alexandria figures prominently in his films, as does Cairo, and it is evoked in its cosmopolitan past and possibility, emblematic of the fruitful mixing of ideas and of peoples.[6] Notwithstanding his depictions of the complexities of Egyptian life, his films, according to Waleed Marzouk, "retain the appeal and energy of mainstream genre cinema. Their combination of popular culture and artistic sophistication give them a certain ambiguity, as well as a rare exuberance and eclecticism."[7]

All his films retain a humanistic and cosmopolitan sensibility. Many of his humorous and filmic flourishes can be seen in his later films, with diverse styles from realism and melodrama to musicals and comedies.[8] While we focus on *Alexandria, Why?*, *Cairo Station*, and *Cairo as Told by Chahine*, films that traverse different periods of the director's career and reveal the span of his art over thirty-five years, many of his other films deserve to be revisited and studies. These films also display very different humoristic modalities and cinematic styles, as discussed below.

Chahine's films, though critically acclaimed, were received with ambivalence by his Egyptian audiences, most scholars attributing this to his formal and thematic experimentations, which include a hybrid of genres, for instance, or the focus on autobiography, or the tackling of sexual identity. His filmography is now archived at the Cinémathèque de France but is not readily available in Egypt.[9] Chahine, however, was cognizant of the absence of an audience at home: "It's very troubling to enter a theatre to find [only] four guys sitting there. . . . What did I do it for?"[10]

Chahine's modes of humor, especially in such important films as *The Ring Seller* (*Baya' al khawatim*, 1965) and *The Sixth Day* (*Al Yawm al-sadis*, 1986), show the depth as well as the extensive and diverse use of humor in his films, from the spontaneous and light-hearted humor that establishes a close connection between characters to darker humor that signals critique. *The Ring Seller*, for instance, is a musical comedy about a village that is anticipating an annual feast of wedding engagements, where the *mukhtar* or village elder invents a story with a frightening figure named Rajeh to entertain the villagers and keep them in check. The film presents theatrical twists and turns, with the invented figure Rajeh unexpectedly becoming real and arriving in the village as a ring seller on the day of engagements, taking the *mukhtar*'s niece as bride for his own son. In addition to wordplay and rhymed speech throughout the film, humor also ensues from slapstick scenes. Humor in Chahine's films evolved over his career from the physical to the more abstract, from the light-hearted to the melancholic, and from spontaneity to a complex visual language. As an example of a slapstick scene, in *The Ring Seller* villagers throw water at one another, playing insouciantly like children. The humor is hardly elicited from "mechanical inelasticity," as Bergson had proposed. In another example, the sight of characters slapping each other is made all the more humorous by a Foley track featuring exaggerated slapping sounds. Again, the physical humor is lively rather than deadened and suggests a vital humor that expands Bergson's vision. In its happy ending, as befitting a musical comedy with a fairly timeless marriage plot, the film is a celebration of fictional invention. There is in the film's conclusion a wink toward the power of the imagination and of fiction, in which lies fabricated in jest have transformative powers and take hold in reality. Fiction brings magic to the everyday, speaking to people's desires and fears.

Chahine's films are imbued with humor, even when poetically treating such somber subjects as a grandmother tending to her loved ones as they die from cholera. This is the situation in *The Sixth Day*, in which humor adds depth even if it is from social bantering that diffuses tension or excessive emotion. Humor here adds a certain texture and complexity to human relations and sentiments, lending dignity to what may otherwise become overpowering emotion in the face of abject adversity. Humor becomes a distancing device that mitigates powerful emotions while registering the silence of the unsaid.

If Bergson has argued that laughter is fundamentally human,[11] he also seems to have reduced the notion of the human to the mechanized in the context of industrialized societies. Humor, he wrote, ensues from mechanical repetition that signals a certain death in living beings. The comical is characterized first and foremost by *"mechanical inelasticity,"* whether "introduced into nature" or into "regulation of society."[12] Laughter, significantly, is a response to a certain mechanism that we witness or that we elicit. As Bergson wrote, "A really living life should never repeat itself.... This deflection of life towards the mechanical is here the real cause of laughter."[13] So we laugh when someone living resembles something mechanical, or when something mechanical is at the heart of someone living. Ultimately, for him, all humans are prone to rigid habits that turn them against themselves and others.[14]

In the film, however, it is vibrant life that surges forth despite the many deaths that history or time delivers. For Bergson proposes that the comic must also be considered in its relation to life. The last scene of *The Sixth Day* is indicative of this: the smile, the hesitant wave, the held-back tear in the goodbye scene. The grandmother Saddiqa has lost everyone and yet she is able to greet life. In Bergson, death reflects a violence of mechanized life, whereas in the film, death is a fluid continuation of life. Seriousness, Bergson reminds us, may signal the burden of choice, the weight of what is most profound in life. Seriousness for him is an indication of freedom.[15] Rather than signaling an indifference or *"absence of feeling,"*[16] laughter in the film is expressive and constitutes a form of social interaction, a freely entered interaction, as Bergson also argues.[17]

In *Alexandria, Why?*, *Cairo Station*, and *Cairo as Told by Chahine* (1991), humor emerges as multi-valenced, at once spontaneous and profound.

ALEXANDRIA, WHY?

Alexandria, Why? (1978) is the first of an autobiographical trilogy that includes *An Egyptian Story* (1982) and *Alexandria, Again and Forever* (1990). (Sometimes *Alexandria . . . New York* [2004] is considered part of what may be a tetralogy.) The three films contain the themes and techniques emblematic of Chahine's cinema: the struggle against repression, the imbrication of the political and the personal, and the expression of homosexual desire. Humorous ambience permeates the films as does complex plotting and preoccupation with character.

An ironic and self-conscious reflection on representation imbues all three. As Pamela Nice indicates, "There are films within films, plays, performances, and the quintessential 'acting' character, Hamlet."[18] *Alexandria, Why?* is considered the most notable film in the trilogy, precisely because of a historical resonance that gives it more coherence and depth.

Humor in this film is exemplified by ironic self-referentiality and scenes characterized by farce, parody, surrealism, and gaiety. In fact, laughter becomes part of the formal experimentation in the film, as shown below, and allows for new understanding. Laughter is accompanied here by the perspectives of the colonized and the minorities, thus becoming critical in deconstructing dominant visions of history; but laughter is also humanistic in that it allows the audience to go beyond the demarcations of history. Thus we relate to characters and we laugh with them, not on the basis of how they are situated in history and not on the basis of their collective identity.

Alexandria, Why? constitutes a departure from Chahine's other work of musicals, melodramas, and epics.¹⁹ It is a hybrid, eclectic, and introspective work with complex and multiple stories and styles, utilizing autobiography, history, drama, farce, parody, surrealism, realism, and performance.²⁰ It is this striking emphasis on parody, the farcical, and the ironically self-referential that constitutes this humorous and subversive vision of history, providing another perspective on an important period in Egypt's history and deconstructing other received narratives.

Set in Alexandria during World War II, when the Egyptians are under British occupation and the Germans are advancing on Alexandria, Yahya, the main character in the film, is loosely based on Chahine: he is a student who wants to be an actor and finally leaves to study in the United States. Growing up in a context of Egyptian nationalism in Egypt, we follow through his life other historical developments. For instance, we are introduced to an Egyptian aristocrat who kidnaps and falls in love with a young man from Dover who is eventually killed, and a Jewish woman who flees Egypt and the advancing Germans with her family and who is disillusioned by Zionism in Palestine.²¹ The characters and their predicaments are very serious, for they are living through war, exile, economic harship: but the filmic representation of these lives is what elicits the humor.

The coming of age of Yahya/Chahine is paralleled by the story of Egypt coming into its own after World War II. The personal and national stories reflect one another in revealing losses and disappointments as well as people caught in the devastating upheavals of history. We see this in terms of the effects on Yahya, Yahya's father, and on the lives of those around them: the father loses his livelihood and possessions (the house furnishings, most visibly); the lovers are separated by war; Yahya leaves.

The coming of age of the cineaste is also a coming of age of cinema in Egypt. This coming of age cannot be extricated from a colonial history and an imperial transition from a European hegemony to an American one. Nascent in this film are many of the themes and questions that preoccupied the filmmaker: the question of Palestine, the ruling classes of Egypt, gender identity, relations to others, and self-realization.

Malek Khoury sees the film as highlighting national identity that embodies social and cultural diversity: "Chahine's cinema of the late 1970s and beyond helped initiate a bold cinematic examination of Arab national identity with an eye for celebrating its social and cultural heterogeneity."[22] For instance, Chahine's evocation of anticolonial struggle reveals this struggle in all its complexity. As Robert Stam and Ella Shohat write: "Subplots offer a multi-perspective study of Egyptian society, describing how different classes, ethnicities, and religions—working class communists, aristocratic Muslim homosexuals, middle-class Egyptian Jews, petit-bourgeois Catholics—react to Egyptian experience."[23] The film also coincided with the Camp David Accords (1978) and the formal Egypt-Israel peace treaty (1979). The accord was a bilateral agreement between Egypt and Israel, ultimately diminishing the capacity of Palestinians to negotiate and further marginalizing them.[24]

In the question that Chahine poses in the title of his film, there is an address to the city—the city as place, as history, and as a cartography of a certain subjectivity. The effect of such an address leaves the future open and uncertain. But there is also an interrogation, left open-ended, the nature of which cannot be fully fathomed. There is, furthermore, an accusation in that interrogation: Why? All these are inextricable from the question of cinema's relation to the place, to myth, and to history. This aporetic question reflects the aporetic humor we witness in the last scene with the laugh of the Statue of Liberty. The laughter is enigmatic, aimed at both the new arrivals to Ellis Island and, with some bitterness, at the turns of history, mainly the turn from British colonialism in Egypt to an increasing American dominance in the region.

In all his films, a certain humor meets a solemn history. One finds a gaiety in his cinema, no manner how dire the historical. The opening scenes of *Alexandria, Why?* are emblematic: long panoramic shot of the sea in Alexandria, the sounds of waves, laughter, echoes of distant conversations, sights of people relishing the day in the sun at the beach and diving into the sea, eliciting a light, gay exuberance in juxtaposition with black-and-white footage of war mobilization in Great Britain and Germany. The distance between those realities is collapsed later in the film in the school play that has the war as its theme, as the ambassador of Great Britain watches in an atmosphere of almost juvenile hilarity as the city outside is being shelled. While the cinematic juxtapositions are stark, as are the farcical effects of humor, the engagement of emotions between the solemn, the sad, the lighthearted, and the exuberant are so subtle as to be barely distinguishable.

Humor follows the same flitting movement as dance in the film. Dance scenes abound in the film. For instance, the scene in which the family's furnishings are confiscated begins with the father frustrated and venting. He is alone with the mother in their room as their possessions are being confiscated; feeling powerless, he expresses his anger about the fact that the son wants to be an actor and not an engineer, about the high cost of living, including the expense of their son's private school education. As he wonders aloud with his wife about how things got to be so wrong, the son and daughter burst into the room. The daughter announces that Nona, the overtaxing grandmother, is trying to make jam but lacks sugar. The son jumps in by telling the others that Nona is missing other ingredients as well. The atmosphere has already shifted into one of farcical but realistic hilarity following the father's rants and raves. Then he continues in this vein, shouting that not only does Nona lack the ingredients necessary to make the jam but she will soon lack the chair on which to sit as she makes it. He asks the son and daughter if she had told them about the confiscation of the furniture, to which they both burst out, "You bet!" Everyone collapses in sympathetic laughter, a moment of family bonding against adversity.

In another scene, the son, Yahya, declines to go to a friend's party since he does not have and cannot afford the right clothes. His mother insists that he should go. The scene is somber when the son sees that the money for his blazer that he was expecting went toward the purchase of his sister's dress. Moved when he sees that she looks quite beautiful in it, he dances with her, an exuberant and light-hearted dance that transforms the scene from sadness to gaiety.

While the film abounds with such subtleties and complexities, its interpretation of history comes dangerously close to farce, implying a certain amount of buffoonery, play, and crudeness in how history has played out in Egypt and in the region. This farcical humor is exemplified in the last shot of the film. After a heart-wrenching departure in which the son leaves home and family for the first time in order to pursue his dream of studying to be an actor in America, and after a long and wearisome crossing of the ocean, we see the Statue of Liberty as the ship approaches the shore of Liberty Island. At that moment we have a vivid impression of the distance between the two worlds as we gaze at both the solemnity of the statue and of the young man looking up at it; then, before our eyes, the statue becomes animated with a frank éclat of laughter, like a toothless bon vivant, almost like the Egyptian woman in the cabaret scene who sings while the soldier from Dover wanders around inebriated before he meets his destiny. And we wonder: Is America having the last laugh? Is Chahine laughing in the face of history?

The effervescent humor from earlier in the film, some of which coincides with dance scenes, is juxtaposed here with this almost insolent laughter of Lady Liberty. Perhaps this is really what is most intriguing here in terms of humor: how do we understand this unexpected laugh that jolts us from the scene in which we see this promising arrival? The first glimpse of this figure of freedom is veiled in an aura of reverence and hope. Her beacon of light is suddenly transformed through the animation of the statue's laughter into bitter, incomprehensible disappointment. The promise that the young man sees in this statue is altered before our eyes into rigid animation: the lofty bearer of ideals becomes a toothless crone! The laugh of the animated statue is not a gay laugh; it is sordid and disturbing, aggressive and overpowering. After the trials of his trip away from home, from family, from the world he has known, Yahya is confronted with laughter that is solitary and derisory, frank and denigrating, in contrast to the laughter in most of the film that affirms togetherness and relatedness. The film shows laughter primarily as a way to connect, to endure together, to express gaiety, and to release tension. And yet, the ending shows the dark shadow of history cast over many little lives. Samir Farid insists, however, that *Alexandria, Why?* is about "human connection at a time of war."[25]

Laughter in this final scene is not one of pleasure, nor does it induce pleasure. This laughter is jarring amidst the music we hear, a music that reinforces the solemnity and romanticism of the occasion. Humor is also part of the culture of enjoying jokes and laughter, a way of maintaining a certain bearing in a war enmeshed with tensions. For instance, laughing at oneself, as the father does after venting his anger as his goods are being confiscated, is a way to maintain dignity in the face of adversity. In this final, aggressive laughter of the Statue of Liberty, we may be seeing Chahine's evocation of the triumph of history over the little stories of Yahya and his family.

While Chahine made many films after this one, *Alexandria, Why?* remains one of his signature works, as well as a landmark of Egyptian cinema and of cinema's representation of history. Humor affects our own reading of the film and our response to it: it engages us despite the sometimes heavy autobiographical moments, and despite a particularly difficult period of history, the period in which the film takes place. It allows us to respond to the film's critical position with more openness, and it wills us to ask questions at the end about cinema's engagement of history through humor. It also allows us to enjoy the inventiveness of the filmmaker and his characters.

CAIRO STATION

Cairo Station (1958) is another landmark film in Chahine's career, an experimental work that represented a departure from Arab cinema of the time. The film's formal experimentation alienated audiences, however, and Chahine would later speak about the film's painful failure upon release.[26] But the negative response from audiences, which led to the film being banned for the dark image it purportedly presents of Egypt, was not shared by multiple critics, who described the film as "a jewel in the history of Arab cinema," "the single most influential film in that cinema's history," "revolutionary at the time in both its form and its content," and "an idiosyncratic mixture of neorealist social commentary, grotesque horror, and lighthearted comedy."[27] Like *Alexandria, Why?* the film is notable for its social preoccupation, but it differs in that here the humor cohabits with the horrific. If *Alexandria, Why?* was framed by the lighthearted laughter on the beach before the war and the sinister laughter of the Statue of Liberty, with laughter indicating the turns of history, humor in *Cairo Station* withdraws in the face of the abject. If in *Alexandria, Why?* humor is exuberant in its everyday nature, lighthearted and aimed at calling attention to social contradictions when it comes to class, gender, generation, and relations of Arab countries with the West, the framing of *Cairo Station* is solemn and dark.

The story centers on Qinawi, a young man who is rendered abject due to his physical lameness and the social handicap that ensues from such a condition. Found at the railway station, Qinawi is given employment and a little kiosk for lodging by the newspaper vendor. Qinawi soon develops a passion for Hanouma, a soft-drink seller engaged to Abou Shri', who is attempting to organize all the workers of the station into a union. While all the characters in the film are struggling to survive in terms of physical necessities, Qinawi is especially frustrated and angry: barely eking out a living, he is outside any social order due to the stigmatization of his physical condition, a disability that limits his hope for love and for his future. He carries a folder filled with pictures of scantily clad women from magazines as he attempts to sell his newspapers. Both sets of papers find themselves fluttering in the air at different times in the station. This has both a comic and tragic effect. It is comical when the newspapers are mixed up with the magazine pictures, as if the serious economic and political news of the country has become comparable to the frustrated desires represented by the photos. It is tragic, too, for these pictures indicate not only Qinawi's withdrawal from the sociopolitical reality he is selling, but also how this reality has no place for him. Intrinsic to Chahine's cinematic art is a social consciousness; as he stated in an interview: "You can't be an artist if you don't know the social, the political and the economical context.... If you talk about the Egyptian people, you must know about their problems."[28] Qinawi's anger, then, seems also to relate to his social frustrations and to his work. In addition to Qinawi's interest in Hanouma and her imminent marriage to Abou Shri' is the rivalry between Hanouma and another character over selling cold drinks and Abou Shri's role in mobilizing workers against their economic exploitation and neglect.

In this film noir, where hilarity meets horror, there is an overwhelming pathos that emerges from the beginning and ending, which are shot in black and white and overshadow the humor in the rest of the film. The humor functions to reinforce a social critique. The film's music, as well as its somber beginning and ending and the narration of 'Am Mabtoul, the newspaper vendor who finds Qinawi in the station, already anticipates the tragic end of Qinawi. The voiceover prologue narrated by the newspaper vendor concludes with the narrator asking this ominous if rhetorical question to the absent Qinawi: "Who would have thought that what happened to you would happen to you?"[29]

Humor occurs throughout the film in both the physical language of the characters and in their verbal bantering, especially of Hanouma. Humor emanates from her body language, from her coquettishness, from an awareness of her sensuality and her exaggerated movements that deploy it. Humor here is found in not taking oneself seriously but also in expressing a certain joyfulness and vivaciousness even in the context of deprivation. The women, for example, banter with one another on marriage and marriage partners as a way of bonding. In one scene, the women are relaxing in a group when Hanouma joins them. They tease her about Qinawi, how he only has eyes for her, how she is leading him on, how she will leave Abou Shri' and marry him. The feigned indignation of Hanouma only adds to the atmosphere of hilarity. In another scene, they taunt her good-naturedly about her marriage to Abou Shri' and how lucky she is, and as she taunts back the scene develops into a playful water fight.

However, in contrast to the above instances of bonding, humor is most complex when connected to Qinawi, who thinks Hanouma will break her engagement with Abou Shri' and marry him instead. This expectation, given the social obstacles he faces—including Hanouma's lack of desire to leave Abou Shri' and to live in a village, not to mention Qinawi's poverty—renders him tragic. Qinawi seems physically influenced by the tramp character of Charlie Chaplin, an example of humor elicited from a certain mechanism of inelasticity. The locale of the train station, with its historical association with colonialism, industrialization, and capitalism, is presented visually in the mechanics of the train's regular movements while passing by, as a space of dislocation, away from home, and a locus of unfulfilled longing and deprivation associated with Qinawi, a loss of hope and of future. Qinawi's dream of being with Hanouma subjects him to ridicule, and his refusal to adapt to the social reality around him and his place in it will lead to his institutionalization. It is such blind mechanization that leads to destruction, the film insinuates. Qinawi attempts to kill Hanouma twice after she rejects him, once when he attempts to dupe her to pick up luggage that she needs for leaving the next day, and later in the train as he chases her. This introduces in the film elements of horror, but this horror is partially exaggerated and parodied. The chase scenes create tensions in the viewer who fears for Hanouma but also laughter for reproducing familiar horror scenes in exaggerated form. When we meet Qinawi the first time, he appears half-dead, as if something has died within him. This is reinforced by the first image we see of his face, through the glass of the kiosk that distorts it into something almost cartoonish. His face is a combination of profound sorrow and humor, but others see him only through his lameness, a metonymy that characterizes his whole being and that places him outside the social order.

Sorrow imbues all humor associated with Qinawi. This in itself is a subversion of the Aristotelian take on comedy. Those who are physically maimed are often subjected to ridicule and comic laughter, but Chahine presents us with a sympathetic figure. Humor is ethical here, in its shroud of sorrow and pathos. While the scene in which Qinawi confesses his love to Hanouma includes hilarity and verbal bantering, it also contains a tinge of bitterness. At first the humor between them suspends harsh reality for Qinawi, but then she recalls him to his circumstances. Qinawi then follows Hanouma and insists that he needs to talk to her. After a few jabs at his lameness—she jokes that if she waits for him, they will need a year to arrive at their destination, to which he retorts, "Do you want to race?"—she sits down by the water and he joins her. He presents her with his mother's necklace as a way of proposing to her. She first teases him about whether it is genuine gold and then comments on its *baladi,* country style. As he expresses his affection for her, she becomes dreamy and plays along. When he tells her that she is more beautiful than even the girl in the magazine that he shows her, she responds, "No, you are." They break into uncontrollable laughter when she finally brings him back to the rude reality of his being penniless and that she will never leave Abou Shri'.

The only humor in the film that is purely aggressive and goes unanswered is the tangential joke at the expense of the religious fundamentalists, when we see them crossing paths with Abou Shri' who carries luggage for them as a porter and his uncomprehending facial reaction when he sees them verbally condemning the dance scene before them as if chastising the devil himself. The use of tendentious humor is reserved only for what Abou Shri' perceives as fanatical, reflecting Chahine's sociopolitical critique in the film, aimed at both the exploitation of workers and the denigration of their spiritual lives. Humor in the film is most often melancholic, with an ethical bent. Moreover, humor is part of relating, just as when Hanouma and Qinawi dance and improvise. It is often linked with dancing for Chahine. Dance, like humor, is a particular and intense expression that reinforces relating to another person. However, as in the dance sequence, that possibility is effervescent and provisional, quickly disrupted by others. In the scene, Hanouma is selling soft drinks in the train and moving to the music that is playing when she spots Qinawi watching her. Each begins to dance, she in the train and he outside watching her. As they are carried away by playful gaiety, lost in their dance, a spectator, her soft-drink competitor, calls to Abou Shri', who drags her away unceremoniously.

The last image of the film is of a girl we glimpsed earlier in the film who waits interminably at the station for her lover so she can see him for a few moments as he arrives with his family and leaves on a train. She is now standing alone waiting for her lover. She is also carried by pathos, and she is a parallel figure to Qinawi. She cannot accept that her lover is no longer hers as she waits for him hopelessly. Although he is clearly leaving and can only see her for a few brief seconds at a train station, she cannot accept the reality of their situation, arrested by melancholic rigidity. And so Chahine ends *Cairo Station* with the girl standing alone, an image juxtaposed with humor in a film associated with a certain liveliness, lighthearted bantering, dancing, and connection. If Hanouma depicts a certain desirability and is emblematic of light-hearted laughter and its pleasures, corresponding to the film's light parodies of horror films, the dark aspects of critique are associated with Qinawi and with what robs one of liveliness.

NAJAT RAHMAN

CAIRO AS TOLD BY CHAHINE

Whereas in *Cairo Station* the focus is on one locale on one particular day, here the focus is on an entire city in its teeming vibrancy from dawn to dusk. In this short film, humor is an intricate part of the filmmaker's tribute to the people of Cairo, a people he recognizes for their humor, vitality, endurance, inventiveness, and resourcefulness. Humor here is a way of living with the messiness of life, wrestling with indignity in the face of deprivations, difficulties, and denials, as we witness the monstrosities of urban developments in the city. The humor of Chahine is never an aloof or autonomous expression, but is intermingled with emotion: love and laughter, loss and laughter. The film's title speaks to an intimate vision of Cairo by its leading filmmaker, who is conscious of the history of Western perceptions of the city. After informing a group of students that he has been commissioned by the French to do a film on Cairo, he asks them, "What do you think they expect from us?" The group, wary of depicting Cairo as exotic with its belly dancers and pyramids, offers all the stark details of a reality they consider to be tragedies of the city. The counternarrative to the exotic expectations includes fundamentalism, unemployment, drought, open sewers, housing shortage, and so on. While Chahine's camera does not avoid these problems, he chooses to pay tribute instead to its people rather than to its stones, as he says. Even in the coffee shop, where Chahine smokes his *shisheh,* as mostly old men listen calmly and plaintively to Oum Kalthoum, the camera follows each face, weather-beaten maps of pain and resignation; each face has its own vitality. All the men listen intently to the diva's song, while one young couple is oblivious to both the music and the place, absorbed only in each other.

While humor may function for individuals as an expression of self-assertion or aggression, Chahine shows how humor establishes a social balance, keeps interactions fluid, and gives life dynamism. The sweeping panoramas of the city and its people include personal vignettes. The sounds of roosters announce the dawn, and eclectic music in the streets accompanies the sound of news and the bustle of the market. The film then focuses on a young boy getting ready for school and contending for time in the bathroom with his ill-humored grandfather; the lost time means he misses breakfast. He runs out the door without having eaten, but his mother lowers a bucket into the street with a breakfast sandwich to go. Earlier, everyone else in the family found time to consume their breakfast, including the grandfather. Later, the doting mother boasts about how her son is the best mechanic in the city. as the grandfather sits on a chair in the street facing the window in which the mother appears. As he reads the newspaper, he retorts that the son is "ignorant, incapable of deciphering alphabets!" It is a random vignette in a day in the life of Cairo; we do not encounter these characters again.

The other main vignette is of a brother and his family joining a young (newlywed?) couple in their already cramped studio right next to the train tracks. No private space exists for the young couple. Their lovemaking is a stolen moment in an adjacent space while the family is watching a football match. We glimpse an expression of raw vitality, almost romanticized, in the harsh reality of deprivation. Chahine narrates that what he loves the most is the ability of Cairo's people to be together in cramped spaces without disturbing others. Humor becomes a vehicle and an expression of this exuberant togetherness despite the harsh reality.

The filmmaking itself is humorous: one visual image blends into another, connecting into a powerful narrative. An image of men praying[30] with their shoes aligned next to them triggers images of a woman looking at displays of shoes, which in turn leads to a succession of images following a theme: a publicity photo of women's sexy shoes, women putting on shoes sensually, the sensuality of a foot gliding into a high heel, an unemployed young man, and a lover of English literature who (one presumes has just marketed his own sensuality to the older foreign couple eyeing him) is waiting for a *shawarma* sandwich that is being dressed and undressed sensually at a *shawarma* stand. We then see the young man, after eating the coveted sandwich, watching a movie in a cinema, a movie that reflects on the cynical social disparity between rich and poor.

This is perhaps the most intriguing aspect of Chahine's humor, the visual development, the manipulation of sounds, and the balance he strikes between pathos and hilarity, gaiety and horror, spontaneous laughter and melancholy, all of which constitute his humor in addition to the verbal and physical humor that abounds in his cinema. Humor is so much part of daily life in the city that he chooses to portray it in its most difficult moments. When he portrays humor in relation to the middle class, the humor seems to socially indict: for example, a man advertising apartments for $250,000 on the twenty-third floor so that one does not have to hear all the "ants" below. The humor only serves to make him appear ridiculous; and he is certainly the object of the joke. The man is exaggerated in his clichéd quest for luxury and comfort, it seems. Chahine never seems to lend this quality of ridicule or aggression to the humor emanating from the poorer classes, however. On the contrary, that humor primarily shows the intelligence and self-affirmation of the poor. The commentary in the film that the unemployed English literature student watches at the cinema further reinforces the film's reflections on class issues.

Perhaps theories of humor like that of Bergson have tended to reflect the mechanical individualism of long industrialized societies. In the context of Egyptian cinema, it seems that humor is also a way of expressing, constructing, and reinforcing social connection. As noted in the introduction to this book, many theorists have alluded to the relationship between pain and laughter, to its possibile connectivity; as such, laughter is closely connected to concerns that are larger than social adaptation, to the ethical and the political. If humor can be aggressive and incongruous, it also has the ability to dignify and be meaningful, as in the cinema of Chahine. Since it is the absurd that draws out humor more so than vice, as many have noted, it is against the absurd that this humorous aesthetic finds its expression. Indeed, in Chahine's film, it is the humorous aesthetic that triumphs over repressive social and political structures and norms. In this way, the humorous aesthetic carries a promise of transformation and of genuine freedom.

NOTES

1. On the cinematic legacy of Youssef Chahine, see also Mustafa Darwish, *Dream Makers on the Nile: A Portrait of Egyptian Cinema* (Cairo: American University in Cairo Press, 1998); Ibrahim Fawal, *Youssef Chahine* (London: British Film Institute, 2001); Hamid Hamzaoui, *Histoire du cinema*

Égyptien (Marseille: Éditions Autres Temps, 1997); Viola Shafik, *Popular Egyptian Cinema: Gender, Class, and Nation* (Cairo: American University in Cairo Press, 2007); and Magda Wassef, ed., *Egypte: 100 ans de cinéma* (Paris: Institut du monde arabe, 1994).

2. Chahine, who was influenced by international filmmaking, inspired and influenced in turn a generation of younger filmmakers, including Yousry Nasrallah and Atef Hetata. For a succinct discussion of the history of Egyptian and Arab cinema as well as the film industries in Turkey and in Iran, see the work of Terri Ginsberg and Chris Lippard, *Historical Dictionary of Middle Eastern Cinema* (Toronto: Scarecrow Press, 2010). Ginsberg and Lippard write: "The success and favorable reception of these films led to the establishment of a series of increasingly influential studios, notably Studio Misr, the first production of which, in 1936, positioned Egyptian cinema as a purveyor of genre films, . . . an industry that became, by the 1940's, one of the world's largest and a significant exporter to the neighboring Arab countries." See Terri Ginsberg and Chris Lippard, *Historical Dictionary of Middle Eastern Cinema* (Toronto: Scarecrow Press, 2010), 84. In the wake of Gamal Abdel Nasser's revolution, more socially conscious films were produced. This encouraged a realist aesthetic and the auteur cinema of Chahine.
3. Ginsberg and Lippard, *Historical Dictionary of Middle Eastern Cinema*, 100.
4. Sheila Whitaker, "Obituary-Youssef Chahine: Egyptian Film-maker Who Championed Nationalism and Arab Concerns with an Independent Eye," *The Guardian*, July 28, 2008, www.theguardian.com/film/2008/jul/28/egypt, accessed September 2012.
5. Ginsberg and Lippard, *Historical Dictionary of Middle Eastern Cinema*, 86.
6. A. O. Scott, "Youssef Chahine, Egyptian Filmmaker, Dies at 82," *New York Times*, July 28, 2008. See also Ginsberg and Lippard, *Historical Dictionary of Middle Eastern Cinema*, xiv.
7. Waleed Marzouk, "Love, Anger and Song: Remembering Youssef Chahine, Egypt's Most Eminent Filmmaker," *Ahram Online*, July 15, 2011, english.ahram.org.eg/NewsContentPrint/5/0/16467/Arts—Culture/0/Love,-Anger-and-Song-Remembering-Youssef-Chahine,-.aspx, accessed September 2012.
8. Ginsberg and Lippard, *Historical Dictionary of Middle Eastern Cinema*, 84-85. *Chaos*, Chahine's latest film, was screened at the Venice Film Festival in 2007.
9. Many critics testify to his inventiveness and his resourcefulness: "By founding his own production company, and attracting foreign co-productions (with the Algerian and then French governments) he managed to keep making the movies he wanted to, even as the Egyptian state film system collapsed" (Lindsey, "As Told by Chahine").
10. Chahine was known to say: "I make my films first for myself, then

for my family, then for Alexandria, then for Egypt. If the Arab world likes them, *ahlan wa sahlan* (welcome). If the foreign audience likes them, they are doubly welcome." Quotd in ibid.
11. For Bergson the comic is *human*, both in the sense of not being shared by other species and as a mark of our humanity and its limits. See Henri Bergson, *Laughter: An Essay on the Meaning of the Comic*, trans. Clousdesley Brereton and Fred Rotwell (New York: Macmillan, 1912), 3.
12. Ibid., 10 and 47, emphasis in the original.
13. Ibid., 34.
14. Ibid., 130.
15. Ibid., 79.
16. Ibid., 4, 5, emphasis in the original.
17. Ibid., 6; Igor Krichtafovitch, *Humor Theory: Formula of Laughter* (Denver: Outskirts Press, 2006), 42. Freud has also noted that a social community is constituted around a joke: the teller, the target, and the audience.
18. Pamela Nice, "Youssef Chahine by Ibrahim Fawal," *Al Jadid* 8, no. 41 (2002), www.aljadid.com/content/youssef-chahine-ibrahim-fawal, accessed September 2012.
19. Whitaker, "Obituary-Youssef Chahine."
20. See *Al Ahram Weekly*, July 13–August 6, 2008. See also Lindsey, "As Told by Chahine," and Nice, "Youssef Chahine by Ibrahim Fawal."
21. Ginsberg and Lippard, *Historical Dictionary of Middle Eastern Cinema*, 16.
22. Malek Khouri, *The Arab National Project in Youssef Chahine's Cinema* (Oxford: Oxford University Press, 2010), 124.
23. Ibid., 120.
24. Whitaker, "Obituary-Youssef Chahine."
25. Cited in Khouri, *The Arab National Project in Youssef Chahines Cinema*, 131.
26. Chahine states: "You cannot imagine how it feels when you walk into an empty auditorium in which a film of yours is being shown. I exerted efforts to make this film the like of which I had never made for any of my previous films. My disappointment at its failure was such that for a while I returned to commercial cinema." See *Al Ahram Weekly*, July 13–August 6, 2008.
27. Lindsey, "As Told by Chahine."
28. Scott, "Youssef Chahine, Egyptian Filmmaker, Dies at 82."
29. Whitaker, "Obituary-Youssef Chahine."
30. Chahine did not seem to shy away from criticizing the increasing influence of Islamists in Egypt. Accused of blasphemy and later acquitted for his film *Emigrant* (1994), he was further disturbed by the stabbing of novelist Naguib Mahfouz, both events that motivated his film *Destiny* (1997).

6

COMEDIC MEDIATIONS

War and Genre in *The Outcasts*

SOMY KIM

From across the street of a dark, southern Tehran road we see a woman get hassled by a driver. Suddenly, a man who has been watching the scene on a motorcycle takes a chain, smashes the driver's car window, and pulls him out of the car. From the commotion of the scene we are taken to a prison where the man receives a warm welcome from crowds of inmates chanting repeatedly, "Bravo, brother Majid!" This opening scene of *Ekhrājihā*, or *The Outcasts*, introduces the protagonist of the film, though, as we follow his steps from behind at ground level, he has yet to be unmasked. Significantly, our protagonist is revealed only when he steps out of a car into his neighborhood where he receives the same chanting welcome from his neighbors, who think he has been away on the *hāj* in Mecca.[1] These two scenes stage the main conflict of the film, between Majid's *lūtī*, or thug life, and a pious existence. This tension allows simultaneous critique of and support for the Islamic ideals of the revolution that have been under great debate in Iranian society since the Islamic Revolution.[2]

The Outcasts premiered in Iran in March 2007, and its popularity astonished critics and viewers alike.[3] It generated more than one billion toman in box office receipts in its first month in theaters, a record for an Iranian film.[4] Thirty years after the Islamic Revolution, many critics asked how a comedy about the propagandistic war of the 1980s could win the hearts of the Iranian public in the 2000s. Their surprise was based on the assumption that support for the ideology of the revolution had waned in the past several decades. The first, most visible form of this discontent took the shape of the mass protests and student revolts of 1999. Locally known as "*hijdah-e tir*," or the 18th of Tir, students were killed and imprisoned for their dissenting actions, and many thousands were injured.[5] So what could have appealed to this post-revolution generation of Iranians in a movie about a wayward son finding his way to martyrdom in the Iran-Iraq War? Most reviewers did not take the film seriously enough for critical study, while one scholar located its significance in the way that the film attempted to collapse generational differences and instill a renewed belief in the Islamic Revolutionary ideals through the figure of a marginalized "other" in Iranian society.[6] I elaborate on Narges Bajoghli's claim of reading that difference, but in terms of social class; furthermore, I analyze how the generic conventions of comedic melodrama enabled subversive critique of class difference while maintaining a respect for war veterans. Ultimately, through the incongruity principle of comedy, the film is able to balance the critique of the clerical elite through jokes revolving around religion while still preserving a respect for the cultural memory of the Iran-Iraq War and, consequently, its war veterans.

The Outcasts is a comedic melodrama, set in the 1980s during the Iran-Iraq War. Majid (Kambiz Dirbaz), a local thug from southern Tehran, decides to go to the front in order to prove his worthiness to the father of Narges (Niousha Zeyghami), the girl he wants to marry. His close neighborhood friends, Amir (Arzhang Amirfazli), Bayram (Akbar Abdi), and Bijan (Amin Hayai), and his uncle Mostafa (Alireza Osivand), decide to go with him. However, they are tested and scrutinized by Haj Saleh (Mohammad Reza Sharifinia) on their Islamic knowledge and motivations for going to the front. After a series of antics they are allowed to go, only to be kicked out of training for inappropriate behavior. After Morteza (Javad Hashemi), a neighborhood friend, vouches for them, they are allowed to come back, and Morteza attempts to reform the group. Ultimately, Majid volunteers to go through a minefield and eventually dies a martyr in a tank raid at the end of the film.

Martyrdom in Iran has played an especially formidable role in shaping the popular and visual culture of Iran since the Iran-Iraq

War.[7] During and after the war, the Islamic Republic's culture industry projected images of martyrs onto billboards, films, television shows, textbooks, and postage stamps.[8] Within this national narrative, the soldiers of the war were likened to Husayn, the Prophet Muhammad's grandson, who according to the Shi'i branch of Islam was martyred in what is known as the Karbala massacre. As the war industry appropriated the Karbala narrative, the Iran-Iraq War itself was called the "Sacred Defense"—a defense from the Iraqi enemy. From this ideology emerged the film's director, Masud Dehnamaki, a religious youth who volunteered to go to the front (*jebhe*) when he was sixteen years old; he had hoped to go when he was fourteen.[9] The Advancement of Documentary and Experimental Cinema, which was one of the film production centers created during the period of the establishment of the Islamic Republic, produced *The Outcasts*, Dehnamaki's first feature film. Therefore, those familiar with his work connect him with Islamic revolutionary ideals.

In fact, the more controversial part of the success of *The Outcasts* lies in the tri-partite tension between the religious background of the director, the negative portrayal of the clergy, and the religious reformation of the main characters. Dehnamaki was the former general commander of Hezbollah, notorious for beating students publicly for un-Islamic behavior. While he has denounced his previous extremist actions, critical reviews of his work emphasize his ties to the Revolutionary Guards and his religious devotion. Thus, a film about the reformation of misfits into exemplary martyrs and veterans of the war has highlighted the tension between critical voices and the public at large.

Significantly, however, the generic conventions of comedy enabled *The Outcasts* to appeal not only to audiences otherwise critical of the hegemony of the Islamic Republic's policies, but also to those who could identify with the film's characters. Some identifiable antics are, for example, going through the motions of prayer, frequently misunderstanding religious language, and acting inappropriately carefree in a religious or war environment. While the film's melodramatic aspects and its eventual denouement indicate a kind of glorification of piety and martyrdom, the film's critique of the clerical elite and societal norms, through comedy, offers a parallel reading to the more melodramatic tenor of the film. According to the United Nations, the unemployment rate for youth ages fifteen to twenty-four in Iran in 2007 was at 22.3 percent.[10] Therefore, Amir's drug addiction and Bijan's thievery, along with the group's overall class status, attend to contemporary issues of a failing economy combined with dealing with the cultural policies of the Islamic Republic's rule. Furthermore, while the generic qualities of the comedy appealed to the audiences, its melodramatic traits enabled its public release and approval by the authorities.[11]

Combining elements from comedy and melodrama, *The Outcasts'* popular success came with controversial implications. Along with the film's popularity, its comedic style distinguishes it from other war films that valorize war and martyrdom. A combination of narrative elements results in a layered effect, appealing to the audience more than simply for its denouement. Thus, the continual criticism of the clerical elite, the melodramatic effect of war life, and the brotherhood of the main characters offer an affective panoply of appealing entertainment that contests a reading of the film as merely upholding the ideology of martyrdom and religious reformation.

The lack of serious studies on film comedy in Iran demonstrates that comedy has been traditionally dismissed in critical circles. Significantly, comedy has the potential to be critical of society, not despite but because of its seemingly safe and non-political topics. This innocuous and attractive trait of comedy has allowed it to combine with other genres to create hybrid forms of entertainment. Hence, Geoff King in his book *Film Comedy* argues that comedy is more of a mode than a genre based on its ability to traverse all genres of cinema.[12] For example, the ability of westerns and romances to be comedic has resulted in comedic westerns and romantic comedies.[13] I consider King's definition an apt description for *The Outcasts* being a comedic melodrama.

In Iran, the genre of comedic film has focused on criticizing high society and poking fun at the low, usually the poor. In *Ganj-e Qarun* (Qarun's Treasure, 1965), a poor youth befriends an old man who attempts suicide and discovers that this man is the richest man in town and, incidentally, the father who gave him away as a baby. Like *The Outcasts,* this blockbuster hit of the 1960s criticized the elite through the comedic but heart-warming antics of the protagonists who mean no harm, unlike their elitist counterparts. Significantly, during the period of *filmfarsi,* or popular cinema, alternative cinema began to take shape and formed what critics now consider "New Iranian Cinema" or the "Iranian New Wave."[14] A majority of these dramas, such as Ebrahim Golestan's *Khesht o Ayeneh* (Mud Brick and Mirror, 1965) and Dariush Mehrjui's *Gāv* (The Cow, 1969), criticized the elite as well, but because of the avant-garde nature of the films, they did not appeal to popular audiences the way *filmfarsi* films did. Interestingly, criticizing the elite has endured as a particularly compelling theme in both dramatic and comedic Iranian films.

The main principle guiding the comedic effects of *The Outcasts* can be explained through the concept of incongruity. The incongruity principle constitutes one of the three main attempts at theorizing the function of the comic. While superiority theory reads humor as ensuing from one entity feeling superior to another, such as audience members feeling a sense of superiority over the characters in the film, relief theory argues that humor relieves tension in the film. Incongruity theory, unlike these other two, locates the power of humor in the dissonance between the expectations of the viewer and the occurrence of the humorous response. One of the earliest incongruity theorists, Immanuel Kant, defines laughter as "an affection arising from the sudden transformation of expectation into nothing."[15] In *The Outcasts* the melodrama of the story is punctuated by various incongruous moments of unexpected situational impropriety.

While comedy hinges on the delicate interplay between cinematic devices and social norms, comedy as a genre has been generally understudied in the realm of Iranian film studies. Significantly, numerous critics of Iranian cinema have noted the attention paid to art cinema over popular cinema, such as popular drama and comedy; but that contentious issue is one repeated in film studies as a whole, and has much more to do with the establishment of films studies as a legitimate field in critical studies than with the particularity of Iranian cinema studies emphasizing art films. Along with its non-elite status as a comedy, *The Outcasts* has been dismissed by critics who consider it to be merely a crowd-pleasing movie directed by a former Hezbollah general. Dehnamaki, a war veteran and ardent supporter of the revolution's founding principles, had produced only two documentary films before this feature. *The Outcasts* imagines the narrative of the everyman, reflecting the director's roots in the poor eastern district of

Tehran. And this everyman narrative indexes the genres of comedy, melodrama, and war, all under the umbrella of *filmfarsi*.

Filmfarsi began as a derogatory term and still carries with it a judgment in critical Iranian circles. First coined by the film critic and historian Dr. H. Kavoosi, the term refers to mainstream cinema without any philosophical message, merely produced for entertainment.[16] This sentiment echoes contemporary critics' assessments of comedy in Iran. In a special issue of *Soureh Cinema* on comedy, critics decry the state of dismal affairs in Iran concerning their comedy. Jamshid Sedagatnejad claims Iran has no comedy because this genre is rooted in comedians like Charlie Chaplin, and in the case of Iran the censorship of comedians prevents them from expressing their full creativity.[17] Because of this drawback, Sedagatnejad claims there are "funny films," but not comedic films in Iran, a critical stance on comedy in Iran shared by other writers in the special issue. However, the claim that the genre of comedy does not exist in Iran is largely based on its comparison with the history of comedy in the United States.

The *filmfarsi* comedies of the Pahlavi period saw a history of popular success that came under scrutiny during the transition period under the Islamic Republic. For example, two comedic films, *Shabneshini dar Jahannam* (A Party in Hell, 1957) and *Mohallel* (The Go-Between, 1971), were the basis for imprisoning the film producer Mehdi Misaqiyeh. Not only did revolutionaries burn down his Capri cinema, but he also was arrested and beaten for "insulting Islam by parodying it."[18] These films, in particular, "made fun of the religious haji types' greed, parsimony, and duplicity."[19] The shift from a newly minted Islamic republic needing to establish its legitimacy to the incumbent government attempting to hold on to any credibility serves as one of the differentials between these contexts. This historical and political difference can explain the formal necessity of *The Outcasts* to set up a hierarchy of piety that contrasts "good" religious figures with "bad" or misguided ones. In contrast with the former comedies directly critiquing and parodying religious figures, *The Outcasts* attempts to rectify the caricaturish representation of religious characters and thus provides a more nuanced and believable set of characters, while pleasing both the authorities and more moderate filmgoers.

Significantly, the main theme bearing on social class in *The Out-*

casts dominates the controversial criticism surrounding it. Thus, reviewers were disappointed with its enormous success and appeal to the general public, for both its lack of aesthetic merit and its threat to the sanctity of the "Sacred Defense."[20] Indeed, those reviewers who took issue with its lack of artistic quality conceded they "must not understand [their] people at all" if such a "simple" comedy could be so entertaining.[21] While this particular reviewer wrote for a youth-directed critical culture magazine, *40cheragh*, a reviewer for the popular film magazine *Donya-e Tasvir* was offended that the film desecrated the sanctity of the war by joking about it.[22] This implies the film is offensive not only to the memories of those who died, but also to the living war veterans. The reviewer attributed the success of the film to the novelty of hearing jokes made about the war, something he found did not make up for the weak plot and lack of character development.[23] All these reviews highlight a particularly significant difference, based on social class and cultural capital, within the cultural makeup of Iranian critical discourse. Pierre Bourdieu's central thesis in *Distinction: A Social Critique of the Judgment of Taste* resonates in this instance, whereby taste "functions as a sort of social orientation, a 'sense of one's place,' guiding the occupants of a given . . . social space towards the social positions adjusted to their properties, and towards the practices or goods which befit the occupants of that position."[24] For these reviewers, comedy as a genre is either not conducive to critical study or not an appropriate mode or genre for serious topics. Interestingly, the former sentiment is expressed in a critical cultural magazine with a more secular, upper class base, while the latter represents a magazine with a broader, more popular audience with concerns about religiosity. Ultimately, disagreements in critical circles concerning the film had much more to do with the ways those communities defined their own social orientation in relation to the film. These disagreements around the film, regarding offensiveness and lack of artistic merit, suggests not only that it has meant something different for different audiences but that the difference has, at some level, been delineated through differences in social class.

Along with comedy and *lūti*-themed cinema, *The Outcasts* builds on the war cinema that preceded its release. During and after the Iran-Iraq War, the Islamic Republic created cinematic institutions like the Farabi Cinema Foundation and Ayat Film Studio[25] in order to support local filmmaking in Iran and to capitalize on the ability of cinema to reach mass audiences. Thus, the beginnings of a formidable film production emerged out of a war culture industry and the Islamic Republic's efforts to legitimize its power during this period.[26] However, while the melodramatic parts of *The Outcasts* share some dramatic characteristics with standard war films like *From Karkhe to Rhine* (1993) or *Ajans-E Shisheh-I (The Glass Agency)* (1997), both directed by Ebrahim Hatamikia, the comedic parts enabled the film to gain a popularity surpassing any other before it. Furthermore, it is worth noting that *The Outcasts* shares the audience appeal of *Marmoulak (The Lizard)* (2004) by Kamal Tabrizi, a film about the comedic antics of an ex-con who poses as a cleric. *The Lizard* was the highest grossing film in Iran before *The Outcasts* and was banned only a month after its release. So, while *The Lizard* did secure popular appeal, it did not provide enough ambiguity in its narrative to ensure its longevity in theaters. In contrast, the most accepted reading of *The Outcasts* considers its denouement as resolving this ambiguous tension, whereby the narrative arc is reconciled with the ideological reformation of the hero.

The characters portray their lowness principally through their acts of impropriety. While ethnic differences come up in the film, like Majid's mother who speaks with an Azeri Turk accent, its presence is secondary to the main source of laughter, which is the group's lower-class status. The best-known comedic characters in Iranian comedic history come from the *Samad* series of the 1960s, in which Parviz Sayyad plays a bumbling *dehāti*, or villager, navigating city life. While his status as an outsider plays a great part in what makes him comical, it is his ignorance and low station that carry the narrative and the humor of the shows. Likewise, in *The Outcasts*, Majid and his neighborhood friends, who speak with accents from the southern suburbs of Tehran, a lower-class neighborhood, are comical insofar as their caricature represents their low status. While Majid's accent informs the audience of his roughness and masculinity and marks him as a *lūti*, his friends' similar street accents are less masculine and more uneducated.

The degree to which Majid performs masculinity, in particular, differentiates him from his fellow "outcasts." Since the 1960s, the figure of the *lūti* or thug has been infused with the added element of protector and hero of the common man. *Qeysar* (*Caesar*, 1969), a film about a man who seeks revenge for a raped sister and murdered brother, also revolves around a *lūti* figure who enacts his masculinity with honorable intentions. In this way, Majid functions as our typical *lūti* figure who becomes grafted onto the figure of the war martyr, a hyper-visible figure of masculinity in postwar Iranian popular culture. An example of this juxtaposition takes place in a scene from their military training; amongst a battalion of soldiers, Majid is compared to a weak soldier. Morteza is lecturing about using hand grenades and asks for a volunteer. A young soldier volunteers, but Majid teases him and says, "This kid stutters. By the time he gets to three we'll be dead." Everyone laughs. Morteza asks one of them to volunteer, and, playing cool, Majid offers the fearful Bayram, who walks forward hesitantly. Bayram accidentally pulls the clip too soon, and, in slow motion, the soldiers try to disperse. However, the stuttering soldier jumps on top of it, but nothing happens because Morteza used a non-functioning grenade for the exercise. In this scene the soldier bears the mark of a real man in the film, in contrast with Majid, who was not willing to sacrifice his life. He says, "Manhood is not defined by . . . yazdi bandanas. You can find real men like him at the front in great numbers." Majid's role as the heroic male *lūti* figure becomes the crux upon which the film is able to balance its appeal as both a comedic melodrama and typical war film.

Significantly, Majid carries the melodrama by being neither the butt of the jokes nor the one who tells them, while his friends Amir, Bayram, and Bijan are fodder for the film's comedic parts. Each of the friends exhibits typical stereotypes of low-class characters: Bijan is a thief, Amir is a drug addict, and Bayram is especially unintelligent. This kind of exaggeration is the most commonly known method of achieving comic effects, but Geoff King also indicates incongruity as a productive means of understanding the highly potent and subversive possibilities of this mode on audience members.[27] The characters' ignorance of social norms and acts that create incongruous moments in the film come directly from their low status in society. Narges Bajoghli argues that what drives the film is the reformation of an "other" in Iranian society to learn the true Islamic (revolutionary) way.[28] The making of this film seems all the more significant, since it takes place at a time when members of the Revolutionary Guard and Iran-Iraq War veterans begin to enter the political stage.[29] However, does the intent of the propaganda machine or the intent of the filmmaker necessarily signal the success or acceptance of the intended message? Considering Roxanne Varzi's study on the post-revolutionary youth's disillusionment with the current regime, a message about the virtues of martyrdom and piety would not be popular with a youth rejecting the restrictive policies of a regime that has consistently come up against popular resistance. However, Varzi's illuminating study focused on the discontent of upper-class youth in northern Tehran, a study that could account for a portion of the moviegoers but hardly the majority. This is particularly important to consider when balancing critical reviews with popular reception.

In a typical good cop–bad cop routine, the soldiers are managed by religious authorities who argue frequently about the presence of the group of outcasts on the frontline. When Majid and his friends attempt to sign up to go to the front, their knowledge of Islam is tested by the authorities asking how many prostrations are in a prayer, how people get buried, and with which foot you enter the bathroom. These questions result in comedic answers as they fumble through wrong answers, and the scene culminates with Amir, the drug addict, saying he would go headfirst into the bathroom if they let them go to the front. Everyone bursts out laughing while Amir looks baffled. A typical instance of incongruity, the humor in this scene is caused by the unexpected nature of Amir's response to a religious question. Haj Saleh is taken aside by Mirza and an older cleric who chastise him for asking such questions and expecting soldiers to be as pious as angels from heaven. Along with Mirza's talk with Abbas earlier in the film, this scene highlights the tension between the original ideals of the revolution and the way it has manifested in the minute details of everyday actions and ritual.

In fact, the central way the film pits "good" piety against "bad" piety was through the arguments between Haj Saleh and the cleric. Haj Saleh and other commanding officers decide to send Majid and company back to Tehran, claiming they belong in the city square and not on the front where the ground is pure. But the cleric protests, "Those are your words and not the words of religion." The rigid expectations of the misguided religious authorities are voiced by the two older religious figures of the film, Mirza, Narges's father and the cleric. These voices of reason are what Bajoghli claims propel the film's message—that is, the ideals of the revolution have not been upheld by the current regime, and the marginalized in society suffer as a result. The elders promote a more lenient approach to those less pious in the service of the higher purpose of fighting the war.

Along with this contrasting of clerical elites, the development of Majid and his friends in the film challenges the notion that the ultimate martyrdom in the film indicates some kind of resolution. Rather, looking at how Majid and his friends Amir, Bayram, and Bijan are being represented as lower-class *lūti* figures illuminates the class critique in the film. Particularly resonant here is King's claim in this regard:

> As a social product, comedy is often involved—implicitly and explicitly—in the politics of representation: the way one group or another is identified, distinguished and portrayed. Who and what we laugh at, and why, has implications in terms of both how we see others and how we define ourselves, the two often closely interconnected. Gender, race/ethnicity and national identity are three major sets of grounds (although not the only ones) on which such distinctions and identifications are constructed and articulated; as such, it is not surprising that they should be recurrent sources of comic material in film as elsewhere.[30]

Majid's identification or lack thereof with the nation contrasts with the pious soldiers. On the jeep ride to the front, Majid shows ownership of his difference by distancing himself and his friends, speaking of Iran as *mamlakat-e shomā* to Morteza. By assigning the role of devotee to "your country" to Morteza, Majid further reveals his lack of allegiance to the "sacred defense" and instead highlights his ulterior motives for being there. Thus, part of his reformation must include his eventual incorporation into the body politic and identification with the status quo.

In the film, Majid's shoes, an old pair of *giveh*, emphasize the fact that he is a common man; it is a class-based rendering of his identity. *Giveh* are recognizable shoes from the poor parts of Tehran and the rural areas of Iran. In the film, Majid's *giveh* are highlighted when he first enters the prison and when he exits the car to step into his neighborhood. Connecting two disparate places through the common element of his shoes connects the prison and his home to his precarious identity. Furthermore, throughout the film, his shoes take him to the front and, most heroically, through a minefield and finally to his death when a tank charges through his barracks. The Tehran streets, the prison, and the front meet in the footsteps of our hero. What is striking about his steps is not that they are the steps of a war martyr; rather, they are the steps of an ex-prisoner, liar, gambler, smoker, and poor local boy. Therefore, *lūti* identity becomes the crux upon which audience identification rests.

The concept of *ādamsāzi,* or moral development, is central to understanding the function of reformation and the implications of martyrdom in the film. *Ādamsāzi* comes from *ādam,* signaling the first man, meaning human, and *sāzi* comes from *sākhtan,* 'to build.' Thus, when the cleric says that the war front is not for the angels, rather for the *ādamsāzi* of people like Majid and his friends, he indicates his belief in the active intervention in the moral development of Majid, the building of his humanity. As mentioned, this attempt at reforming Majid and his misfit friends forms the main tension in the narrative, with old clerics embodying the ideals of the revolution, on the one hand, and the new clerics concerned with the rituals of Islam, on the other. However, the way this education or reformation unfolds signals a disjuncture between the conventional concept of *ādamsāzi* and one that the narrative of the film suggests, and moreover, signals a critique on reformation as a viable possibility for our hero.

What kind of reformation takes place in *The Outcasts*? The attributes most distinguishable and referred to in the film are Amir's drug addiction, Bayram's cowardliness, and Bijan's thievery. The new clerics criticize their ignorance of Islamic rites and, based on this, deem them unfit to go to the front with pious men. Thus, a solid reformation of the characters involves their cessation of these particular unfit acts along with their education in the Islamic rituals of which they are so ignorant throughout the story. However, there is no expression of their education process, resulting in some kind of ultimate, enlightened version of themselves. Furthermore, Majid bears no recognizable vices that necessitate cessation as with his friends. However, in contrast with the other characters, Majid's sole mark of difference, his non-allegiance to the nation, carries the film's central weight.

In terms of reformation, Bijan, the thief, is the only character who exhibits actual moral reformation as a result of the war experience. From stealing shoes at the mosque to prayer beads from clerics, Bijan's thievery is represented as compulsive. Thus, when they arrive at a bombed village, he begins to loot the houses and schools. However, when he unexpectedly finds a dead girl in a closet, he is distraught from the sight, weeping as he carries her to the other soldiers. After this dramatic scene, back at the camp he returns all the stolen goods to their owners. Therefore, Bijan's change occurs in his *ādamsāzi* as a result of the impact and harrowing reality of war. We see no similar kind of reformation or epiphany with the other characters, including Majid. While Majid does sacrifice himself by walking through a minefield and finally being run over by a tank, he does so for Narges, her father, and his friends, connecting his community to his martyrdom.

Amir is particularly significant as Majid's foil in this comedy about masks and false piety. As a drug addict, Amir speaks his mind, and thus he serves as the uncensored mouthpiece for the audience and characters in the film. He unknowingly unravels Majid's plan when he runs up to him just as Majid is giving Narges's father water from the holy spring of Zamzam, which he purportedly brought back from his pilgrimage to Mecca. At the front Amir offers drugs to soldiers with head injuries, marking his impropriety not only in public but also on what the clerics consider pure ground. While his actions in these scenes reflect socially unacceptable behavior, most boldly embodied in his drug use and physical countenance, Amir challenges these notions by being ignorant of their controversial nature. Ultimately, he serves as Majid's unprotected, unsober self who speaks through the mask of masculinity.

If Majid's death inscribes the impossibility of a lower-class figure integrating into a postwar, Ahmadinejad-led Iranian society, then the integration of Bayram must signal a conditional aspect of this impossibility. By the end of *The Outcasts* Majid becomes a *shahīd* (martyr) and consequently does not reunite with Narges; rather, he becomes memorialized as a lover of his nation. Significantly, Bayram acts as Majid's foil in regards to pursuing their love interests. When Majid first comes back from prison and his neighbors think he came back from *hāj*, Bayram attempts to kill a lamb for the welcoming rite. This scene introduces Bayram's interest in Majid's sister Marziyeh as they exchange looks, and Majid shows his disapproval by storming off. Two scenes that compare the relationship of Marziyeh and Bayram with that of Majid and Narges occur at places of delivery, one at the bus stop and the other at the phone station at the front. At the scene when they depart for the front, Bayram hesitates about going and instead proposes that he marry Narges and that when Majid comes back he can replace him. To further its comedic effect, Marziyeh momentarily ceases her lamenting over his departure in order to scold him for being cowardly, resuming crying when he quickly agrees to go. Immediately following this scene is Majid's nervous goodbye to Narges, who says she will wait for him. The evident relief and joy in his face underscore the hope and motivation that drives his action in the film.

The complementary positioning of these two couples is further developed in the scene in which the men telephone the women from the front. Bayram calls Marziyeh only to have Majid pull the phone away from him. Marziyeh hangs up after hearing her brother's voice. Afterward, Majid dials Narges's number and, just as she is about to pick it up, her brother Abbas picks up the phone instead and greets the caller with a resounding religious greeting, *Assalām w'aleikom*! Majid hangs up. Here, the two brothers' interventions in the phone calls from their sisters' love interests indicate a connection being drawn between social norms and social propriety, and not so much with religious propriety. Their actions parallel one another and suggest a critique of social norms and not of religion. Majid, however, ultimately dies and does not reunite with his lover, while Bayram lives and does. Having Bayram overcome death and eventually reunite with his love interest casts doubt on Majid's supposed reformation, which is presumably reached through martyrdom.

While the denouement of the film suggests the ideological reformation of Majid and his deviant gang of friends, it is significant only insofar as we place the gravitas of the film at the end, and we assume reformation of moral values based on the death of the hero. Instead, the film shows that the comedic mode, which typically capitalizes on mockery of higher groups (groups in power) and an investment in lower characters, enables a reading that in fact critiques the resolution of a martyred ending. Iranian war films only recently began to criticize the reasons for the war and its subsequent effects. Ebrahim Hatamikia's melodramas in particular have been the hallmark of war films after Morteza Avini's films of the "Sacred Defense." While Avini's films promoted the heroism of soldiers and the necessity of fighting for the Islamic republic, Hatamikia's films centered on the trauma of war veterans and the destitute lives they have lived in the postwar period. However, both directors have upheld a somber vision of the war hero, one that is challenged by the comedic characters in such comedies as *The Outcasts*. This interplay between genres highlights the tensions that have arisen around the popularity of *The Outcasts*. While the melodramatic martyr narrative allowed its government-approved release, the comedy and its attendant social critique are what appealed to an Iranian audience struggling to accept the strictures of an increasingly restrictive government.

NOTES

1. The *hāj* is an annual pilgrimage to the city of Mecca in Saudi Arabia, a compulsory rite for all able Muslims.
2. Various critics debate whether to refer to the revolution of 1979 as the Iranian Revolution or the Islamic Revolution. Since this essay deals with the Islamic values espoused by the Islamic Republic and its policies, I refer to the revolution as the Islamic Revolution.
3. See Borzou Daragahi, "The World; A Different View of Iran's Soldiers; A Movie Takes on the Myths That Underlie the Islamic Republic: Who Fought in the War with Iraq, and Why," *Los Angeles Times*, September 14, 2008, A16.
4. See "Ekhrājihā Passes One Billion," *Cinemā ye mā*, April 6, 2007, www.cinemaema.com/NewsArticle2074.html.
5. The 18th of Tir occurred in July 1999 in protest of the closing of the Iranian reformist newspaper *Salaam*. It was the largest demonstration of anti-regime sentiment at the time and is mourned every year for those who died, were beaten, or were arrested as a result. The clashes of 2009, following the upheaval of the tenth presidential election of Iran, were especially resonant because of this anniversary.

6. See Narges Bajoghli, "The Outcasts: Reforming the Internal 'Other' by Returning to the Ideals of the Revolution" (M.A. thesis, University of Chicago, 2008).
7. The Iran-Iraq War began less than two years after the establishment of the Islamic Republic and lasted from September 1980 to August 1988.
8. See Peter J. Chelkowski and Hamid Dabashi, *Staging a Revolution: The Art of Persuasion in the Islamic Republic of Iran* (New York: New York University Press, 1999).
9. Interview in *Māhnāmeh-ye Sinemāi-ye Fīlm*, March 2007.
10. See www.indexmundi.com/iran/youth-unemployment-rate.html.
11. Dehnamaki claims he had to cut the screenplay considerably to get it approved by the censors.
12. Geoff King, *Film Comedy* (London: Wallflower, 2004), 5.
13. Ibid.
14. See Richard Tapper, *The New Iranian Cinema: Politics, Representation and Identity* (London: I. B. Tauris, 2002).
15. Quoted in Jonathan Lippitt, "Humour and Incongruity," *Cogito* 8, no. 2 (1994): 147-53.
16. See www.massoudmehrabi.com/articles.asp?id=659039788.
17. Jamshid Sedagatnejad, "Dast o Bal-e Ma Baste Ast," *Soureh Cinema* 23 (2008): 42.
18. Hamid Naficy, *A Social History of Iranian Cinema, Volume 3* (Durham, N.C.: Duke University Press, 2011), 33.
19. Ibid.
20. Bajoghli, "The Outcasts," 31.
21. Ibid.
22. Ibid.
23. Ibid.
24. Pierre Bourdieu, *Distinction: A Social Critique of the Judgment of Taste* (Cambridge, Mass.: Harvard University Press, 1984, 466).
25. For a comprehensive history of the institutions and policies concerning cinema in this period, see Hamid Naficy, *A Social History of Iranian Cinema, Volume 3* (Durham, N.C.: Duke University Press, 2012).
26. See Roxanne Varzi, *Warring Souls: Youth, Media, and Martyrdom in Post-Revolution Iran* (Durham, N.C.: Duke University Press, 2006).
27. King, *Film Comedy*, 5.
28. Ibid., 3.
29. Bajoghli, "The Outcasts," 3.
30. King, *Film Comedy*, 129.

7

HUMOR AND THE CINEMATIC SUBLIME IN KIAROSTAMI'S *THE WIND WILL CARRY US*

GAYATRI DEVI

The title of Abbas Kiarostami's film *The Wind Will Carry Us* (*Bad mara khahad bord,* 1999) directly alludes to a poem by one of Iran's most famous modern poets, Foroogh Farrokhzaad. The title of the poem and, by extension, the film, conjures up visions of a flight to freedom, a welcome ejection from this world in which one is jettisoned by the pure energy of a natural force. The poem opens with an intimidating scene containing two unequal entities, one small and the other very mighty: a personalized night, "my small night," and a seeming antagonist, "the dark hell wind" roaring outside:

> in my small night, what mounting regret!
>
> wind has a rendezvous with the trees' leaves
>
> in my small night, there is terror
>
> of desolation
>
> listen! Do you hear
>
> the wind of darkness howling?
>
> I watch breathlessly
>
> and wondrously this alien happiness
>
> I am addicted to my own hopelessness

> listen! listen well!
>
> can you hear the darkness howling?—the dark hell
>
> —wind scything
>
> its way towards us?[1]

It is not merely the juxtaposition of the small against the mighty that evokes the split feeling within us; it is also the poet's response to the scene as she experiences it. Her response is colored by several semantic contradictions that gravitate toward a certain kind of paradox: "mounting regret," "terror of desolation," "alien happiness," and "addicted to my own hopelessness." The contradictions appear to engender both terror as well as a seemingly strange sense of calm and happiness, as evinced by the adverb "wondrously." The terror is further personified as an unknown entity that the poet senses intuitively as both a figure of care as well as mysterious and menacing: "behind this window an unknown / something fears for me and you."[2] In the concluding stanza of the poem, the poet invites a mysterious figure, "you who are green from head to toe," perhaps *al-Khidr*, the "Green Man" of Sufi belief, to approach her like a lover, so that their union might prove stronger than the fear, as expressed in this injunction: "the wind will carry us with it / the wind will carry us with it."[3] From an opening scarred with terror, the poem concludes on this note of mystical flight.

The experience described in this poem resembles what Kant termed as the encounter with the sublime in his *Third Critique*,[4] a disorienting perception of magnitude and power that induces both terror and relief in us successively. This encounter puts us directly back in touch with our faculty of reason or morals that provides the only counterbalance that contains and conquers this externally induced sensory disorientation. In this essay, I discuss Kiarostami's *The Wind Will Carry Us* as exemplifying a Kantian engagement with the sublime, which not only has implications for a political reading of the film, but also issues a direct challenge to the cinematic art's generic reluctance to engage meaningfully with spiritual themes, preferring instead to serve as a "metaphoric crucible" that can "reveal truths that everyday convention prevents our perceiving," and that may then be imagined to be the basis for some form of social action.[5] However,

I contend that the numinous is not beyond representation in film, nor is the repressed content in a third-world artifact always servicing the national allegory.[6] Further, it can be shown that the very fact of iterative, mechanical reproduction that Walter Benjamin bemoaned as being instrumental in depriving the "aura" of a work of art[7] may be seen to be equally instrumental in pursuing the emergence of "the gap" to make the numinous visible in a subjective experience that may be disorienting to social reality, but is, at the same time, profoundly truthful, moral, and ethical from a spiritual perspective.[8] Abbas Kiarostami's films may best be read as films experimenting with such an investigation into the nature of what the cinematic medium privileges as "reality," and whether the contours of this "reality" may be altered in dimension and depth through filmmaking. Is it possible to speak of "the invisible" in a medium whose very reputation rests on its power to penetrate anything and everything and to render everything visible? In *The Wind Will Carry Us,* the lost "aura" of the cinematic artifact is restored through a series of structural disruptions that end up realigning the mode of cinematic realism with the modes of comedy and humor. The effect is one of an augmented moral agency in the subjectivity of the protagonist, Behzad, a television producer who is in the small, remote Kurdish village of Siah Dareh to film the death ceremony of a one-hundred-year-old woman. Behzad is on assignment from Tehran with the clock ticking behind him, but the old woman refuses to die, throwing Behzad's plan into disarray. This humorous and sublime paradox is the crux of the plot of this beautiful movie. The submerged vibrations of the cinematic sublime in *The Wind Will Carry Us* repeatedly make incremental eruptions on the realistic surface of the film, much like the mechanism of repetition in humor, until the eruptions make the hidden numinous content visible in a radical realignment of the subjectivity of the characters. Not only are the conventions of cinematic realism debunked in this attempt to isolate the sublime, but the resultant apprehension of the sublime has the same salubrious effect of encountering an instance of liberatory and ethical humor.

Long before Kant made the sublime an important aesthetic category with political potential, the Greek theoretician Longinus defined the sublime as a text that contains "a certain loftiness and excellence of language."⁹ "A lofty passage does not convince the reason of the reader, but takes him out of himself. That which is admirable ever confounds our judgment, and eclipses that which is merely reasonable or agreeable. To believe or not is usually in our own power; but the Sublime, acting with an imperious and irresistible force, sways every reader whether he will or not."[10] In other words, it is pointless to resist the sublime. Longinus also issues this caveat, that if the thoughts "which it suggests do not extend beyond what is actually expressed; and if, the longer you read it, the less you think of it, — there can be here no true sublimity, when the effect is not sustained beyond the mere act of perusal."[11] The sublime, on the other hand, "gains a complete mastery over our minds."[12] The sublime effect is experienced "when a passage is pregnant in suggestion, when it is hard, nay impossible, to distract the attention from it, and when it takes a strong and lasting hold on the memory, then we may be sure that we have lighted on the true Sublime."[13]

In other words, the challenge of the sublime is a form of total takeover of senses, imagination, reason, and the effective content and process of thoughts. In some ways the experience of this effect cannot help but be repetitive, regardless of the particular perspective that engages with it, according to Longinus: "we may regard those words as truly noble and sublime which always please and please all readers."[14] The cause that determines the technique of the sublime, which produces this kind of lofty transport of our senses, Longinus explains, depends on "a law of Nature that in all things there are certain constituent parts, coexistent with their substance. It necessarily follows, therefore, that one cause of sublimity is the choice of the most striking circumstances involved in whatever we are describing, and, further, the power of afterwards combining them into one animate whole."[15] Longinus cautions us against mistaking "amplification" and "repeated insistence" in the manner of "exaggeration" as the path that leads us toward the experience of sublimity.[16]

What is particularly striking about Longinus's theories about the aesthetic category called the sublime is its rather unselfconscious (perhaps regressive and reactionary, from our modern media-for-the-mass public perspective) insistence on the ability, or rather expectation, that a work of sublime art will and should "fall on our ears like the voice of god."¹⁷ Longinus demonstrates through multiple examples from the writers of antiquity the elevated effect of particular syntactic and rhetorical structures, and the use of particular figures and images in creating this "transporting" effect on the minds of the readers. Longinus boldly confers a certain hierophanic and auratic dimension to a work of art, making it possible to speak of the "truth" of a creative work of art. Longinus's careful lexical and syntactic sculpting of the sublime from amongst the copious collection of texts from antiquity is equally quick to bracket the failures of what specific examples lack the constituents of the sublime, the mistakes traced back to particular syntactic, rhetorical, and figurative choices that the writer in question made. Longinus proves through careful discussion specific examples of dishonest writing, and how certain techniques and figures used in writing easily betray the writer's less-than-wholesome thoughts. Longinus's interests are primarily aesthetic, but the truly sublime is also truthful and moral beyond a doubt, according to Longinus. His examples are persuasive. Thus Longinus's essay exemplifies a strong practical belief in the power of art to elevate, affect, and transform the human mind for the better.

Longinus's assertions regarding the sublime are also relevant to our present discussion, as they privilege a singular subjectivity as a valid measure of the aesthetic and we might say the moral power of a work of art. While watching a movie is a highly personal and self-contained experience, the discourse that surrounds films, the critical apparatus that surrounds the film as a cultural artifact, is often reluctant to foreground responses that are entirely subjective in nature. Unlike the individualized contemplation of a painting or a poem, where the subjectivity of the one encountering the work of art *is* the primary measure of the success of the work of art as art, in cinema, such an individual subjective experience is subsumed under the collective, mass, and public objectives conventionally thought to control the making, distribution, and enjoyment of cinema. This is particularly true of the discourse of both lay and critical responses to genre comedies, where, as a rule, the laughter that you hear in the theater is the laughter of the group. When you laugh, when no one else is laughing, then the comedy becomes aggressive and divisive rather than socially cohesive. But if we are to privilege Longinus's views on the topic, sublime laughter is a subjective experience that does not wait for social approbation; indeed, sublime laughter should direct the social, collective response, rather than the social response disengaging with the sublime. Even if one laughs alone at the sublime joke, Longinus argues, the humor in such an instance is purged off all aggression so that the singular laughter might augment the cohesion, or at the very least ward off aggressive responses. In other words, sublime laughter is a quiet laughter, and because of its quietness, it does not create aggression, violence, or hostility, even if one laughs alone. Regarding certain types of comic exaggeration that have sublime effects, for instance, Longinus notes that "these extravagances, however improbable, gain credence by their humour. . . . For mirth is one of the passions, having its seat in pleasure."[18] His example is an amusing comparison excerpted from an ancient text:

> "He had a farm, a little farm, where space severely pinches;
> 'Twas smaller than the last despatch from Sparta by some inches."[19]

Humor mollifies the put-down through an indirect and rather fantastic exaggeration, which actually proves its sublime effect in reverse, by using hyperbole to minimize the magnitude of something. The humor calls attention to itself and makes us marvel at the figure rather than the referent of what the figure represents.

In many key aspects, Kiarostami's films have successfully evolved an idiom to represent such quiet transformative experiences that might seem to run counter to the received wisdom in cinema studies regarding the social and historical imperative of cinema. To some extent, Kiarostami's perceived identity as an auteur filmmaker has made the movie audience, including its critics, welcome his personal vision of cinema and the subjects that he handles. Kiarostami has compared the role "imagination" plays in the apprehension of a movie as similar to the role it plays in the reading of a novel:

> I envy people who read novels since they have much more freedom to use their imagination than a film audience. If a

HUMOR AND THE SUBLIME IN *THE WIND WILL CARRY US*

film could be structured like the layout of a book it would be ideal. For example, the last four lines of a chapter could end at the top of a page with the rest of the page blank and the following page sitting next to it. The new chapter then starts with a short title. This kind of format gives you an opportunity to pause and think. It often surprises me when people say, "I picked up a book and I couldn't put it down until I finished it." How can one see that as a positive quality for an artwork? It's the same superficial excitement that the mainstream cinema imposes on their audiences. Sometimes, as I'm editing my films, I like to insert a black leader instead of an image (like that blank page of the novel) and say, "that's it for now!" . . . One who writes a novel might write it from the very first letter to the end but later he or she divides them into different chapters in order to create desired moods and atmospheres. But conventional cinema doesn't do that since its legacy is to take the audience hostage and dictate to them. In other words, it gives them a pre-packaged deal with determined message and a closed ending. That is why it cannot tolerate open, simple and uneventful moments. And audiences are conditioned by this kind of a cinema! They get lost and confused when they face an open-end. Sometimes you hear them say, "I could understand the film until the end, but I could not understand that very last scene." But I believe even if for some reason you can't watch the film to the end (for instance because of a black out) you should feel content.[20]

That Kiarostami does not privilege the medium called cinema as a technological medium intrinsically different from other "art" forms is evident in the above observation. Besides, Kiarostami did leave the screen dark for about five minutes in *ABC Africa,* unsettling as it was amusing, leaving much speculation about his motives among the critics, the winning response being the "limitations of the medium."[21] In what is at once a serious and amusing thought, Kiarostami admitted in the same interview that "back in the days when I used to watch films, after an impressive or moving scene or sequence I would leave the theatre. Those particular moments could make my day and I felt see the ending."²² This particular interview is noteworthy ...rallel registers of art and cinema used interchangeably by ... viewer to apply to two different forms, and very strictly and ...ally by Kiarostami to refer to his films. To the interviewer's ...on "How much art, philosophy, sociology, and political theory ...ivolved in your creative process?"²³ Kiarostami replies, "Whatever theories had to offer me, they should have offered it long before ...ood behind the camera. One should already have digested what he ... she has read or learned before starting an artistic project,"²⁴ there-..y implying that "art" is not an external influence on his cinema, and that Kiarostami considers himself an "artist," and that he is engaged in the making of "art."

The above subtle but clear self-presentation as an "artist" is particularly relevant when discussing Kiarostami's cinema. Cinema was the choice modern medium positioned as the game-changing "art" form, vis-à-vis any art form's relationship to its matter, materials, and reception, argues Walter Benjamin in his famous essay "The Work of Art in the Age of Mechanical Reproduction." Benjamin's highly ambivalent interpretation of the effect of the penetration of "reality" by cinematic technology not only makes evident certain unique representational gains that only the cinematic form can consolidate, but it also reads these gains in the light of much greater and far more serious losses, such as the form's distance from its tradition, the "aura" of the original versus the copy, the changed relationship between cinema and its actors, cinema's high threshold for audience distraction and absent-mindedness, and, finally, a harrowing spectacle of what such a mass audience is capable of doing when they are given a chance to "express themselves."²⁵ In his polemical conclusion, Benjamin forewarns that totalitarian fascist movements will mobilize the masses and utilize "art" for its destructive ends: "The logical result of Fascism is the introduction of aesthetics into political life. The violation of the masses, whom Fascism, with its *Fuhrer* cult, forces to their knees, has its counterpart in the violation of an apparatus which is pressed into the production of ritual values."²⁶ Benjamin quotes Marinetti's Futurism manifesto to note that fascism "expects war to supply the artistic gratification of a sense perception that has been changed by technology."²⁷ Framed against such a perception of technology as art, Kiarostami's emphasis on the "timelessness" of art might sound reactionary and, perhaps, from a political perspective, as even engaging in bad faith humanism: "I believe true art should be timeless. In a country like Iran, where social and political issues are constantly shifting, the artist should focus beyond these mundane issues, on more fundamental realities like humanity itself, which is more universal."[28]

Indeed, Kiarostami has come under scathing attack from the literary and cultural critic Hamid Dabashi precisely for his failure to adequately capture the "universalization of the Iranian particular."[29] In Dabashi's reading, the controversial "stable scene" in *The Wind Will Carry Us,* in which Behzad goes to buy milk from a house in the village where the ditch-digger's beloved resides, is equivalent to both an "ocular masturbation," as well as "one of the most violent rape scenes in all cinema."[30] Dabashi traces the alleged excesses of this scene to Kiarostami's exploitative claims to particular Iranian realities:

> Over the last three decades, but particularly since he achieved international prominence, Kiarostami's has been the spectacular success story of a Third World filmmaker turning the particular of his native location into the global parameters of an emancipating rereading of reality. If he has richly deserved comparison with such great masters as Satyajit Ray and Akira Kurosawa, it is precisely because of this universalization of the Iranian village. They, as indeed had Kiarostami until this film, restored a universal dignity to the people they redrafted for the world at large. But in this stable scene Kiarostami does precisely the opposite of universalizing Iranian dignity; he begins to particularize a universal indignity. The blank-faced, wide-eyed, imitation-cool, made-in-Tehran protagonist, who may think that his unbuttoned shirt, dirty blue jeans, unlaced boots, Japanese station wagon, and Tehrani accent tellingly distinguish him from the Kurdish villagers, does not realize, in the depths of his own depraved nativism, that, for the global audience, he is as much part of the Third World as the villagers.[31]

While Kiarostami himself would agree that we have the license to interpret his cinema any way we want,[32] since cinema, as a work of art, will engage its viewers in singular ways, much like a poem or painting, Dabashi's vitriolic attack brings to the forefront several issues about cinema's claim to represent "reality," universals, particulars, and so on. In particular, it is possible to argue that the stable scene is an apt exemplum of a possible cinematic sublime, and that it is, in fact, the most "moral" scene in the whole film. Dabashi is correct in identifying the scene as one that produces a bifurcated response within us in equally alternating measures of fascination and discomfort, but it also endures as unforgettable and profoundly memorable in a shocking but edifying manner, as Longinus would say. This scene is so unexpected and singular that we may look toward Kant and his analytic of the sublime to understand our own responses to this scene. Contrary to Dabashi's labels of "rape" and "ocular masturbation," Kiarostami stages the stable scene in such a way that it effectively shuts down our sensory responses, because, upon critical reflection, they reveal themselves to be absurd. Indeed, Dabashi himself admits this absurdity when he notes that Kiarostami uses this "hideous instance" to introduce Foroogh Farrokhzaad's poem "The Wind Will Carry Us," which, Dabashi concedes, sounds "silly" and "graceless"[33] in this particular context. In addition, Dabashi himself has identified the city-boy sartorial buffoonery of Behzad as well. In other words, there is nothing pornographic or remotely prurient in this scene, other than the uneasiness of watching a man make a fool of himself, along with seeming to see something that is not meant for our eyes. The ordinary act of milking a cow that many of us have seen a thousand times becomes tendentious in this scene with the only light source in the scene fixed on the full teats of the cow and the girl's hands milking them. We are forced to turn to our reflective judgment, to our own faculties of reasoning in order to comprehend the profound disorientation the scene produces in us. I argue that this intentional discomfort in the viewer and our eventual transcendence of it by realigning ourselves with the "moral" is the only way in which cinema can lay claims to represent "reality." I further contend that the deep discomfort that clings to us from witnessing this scene rises from our inability to understand the utter unpredictability of Behzad's conduct in a rational manner. However, our understanding of this scene may become more lucid when we consider it as part of a particular list of scenes Kiarostami makes visible through the course of the film: all are necessary eruptions in the protagonist Behzad's interactions with the villagers and the surface-level reality of the lived life in the village of Siah Dareh.

If there is a moral center to *The Wind Will Carry Us,* it makes its unmistakable and ineluctable presence felt in the stable scene. It is possible to see that something invisible and ineffable—the sublime—has been tracking and discomforting Behzad, the protagonist, from the moment he arrives in Siah Dareh. Behzad is pushed toward reflective thinking and moral action in Siah Dareh, in every encounter he has with the village, though he tries hard to resist it. These interactions form the basis of the humorous critique of Behzad and all that he represents. Furthermore, Kiarostami characterizes Behzad as a human being who acts like an automaton, in contrast to the villagers who are shown to live and relate to each other and Behzad in the living present within the diegetic framework of the film, and with variety and intimacy. In small increments, Behzad's automaton-like performance of life in Siah Dareh is contrasted comically with the genuine and authentic lives of the villagers, particularly the village women. The stable scene symbolizes Behzad's one final attempt to blind himself to the transformation that calls out to him, and the growing critical judgment within him, but already it is too late; the scene clearly establishes Behzad's lowest point as an authentic human being. Behzad's life unravels quickly beyond this point, and we gradually see Behzad being integrated back into life on earth, through a lesson that is as hard-learned as it is humbling, though he had come to Siah Dareh in order to meet and photograph Death.

In his *Analytic of the Sublime,* Kant describes the sublime through a series of cumulative propositions. In its simplest form, the sublime is to be found in a "formless object,"[34] which represents "boundlessness" and "quantity."[35] The boundlessness of a sublime object, then, is "not only great, but absolutely great in every point of view (great beyond all comparison)," which leads Kant to expand the proposition thusly: "It is a magnitude which is like itself alone. It follows then that the sublime is not to be thought in the things of nature, but only in our own ideas."³⁶ The perception of magnitude in things of nature, Kant says, is always relative; thus, he amends the definition of the sublime as "the mere ability to think which shows a faculty of the mind surpassing every standard of sense."³⁷ Postulating this essential connection between the "boundlessness" of the sublime "object" with a concurrent rational (subjective) faculty of the mind to apprehend its boundlessness allows Kant to arrive at a hypothesis of the "noumenon," here, the "infinite":

> Nevertheless the bare capability of thinking this infinite without contradiction requires in the human mind a faculty itself supersensible.... The faculty of being able to think the infinite of supersensible intuition as given (in its intelligible substrate) surpasses every standard of sensibility and is great beyond all comparisons even with the faculty of mathematical estimation, not, of course, in a theoretical point of view and on behalf of the cognitive faculty, but as a practical extension of the mind which feels itself able in another (practical) point of view to go beyond the limits of sensibility.³⁸

While Kant's use of the terms "noumenon" and "infinity" in the context of his discussions regarding the mathematical sublime do not necessarily imply or call for a hieratic interpretation, such a connotation is really not far behind at all times. This hieratic imperative becomes rather explicit when Kant concedes that mathematical imagination will always come up with an appropriate measure to comprehend infinity, and that it is only the "aesthetical estimation of magnitude in which the effort toward comprehension surpasses the power of the imagination."³⁹ Since it is "self-contradictory" to "comprehend infinity," and since it surpasses all "standards of sense," Kant postulates that such a phenomenon of nature makes us judge it "sublime, not so much the object, as our own state of mind in the estimation of it."⁴⁰

It is the above postulation regarding the limits and processes of the "aesthetic estimation" of infinity, as it constitutes the act of subjective perception, that maximally resonates with the humorous content of most Kiarostami's films, in particular *The Wind Will Carry Us*.

Kiarostami's films do attempt to make visible the infinite, and along aesthetic lines that eschew aggression, humiliation, or fear, and instead explore a humorous exposition. Kant did theorize about the faculty of humor proper in his *Analytic of the Sublime,* where he discusses "wit" as a "play of thought," springing "merely from the change of representations in the judgment." Kant says that this change, however, does not produce any "thoughts," but that it does "animate" the mind.[41] Kant further notes that whatever produces convulsive laughter within us has something "absurd" within it, something for which the understanding can find no satisfaction: "Laughter is an affection arising from the sudden transformation of a strained expectation into nothing."[42] Regarding humor, Kant observes that the humorous manner is closer to the arts that excite laughter, "a mental disposition, in which everything is judged quite differently from the ordinary method (reversed, in fact), and yet in accordance with certain rational principles in such a frame of mind."[43] Kant brackets "the humorous" with "the pleasant," rather than to "beautiful art, because the object of the latter must always show proper worth in itself, and hence requires a certain seriousness in the presentation."[44]

While Kant's theory of humor contributes toward our understanding of the role of "the absurd" and "the incongruous" in producing laughter, what I intend to do in this essay is explore whether there are "humorous" implications in Kant's theories regarding the sublime. Whether Kant intended it or not, I argue that the sublime poses one of the most effective humorous challenges to reality's status quo through its intuitive schema of a potentially frightening loss of power and comprehension that is, however, at the crucial moment revealed to be amenable to our faculties of reason, reflective thinking, and moral judgment.

Kiarostami's movies would benefit greatly from such a reading, having always demonstrated a keen psychological and aesthetic interest in the baser emotions of fear, panic, anxiety, and confusion. *Bread and Alley* (*Nan va kuche,* 1970), his very first short film—only twelve minutes long—is a good example of Kiarostami's approach to these emotions as an aesthetic film problem. Made for the Institute for the Intellectual Development of Children and Young Adults, the movie reveals nothing much by way of plot. A young boy, nine or ten years old, has to walk through an alley to get to his house; he is coming back from buying bread. The only problem is that the alley is narrow and long and in the middle of the alley is a dog. The boy is afraid of the dog. It is a silent film with no dialogue and only background music, one track in particular resembling The Beatles's "Ob-la-di Ob-la-da" from their *White Album* (interestingly enough, the album was released only in 1976, six years after the release of *Bread and Alley*). For the first two or three minutes of the film, the boy walks merrily along kicking a ball of sorts until he is stopped short in his tracks by the dog, whose bark is heard offscreen. We hear the dog before we see it. The dog then makes a quick appearance, coming toward the boy from the direction of where the boy wants to go. The boy runs back and stands against a wall peering in fear toward a curve in the alley, beyond which the dog presumably lies waiting for him. We hear the dog barking occasionally offscreen. We see a few people, older men and women, donkey carts, and so on, pass by, but the boy is rooted to the spot in fear. The dog is nowhere in the diegetic frame for most of the duration of the film. We hear its bark occasionally. The dog is an invisible presence.

This film belongs to the problem-solution genre of films that Kiarostami made for the Institute, and so, in a while, about halfway through the film, we see an elderly man coming toward the boy and going in his direction. The boy removes himself from the wall and walks behind the man. The man is wearing earphones and does not hear the boy at all. The boy walks with the man up until the man reaches his house. The boy is now at a point in the alley where he can actually see the dog lying in wait. The boy has advanced far enough that he does not turn back again. Instead, in the split second that the dog charges the boy, the boy breaks off a piece of the bread and throws it to the dog. Apparently, that is all the dog wanted. He wags his tail and starts following the boy. The sound track, which stopped as soon as the dog first barked, resumes, and a wonderful flute processional now accompanies the boy walking toward the camera and to his house with the dog following close behind. The boy knocks on his door; his mother opens the door; the boy goes in; she shuts the door. The despondent dog lies on the doorstep looking around wistfully. Not for long, though, because another young boy comes toward the dog and the camera, a heavy basket in one hand and a brimming soup bowl in the other. The freeze-frame final shot shows the new boy skidding to a halt at the sight of the dog on the other boy's doorstep. The dog is his problem now.

This short beautiful film tightly captures many of Kiarostami's salient techniques, in particular the long take in real time as opposed to the narrative pieced together through editing, the use of offscreen sounds to add depth and dimension to the diegetic frame, and the judicious use of close-ups to reveal the character's thoughts. The humorous ethos of the film, moreover, stems organically from the boy suddenly switching from one state of mind to another—from mirth to fear—if we are to use Kant's definition of the psychic process of humor. While *Bread and Alley* does not evoke the sublime in us because of its simple subject, we can nevertheless see Kiarostami exploring, even with such a simple story, the resourcefulness of the boy who is forced into reflective thinking by the dog, an entity that is a source of (relative fear) to the boy.

The resolution to the crisis in the plot—the boy feeds the dog—is a didactic element that resembles Freud's definition of humor, for instance, as the loftiest of mind's defensive devices.[45] But *Bread and Alley*, as well as a series of films with nearly similar themes and child and young adult protagonists, such as *Recess* (*Zang-e-tafrih*, 1972), *The Experience* (*Tajrobe*, 1973), *The Traveller* (*Mosafer*, 1974), *A Suit for a Wedding* (*Lebas-i baray-e arusi*, 1976), *Where Is the Friend's House?* (*Khane-ye dust kojast?*, 1987), and *Homework* (*Mashq-e shab*, 1989) all provoke fear, pain, and pleasure in us, but they stop short of the transformative power of the sublime in their reluctance to allow the necessary free play of the imagination to be overwhelmed by a worthy power as an adversary. Thus the challenges that these young protagonists undergo in the form of fear (*Bread and Alley*, *Where Is the Friend's House?*, *Homework*) and desire (*Recess*, *The Experience*, *The Traveller*, *A Suit for a Wedding*) stop short of leading them (and us) out from under these paralyzing emotions. The young protagonists blend back into a society where nothing has changed for them. There is some inevitable pathos in this resolution.

In the two later full-length films, however, *Where Is the Friend's House* and *Homework*, Kiarostami does explore certain bold aesthetic resolutions that approach the Kantian sublime, albeit in a tentative manner, to the harrowing fear experienced by the young boy protagonists. *Homework* ends with a final interview with a terrified young boy who cannot stop crying and calls for his friend while Kiarostami interviews him about his homework. *Homework* is a series of interviews with very young children and some parents about their thoughts on the practice of "homework" assigned from school. Kiarostami asks the children questions like these: Do they like doing homework? Do they get help? Who helps them? What is the consequence for not doing homework? What is the consequence of doing homework on time? What is the punishment for not doing homework? What is the reward for doing homework? What do they like more—doing homework or watching cartoons? To which child after child replies, "Doing homework."

The boy who does the final interview for Kiarostami has been so traumatized by the whole experience of doing homework that he cries in front of the camera the entire time. (If Dabashi found the stable scene one in which Kiarostami particularizes human indignity as Iranian, then this scene runs a close second to the same charge. It is like watching an execution.) The despair and terror of this scene is of a very high magnitude, particularly when we consider the fact that their mouthpiece is an eight- or nine-year-old child. Kiarostami concludes the film by inviting the child to come nearer to him and asking him to say something that they are learning in the religion class, a class that the child is afraid to miss and fears because of the punishments. The boy asks Kiarostami, "Can I recite 'O Lord'?" Kiarostami says yes, and the boy recites the following prayer:

> O, Lord of the beautiful stars,
>
> O, Lord of the many-colored universe,
>
> Thou, who created Venus
>
> Thou, who created the Sun and the Moon,
>
> The mountains and the oceans,
>
> The lovely colors of the trees
>
> The tiny wings of butterflies,

HUMOR AND THE SUBLIME IN *THE WIND WILL CARRY US*

And the nest of birds,

Eyes for us to see them,

Rain and snow,

Heat and cold,

Thou, who made all these things,

Thou who granted all my wishes,

Fill our hearts with joy and happiness.

It is an extraordinary ending to a harrowing film that systematically and with great precision reveals a complex web of parental illiteracy, unrealistic educational objectives, harassed, beaten, and overworked children, and no imaginative attempt to understand them at all. In this final scene, when we witness the terrified child reciting the above prayer from memory for Kiarostami, we undergo a state change that dislodges us from the hopelessness and fear we felt for the child to something resembling hope. Why would we want to deny the dignity of this complete protection offered by the prayer to this child? The juxtaposition of this peaceful and calming prayer adjacent to the terrorized cries of the boy creates a transcendent disruption within us that forces us to seek a moral resolution to this terror. This is the moral ground to which our reflective thinking brings us. It is a sublime moment.

Similarly, in *Where Is the Friend's House?* young Ahmad travels twice in frenetic back-and-forth movements between his house and the village of Poshteh in a futile search to find his classmate Mohammad Reza's house. Homework is the culprit in this film as well. Ahmad brings home Reza's notebook, as well as his own, by mistake, and Reza, who has not been doing homework regularly, will again miss doing his homework that night, causing him to be punished and expelled from school. This fear gnaws at Ahmad and, instead of heeding his mother's command to do chores around the house, he goes to the village of Poshteh to find Reza's house. He never finds it, despite attempts on two different trips. It is clear that his mother punishes Ahmad when he returns late at night, though Kiarostami does not show us the punishment. We only see Ahmad sitting with bowed head in his room doing his homework. As David Oubina has noted, "Kiarostami decides not to show the scolding, not in order to eliminate a dead time (the event is of central importance), but in order to recover it as contained violence."[46] The next morning, we see Ahmad surreptitiously returning the notebook to a stunned Reza. Unbeknownst to Reza, Ahmad has copied his homework into Reza's notebook as well. The teacher checks it off. The only proof of Ahmad's "cheating" remains in the form of a flower that he leaves in Reza's notebook, the flower the old carpenter had given him the previous night when he tried to find Reza's house. As in the prayer that ends *Homework*, the flower represents the way out for the two young protagonists, a symbol from a world Ahmad has visited, parallel to this world. It also indicates a mental change in the magnitude of Ahmad's concern for Reza, his guilt for violating his mother's instructions, and the disorienting events that he encounters in his fervent attempts to find Reza's house in the increasingly dark and mysterious night.

Repetition, as a trope, is powerfully used in this film not only to signify the exhausting, ritualized effort Ahmad puts into searching for Reza's house, but also to disorient the viewer's expectations about the nature of the real world that cinema represents. Alberto Elena notes that Kiarostami carefully reconstructed all the settings in *Where Is the Friend's House*: "Streets, houses and even the landscape were redesigned to meet the needs or simply the demands of the director, whose objectives were undoubtedly clear and which definitely did not include yielding to realist dogmas."[47] Ahmad's search for Reza's house takes on increasingly symbolic and mystic undertones—the quest, the suffering, being lost, encounters that hinder and help, and the flower at the end of the journey all partake in this mystical layer of the film. Moreover, the title *Where Is the Friend's House*—taken from the modern Iranian poet, Sohrab Sepehri, who writes in the Persian mystic tradition—speaks of an imaginative and aesthetic resolution to the seemingly "real" problem faced by the young protagonist. "Friend" is another name for "God" in the Sufi tradition in which Sepehri writes. Ahmad is literally searching for his "friend" Reza's house in the film, the one house he cannot find. This choice of the title along with Kiarostami's "tampering" with the "reality" of the natural setting point toward a radical attribution of the nouminous

HUMOR AND THE SUBLIME IN *THE WIND WILL CARRY US*

to the real. As in *Homework,* the resolution approaches the sublime, not merely because of the film's stated interest in the infinite, but also, as discussed above, because the movie, as well as our perception of the conflict, progresses from a dense and overwhelming magnitude of fear and despair that hangs over the mise-en-scène to the relieved faces of the two boys, and the image of the flower in the resolution. The sublime resides within this scale difference in the expenditure of our emotional energy.

The natural world itself becomes imbued with a sublime spirit in *The Wind Will Carry Us,* in which the hero, unlike the innocent young adult protagonists of these earlier films, is a reluctant initiate into the spiritual path. *The Wind Will Carry Us* has a simple plot: Behzad and his crew arrive in the remote Kurdish village of Siah Dareh to film a death ceremony. One of the oldest women in the village is dying of an unexplained ailment. Almost as a joke to Farzad, the young boy who becomes their village guide, Behzad describes their visit as a secret treasure hunt. Nothing happens in the village as far as Behzad and his crew are concerned; we hardly see the crew at all. They languish in boredom in an inside room, making slightly smutty comments about women and eating strawberries. Behzad spends time either shaving his clean face even more cleanly or in frenetic drives to a hilltop cemetery to receive cellphone calls that are always perilously close to being dropped. On one such visit, Behzad makes the acquaintance of a young man digging a ditch for "telecommunications"; if cabling for telecommunications comes to our mind it is rightfully so. The villagers often refer to Behzad as an "engineer," a sign of his education, perhaps. Behzad discovers what appears to be a clandestine romance between the ditch-digger and the village girl Zaynab, who brings milk for her lover to drink. Behzad decides to get some fresh milk for himself and participates in the infamous stable scene that elicited Dabashi's wrath. As the movie concludes, Behzad falls out of favor with the boy, the ditch-digger collapses under rocks that fall on him, and Behzad plays a small part in rescuing him. There is some indication that the old woman dies, but Behzad's crew leaves him and in the end Behzad himself departs Siah Dareh after photographing the women coming out in force into the village, presumably to arrange the funeral ceremony of the dead woman. We do not see the ceremony itself.

However, this plot summary may also be read as containing challenges that are specific to the inevitable growth and transformation of Behzad, a character rightfully described by Dabashi as a pompous fool from the big city on a self-important mission to the country. Behzad's transformation while in Siah Dareh is presented through a series of ruptures in the surface of the landscape as well as through the superficial exchanges between Behzad and the villagers. The cumulative effect of these ruptures is to showcase Behzad's comic disorientation and confusion, as well as to serve as ocular proof of the presence of the sublime that has targeted Behzad for spiritual growth.

Much of Behzad's disorientation is presented through his unguided engagements with the landscape. For instance, Kiarostami begins the movie with a meandering panorama of the Kurdish countryside vivisected by the roads from Tehran on which Behzad's vehicle labors along with great difficulty. It is not merely the van that is struggling; Behzad and his crew are lost. The conversation in these scenes (all overheard) centers around an unidentifiable landmark where they should have turned: a lone tree. It is ironic that this conversation takes place as we see the van rumbling along a hillside dotted with singular trees. All these trees look the same to the passengers in the van. They are outsiders and the joke is on them. After they arrive in the village, in an exceptionally grand but too-close-for-comfort shot, Kiarostami shows us Behzad's disorientation as Behzad takes in the village. Behzad stands on the rooftop of his host's house and gazes at the alien architecture of the place: we might call the constitution of this village from Behzad's perspective almost cubist, with the surfaces of the roofs, ground, windows, doors, stairs, antennas, and pylons intersecting each other at random angles, an odd flower pot placed here and there. The effect on Behzad is as if he is unable to experience depth. He is overwhelmed by the surface and it shows on his face.

In some respects, Behzad is like any typical city slicker exiled to the countryside. He is impatient, superficial, and demanding in his interactions with the villagers of Siah Dareh, who are largely women and children. But Kiarostami also shows us that there is a perverse streak in Behzad, which might be an existential characteristic specific to him. We first sense this in his jocular but aggressive taunting of the young boy Farzad. Farzad, who is taking an exam, asks Behzad, "What happens to the Good and the Evil on Judgment Day?" To which Behzad replies, "The Good go to hell and the Evil to heaven." He sees the startled look on the boy's face and corrects his answer: "The Good go to heaven and the Evil to hell." But this is our first indication that Behzad is increasingly a man whose relationship to himself and the world is amiss. This is also where Kiarostami weaves into the narrative the thread of a spiritual quest, which comes full-circle in Behzad's final edifying encounter with the Kurdish physician. More callous and gratuitous acts follow; at the cemetery, he picks up a human thigh bone and throws it on the dashboard of his jeep as a curiosity item. Also at the cemetery he sees a turtle inching its way along the rocky, uneven ground. Behzad kicks it and topples it over on its side. After Behzad gets in his jeep and leaves, Kiarostami lovingly shows us the turtle straightening itself up after a couple of difficult attempts and nimbly moving away. It is almost as if the natural world is watching Behzad. One is reminded of the mysterious figure in Farrokhzaad's poem who stands outside looking in. We also see Behzad looking at apples falling and rolling in real time, perceptions that slow him down.

Behzad engages in flirtatious conversations with his host; when she tells him that the young men are off working in the fields since they have to earn their living in the summer and cannot work in the winter, Behzad rephrases her comments as meaning that the men are being "idle" in the winter. He then looks markedly at her pregnant belly and says, "Some seeds are sown in winter and harvested in summer. See, you have not been idle." As the woman blushes and continues to thread the wool on the veranda posts, Kiarostami presents us with a crude man obsessed with sex and death, a subjectivity that is slowly being ruptured in Behzad's encounters with nature and with the people of Siah Dareh.

The estrangement experienced by Behzad and his crew ultimately has an economic reason. They are sent to Siah Dareh to do a job for their boss in Tehran, but they cannot do that job before the old woman dies. We hear constant bickering between Behzad and his crew about their frustration at being unable to film the mourning ceremony for the old woman. At one point in response to his crew's irritation that the old woman has not died yet, Behzad says, "I can't strangle her!" Behzad is constantly hounded by wireless calls from Tehran, and the nature of his conversations leads us to believe that he is being asked to account for their delay in Siah Dareh.

The eruptions through which the sublime makes its presence felt, and which mark Behzad's growing awareness of his self-alienation, begin with the spatial disorientation he experiences while looking for the lone tree on the hillside, and includes his robotic and repetitive meanderings from the village to the hill to take his telephone calls, his callous overturning of the turtle, his patronizing exchanges with the ditch-digger, his attempts to impress Zaynab with Farrokhzaad's poem in the underground cellar when she milks the cow, his angry outbursts with Farzad, and finally his impatience with the old woman who will not die. Collectively, Siah Dareh is an entity that overwhelms Behzad to the point of non-comprehension and complete disorientation, an appropriate incentive to turn his thoughts toward reflective judgment, which is the seat of the sublime.

Every entity with whom Behzad interacts turns away from him. The ditch-digger stops singing when Behzad interrupts his work, though Behzad encourages him to sing. Zaynab does not show her face to him though he asks her to do so, and furthermore tells him to pay her mother for the milk. Farzad refuses to ride in his car after he shouts at him, and to align himself with Behzad in the second half of the film. When Behzad makes small talk about his smoking polluting the atmosphere, the Kurdish physician tells him, "It will take more than your cigarettes to pollute this atmosphere." The villagers only give to Behzad; he cannot take anything from them that they do not give.

Behzad's total exposure as a phony and confused human being takes place in the stable scene. It is here in the stable's darkened interiors that Kiarostami all but erases the materiality of Zaynab when he has Behzad recite Farrokhzaad's poem about desire for union and then depart with his banal comment, "You know writing poetry has nothing to do with diplomas. You can do it too if you have talent." It is instructive here to recall how Zaynab rejects his repeated requests to show her face to him. Zaynab is not a veiled woman; in fact, none of the women in Siah Dareh are veiled. Behzad wants to see her face because he had earlier seen her running away from the cemetery after delivering milk to her lover Yosef, the ditch-digger. It is his curiosity that makes him want to see her face, but Kiarostami does not permit it. When Behzad speaks of needing fresh milk, Yosef tells him that any house in the village would give it to him. But Behzad wants to get milk from the same place that Yosef gets it, from Kakrahman's house, Zaynab's house. There is an internal symmetry to Behzad's stable scene with Zaynab and his cemetery scene with Yosef. It is as if the roof caving in, a central motif in Farrokhzaad's poem, actually happens at the cemetery with Yosef. It is as if the desperate cry of Farrokhzaad's speaker for the wind to lift her out of the caved-in house actually happens to Yosef at the cemetery. "He needs air," the Kurdish physician tells Behzad. There are other parallels as well. It is Behzad who cannot see, first Yosef's face at the cemetery and later Zaynab's face in the cellar of her house. When Behzad tells Yosef that he cannot see him, Yosef answers: "I can see you." Our lingering feeling in watching Behzad's interactions with the villagers is one of seeing him trying to fit in, to get the upper hand, and being denied that opportunity at each turn. He is the one who is in the dark, and he is literally and figuratively in the dark in the scene with Zaynab. Zaynab resists his advances to connect with her the way her lover did at the cemetery. Even after Yosef is rescued from the hole, Behzad does not see his face, though he lends his van to the villagers to rush him to the hospital.

What is ultimately overwhelming about Behzad's isolation and self-alienation is the fact that it is shown to result organically from the mismatch of being out of place in Siah Dareh in every which way possible. In truth, Behzad is a ridiculous character in the Aristotelian sense. We should not feel bad about laughing at Behzad's vain and ignorant antics in the village. But Kiarostami mounts such tremendous incomprehensibility upon Behzad that he is more in the position of one who is ready to confront the sublime and be transformed by it rather than one who simply deserves to be laughed at.

Except for the children and the very old, Behzad is the only adult male in the village, and it appears the only adult who is not engaged in some sort of labor. We see the women in the village engaged in their chores while Behzad drives around frenetically from point to point trying to establish connection with Tehran. The women labor in an unmarked fashion at household chores. Women and children labor a great deal in this village. For instance, Farzad carries and fetches for a host of women, in addition to attending school and also taking care of Behzad's requirements. We see a woman hidden under a huge pile of hay that she is carrying to a shed. Behzad's host, we learn, has given birth overnight; she tells him this herself while washing clothes in her usual fashion. It is interesting that Dabashi would see rape where there is none but does not hear the film's interesting and subtle discussions about women and work. In a critical scene, Tajdolat, the woman who runs the coffee shop, and her male interlocutor argue about the relative weight of labor. Who labors more, men or women? Who accrues the benefit of women's labor? This discussion is particularly telling because Tajdolat speaks of physical labor in all its forms, including child birth. She refers to the lingering psychological weariness that labor brings. The man fills the conversation with sexual innuendos by referring to how men need to labor in order to produce children. This scene is interrupted when Behzad leaves for his sojourn to Kermanshah, and when he comes back we see Tajdolat sitting pensively with her head in her hands and the man leaving. They have obviously had a fight. As he leaves, Tajdolat states with barely suppressed anger, "You are a coward if you come back!"

The signifying of woman as labor is most forcefully articulated in the scenes in which Behzad hears from Farzad's schoolteacher about the origins of the mourning ritual that he has come to document. As Behzad's comic deflation continues, the teacher states that the ceremony is scarring for the women, giving examples of when his mother had to scar her face to express her loyalty and love toward his father when his father's aunt died. She had to scar her face once again when a distant cousin of his father's boss died, he tells Behzad. "So that my father wouldn't lose his job, my mother mourned a great deal," he explains. "There was a lot of competition at the factory between the men to hold on to their jobs. Need and necessity, you see? . . . No question of showing pity or giving in. Everyone displayed themselves, pushed themselves forward to please the boss. . . . When I think about this, it is painful. . . . I think the origins of this ceremony are bound to the economy. What I told you just now has been engraved in their memories." This patriarchal ritual, in which men use the bodies of their women—for men's economic purposes—to express their loyalty to their employer and preserve their jobs, is of course an ironic commentary on Behzad's own presence in Siah Dareh. He is there to shoot the same mourning ceremony for his employer in Tehran, presumably for anthropological "othering" purposes. The ceremony is still an economic one; but the anthropological discourse of the schoolteacher exposes the seamless continuity between the culture Behzad has come to document and that of his own. Kiarostami effectively blurs the outsider-insider anthropological positions by making the requirement of the ritual coincide with that of Behzad's presence in Siah Dareh.

The burden of Behzad's deflation, however, is not of a destructive kind. In the final scene, when Behzad drops into the river the thighbone that the ditch-digger had given him, and we follow the river as it runs toward us, here and now, we see the possibility of Behzad's renewal as a human being who has been transformed by the quest that brought him to Siah Dareh. Every comfortable master-slave binary that Behzad represents exposes itself as a deeply flawed category—city versus country, Tehran versus Siah Dareh, Iranian versus Kurdish, educated versus uneducated, man versus woman, adult versus child, and so on. In its aesthetic and moral insistence on the rejuvenation of a deeply flawed and foolish character such as Behzad, without any aggression but with the pain of knowledge and hope for the future, with both loss and gain, *The Wind Will Carry Us* demonstrates the moral and transformative power of the sublime.

NOTES

1. Foroogh Farrokhzaad, *A Rebirth* (Costa Mesa, Calif.: Mazda Publishers, 1997), 14–15.
2. Ibid., 15.
3. Ibid.
4. Immanuel Kant, *Critique of Judgment,* trans. J. H. Bernard (New York: Hafner Press, 1951), 178.
5. See Jeffrey Pence, "Cinema of the Sublime: Theorizing the Ineffable," *Poetics Today* 25, no. 1 (2004): 33. Pence summarizes the critical trends in cinema studies as replaying "in miniature the oscillation in the modern West between science and religion, reflecting the inadequacy of either orientation to satisfy by itself all of our concerns." Except for

brief periods in the history of cinema studies, contemporary trends in film studies in the West seem to privilege an orientation toward the "social and historical reality." Pence identifies several schools of thought and dominant theorists of cinema at the helms of such an orientation: "Whether in the tradition of German *Kulturkritik* from which Benjamin emerges . . . , or in the movements of Althusserian Marxism and Lacanian psychoanalysis that accompanied film studies' institutionalization in the 1970s and 1980s . . . , or in what might be understood as cinema studies' dispersal into the more freewheeling explorations of power and identity in contemporary cultural studies . . . a critical perspective skeptical of the social relations and mentalities implied by cinematic conventions aligns itself with those aspects of cinema that appear most modern and radical."

6. Fredric Jameson, "Third World Literature in the Era of Multinational Capitalism," *Social Text* 15 (Autumn 1986).
7. Walter Benjamin, "The Work of Art in the Age of Mechanical Reproduction," in *Illuminations,* trans. Harry Zohn (New York: Schocken, 1968).
8. Martin Heidegger, "The Origin of the Work of Art," in *Poetry, Language, Thought,* trans. Albert Hofstadter (New York: Harper and Row, 1971).
9. Longinus, *On the Sublime,* chap. 1, www.gutenberg.org/files/17957/17957-h/17957-h.htm, accessed January 28, 2013.
10. Ibid., chap. 1.
11. Ibid., chap. 7.
12. Ibid., chap. 34.
13. Ibid., chap. 7.
14. Ibid.
15. Ibid., chap. 10.
16. Ibid., chap. 12.
17. Ibid., chap. 8.
18. Ibid., chap. 38.
19. Ibid.
20. "Abbas Kiarostami," *Firouzan Films,* www.firouzanfilms.com/HallOfFame/Inductees/AbbasKiarostami.html, accessed January 28, 2013.
21. See A. O. Scott, "A Darkness Cast upon Childhood," review of *ABC Africa,* directed by Abbas Kiarostami, *New York Times,* May 3, 2002, movies.nytimes.com/movie/review?res=9902E4DA1331F930A35756C0A9649C8B63&partner=Rotten%20Tomatoes. Scott interprets the "blank screen" as indicative of "the medium's limitations and to its power, to the objectivity of the camera and to the artifice involved in even its simplest use." It could very well be that in countries like Uganda and many others, electric power goes out very often, and Kiarostami was accurately capturing the event in real time.

22. "Abbas Kiarostami," *Firouzan Films*.
23. Ibid.
24. Ibid.
25. Benjamin, "The Work of Art in the Age of Mechanical Reproduction," 241.
26. Ibid.
27. Ibid., 242.
28. "Abbas Kiarostami," *Firouzan Films*.
29. Hamid Dabashi, *Close Up: Iranian Cinema Past, Present and Future* (New York: Verso, 2001), 252.
30. Ibid., 254.
31. Ibid., 255.
32. "Abbas Kiarostami," *Firouzan Films*.
33. Dabashi, *Close Up*, 253.
34. Kant, *Critique of Judgment*, 82.
35. Ibid.
36. Ibid., 88.
37. Ibid., 89.
38. Ibid., 94.
39. Ibid.
40. Ibid.
41. Ibid., 176.
42. Ibid., 177.
43. Ibid., 181.
44. Ibid.
45. Sigmund Freud, *Collected Papers, vol. 5*, ed. James Strachey (New York: Basic Books, 1959), 217.
46. Quoted in Alberto Elena, *The Cinema of Abbas Kiarostami*, trans. Belinda Coombes (London: SAQI, 2005), 71.
47. Ibid., 72.

8

AMERICA THE OPPRESSIVELY FUNNY

Humor and Anti-Americanisms in Modern Turkish Cinema

PERIN GUREL

In the last decade, the Turkish Ministry of Culture and Tourism has supported the country's rising movie industry as a strategic tool for reaching the rest of the world.[1] However, all genres have not benefited equally from this public relations investment. Comedies like the gross-out slapstick series *Recep İvedik,* which are the most successful films in Turkey, have received little or no support from the Turkish government and little attention abroad.[2] While there is increasing interest in Turkish auteurs such as Nuri Bilge Ceylan among Western art house audiences, Turkish comedy has not generally traveled beyond the borders of the Turkish language. In countries with large diasporic Turkish populations such as Germany and Austria, some theaters do screen popular Turkish comedies.[3] In the United States, however, where Turkish communities are much more dispersed, festivals organized by Turkish American cultural associations constitute the primary venues for the screening of Turkish films. These occasions have understandably prioritized art house movies and the so-called classics.[4] The dearth of Turkish comedies in the United States is, of course, in direct contrast to the daily streaming of U.S. sitcoms, adult cartoons, and comedies into Turkish living rooms. Turkish comedies about America and Americans often address and contest precisely this inequality of access and laughter.

Westerners have ignored Turkish comedy, but Turks have gained a lot of ideas about the West from Turkish comedy. This lowly genre is important not only for combining folkloric elements with appropriations from Hollywood but also for constituting one of the most popular sources of contemporary representations of America and Americans in Turkish culture. In line with comedy's potential for inversion and subversion, U.S.-based signs, symbols, and tropes are often broken down and reassembled to meet Turkish needs in an imperfect and uneven reversal of "cultural imperialism" in Turkish comedies. Adapting a "critical transnationalism," this essay pays attention to local agency and transculturation as well as structural inequality, such as the near-domination of Turkish film distribution networks by U.S.-led multinationals following the privatization of the Turkish economy in the late 1980s.[5] Not only are such inequalities rarely lost on the producers, audiences are often keenly aware of them as well. Thus, this essay traces the development of America and Americans as instruments of comedy in Turkish film from the 1970s to the contemporary era, balancing humanistic exploration of representation with sociohistorical notes on the relation of popular Turkish cinema to Hollywood.[6] It proposes a preliminary critical transnational trajectory from populist left-wing comedies of the 1970s, to the conflicted neoliberal parodies of the 1990s, to the complexly globalized cinemascapes of the early twenty-first century. These are exemplified by three top-grossing personality comedies featuring each era's most famous comedian: *Köşeyi Dönen Adam* (The Man Who Turned the Corner, 1978) with Kemal Sunal, *Amerikalı* (The American, 1993) with Şener Şen, and *Yahşi Batı* (The Mild West, 2010) with Cem Yılmaz.[7]

Turkish comedies often utilize one of three comic figures: the *eiron*, "the mock-modest man" identified by Aristotle who conceals his knowledge to overcome those in power; the trickster, who upsets the prevailing order through shape-shifting and sexualized anarchy; and the wise fool, whose unstudied idiocy unmasks the hypocrisies of contemporary society. All these figures, particularly the last two, have deep roots in Turkish folk culture, having been manifested in important narrative *focusees* such as Nasreddin Hodja, Keloğlan, and Temel the Fisherman. Focusees are vernacular characters "serving as the focus for the attribution of narratives," who, somewhat like typecast actors, maintain some continuity as well as flexibility in their symbolic attributes.⁸ In classical Turkish Cinema, Kemal Sunal (1944-2000) and his well-established character Şaban, a simple, uneducated, but loveable country bumpkin, best exemplify the wise fool.⁹ In *Amerikalı*, Şener Şen, a versatile actor, operates as the urbane eiron. In *Yahşi Batı,* Cem Yılmaz takes his preestablished shrewd peddler and trickster persona to the Wild West.

Comedy films about America and Americans seem aware of the power of the cinematic image, often self-consciously utilizing TV clips, film sets and costumes, and parodic references to Hollywood. The ultimate in such pastiche, transculturation, and Turkification may be the rise of a new crop of media that utilize American actors (including relatively famous ones, such as Chevy Chase, Steve Guttenberg, and Megan Fox) to do Turkey's comic bidding in the early twenty-first century. These seem to declare the final domestification and defanging of the oppressively hilarious American. But as my final example, *Yahşi Batı,* shows, the wish to "laugh back" at U.S. hegemony remains imbued with anxieties about communication, while Turkish language and culture remain the provincial to Hollywood's "global vernacular."¹⁰ Moreover, such anxieties are often expressed in the language of gender and sexuality, most vividly in the lack of a marriage-based resolution, which (in opposition to the conventions of New Comedy and Hollywood-style romantic comedies) refuses to materialize.¹¹

It is no surprise that the West has loomed large in the Turkish cinematic imagery from its earliest beginnings, as the Turkish movie industry was formed through deep transculturation. The first movies were projected on to Karagöz shadow puppet screens, and Turkish comedy developed into what scholars have called "the Cinema of Karagöz," employing common stock characters, such as the rough-hewn Karagöz and the pretentious Hacivat, absurd misunderstandings, and lewd language play.¹² Early films regularly added local scenes to foreign features and stole foreign scenes to add to Turkish movies. This involved Egyptian as well as Hollywood films, but by 1954, 300 of 350 imported films were American.¹³ The Turkish film industry was given a boost by the reduction of municipal tax to 25 percent in 1948, in comparison to 70 percent for foreign films, opening up the space for experimentation.¹⁴ Although melodramas dominated screens, producers experimented with a wide variety of genres. In addition to spaghetti (or kebab) westerns, comedy films proved the most hospitable home for representations of "America" throughout the fifties, sixties, and seventies. These decades represent the first Golden Age of Turkish Cinema, known as Yeşilçam, when the industry became third only to Hollywood and Bollywood in terms of its productivity. By the mid-1970s, an average of 200 Turkish films were being produced yearly.[15] Most of these films were "remakes, adaptations, and spin-offs," quickies made in a few months under stretched budgets.[16] Popular Turkish comedies featuring famous comedians in situations just different enough to simulate interest and similar enough to maintain loyalties fit perfectly under this system; such films advertised each other and functioned somewhat like modern day sit-coms or traditional folk tale cycles, as the audience carried expectations and tacit knowledge from one movie to another.

Shot on location with low production values, dubbed in postproduction to save money, 1970s Turkish comedies combined the plight of the urban poor and slapstick antics with romantic or soft-core battle-of-the-sexes comedy. The 1978 comedy *Köşeyi Dönen Adam*, featuring the famous Şaban character played by Kemal Sunal in sixteen other films, is the epitome of this sub-genre as well as a significant variation from it. Like Charlie Chaplin in his late films, Sunal carries a well-established, downtrodden, simple bumpkin to a left-wing political conclusion. In films such as *Salak Milyoner* (The Foolish Millionaire, 1974), Şaban, the bumbling fool from the provinces, finds love and fortune only through sheer luck, naiveté, and folksy uprightness. In *Carikli Milyoner* (The Millionaire with Sandals, 1983) and *Sosyete Şaban* (High-Society Şaban, 1985), Şaban gets the upper-class girl who had originally scorned and mocked him, even as he confirms the validity of folksy morals he has brought from his village. He thus exposes and personally triumphs over the oppressive Turkish structures of class and upper-class westernization, without directly changing them. The connections and variations between this generic clash-of-classes Şaban plot and *Köşeyi Dönen Adam* are, therefore, as significant as those between Chaplin's character and message in *The Tramp* (1915) and *Modern Times* (1936).[17] In other words, *Köşeyi Dönen Adam* does not just depict the triumph of the upright protagonist despite the power of U.S.-led commercial capitalism in Turkey. It critiques the whole system: capitalism, commercialism, and the United States.

In a perfect exemplification of Turkish cinema's incorporation of folk forms and Western imports, the title of *Köşeyi Dönen Adam* (The Man Who Turned the Corner) is based on a proverbial expression meaning "the man who struck it rich." The film, based on a novel by dramatist Müjdat Gezen, *Esegin Karnindaki Elmas* (The Diamond inside the Belly of the Donkey), depicts the coming to political consciousness of Adem (Kemal Sunal), a member of the *lumpenproletariat*. Adem is a simple-minded office boy working for a Turkish bubble gum company who dreams of striking it rich and marrying the neighborhood beauty—a headscarf-wearing coquette called Şükran (Meral Orhonsay), whose strict and stingy haji father (Ali Şen) is also Adem's oppressive landlord. In order to better his situation, Adem collects coupons from newspapers and ignores the leftist movements. The American in this film is a donkey, Mr. Dörtnal (Mr. Fourfoot). Adem inherits the donkey, and the donkey alone, from his uncle in America, who is said to have owned diamond mines. In a moment of desperation, and urged by a tabloid writer out to make some money selling newspapers, he makes everyone around him believe that Mr. Fourfoot carries a priceless diamond within its bowels. He soon finds all women, including the head-scarfed beloved he had long idealized and the sexy secretary at his factory, to be unprincipled and materialistic. All religious figures, such as the haji landlord, and business figures, such as his unscrupulous boss, prove themselves hypocrites as well. Having treated him like dirt at the beginning of the movie, they try pathetically to get into his good graces and coo over him and the donkey while praising America endlessly. Adem prevents them from butchering the donkey for the diamond, saying they must wait until the diamond emerges "naturally." Toward the end of the movie, all the materialistic characters dive into the donkey's dung, frantically searching for the diamond—clearly a metaphor for American aid, which often involved cast-off weapons from the U.S. Army. In fact, between 1975 and 1978, the year the movie was released, the United States implemented an arms embargo on Turkey, which one of the characters in the movie even references. The film allegorizes this by making the donkey constipated until the end of the movie. As the characters dive into Mr. Fourfoot's excrement in the grand finale, Adem silently leaves, literally turning a street corner in order to join a May 1 workers' parade. The young female workers in the march, gender-neutral and politically committed, are the only women who do not try to seduce him for monetary gain.

Köşeyi Dönen Adam courts audiences with the Şaban character—Adem is a bumbling fool throughout most of the movie—yet the film differs from the formula in significant ways. The most obvious change is in the allegorical significance of the name Adem, meaning Adam, and standing for the everyman, in opposition to Şaban, the stereotypical fool who shows no progressive change within his movies. According to Vadullah Taş, who has written a casual introduction to all eighty-two Kemal Sunal films, *Köşeyi Dönen Adam* also carries the distinctive stamp of its Kurdish Turkish auteur, Atıf Yılmaz, making this "a creative-director film in the Western sense," resembling the works of Pasolini.[18] Yılmaz indeed employs a different cinematic style in contrast to the conventional populist realism of the Şaban films by including bizarre expressionistic scenes that reflect Adem's subconscious. Yılmaz signifies Adem's seduction by the promise of wealth, Americanization, and fast women in several psychedelic, hyper-saturated dream sequences, which contain images from television and resemble the fast hypnotic edits of a TV commercial. A photograph of Adem's uncle cuts into an image of the Statue of Liberty, followed by a clip from a TV variety show, zoom-ins and extreme close-ups of seductive women, and a wide-angle image of his boss chewing gum, layered over an acid-rock sound clip. Although they combine the abject and the grotesque with the element of incongruity, these sequences are far from humorous, because the psychic and emotional distance necessary for laughter is missing. The complete colonization of Adem's psyche has allowed the director to cross the uncanny line between humor and horror. These American wet dreams are then contrasted with the clear, unadorned left-wing graffiti, which Adem sees on the walls of the city upon waking up and leaving his apartment. In contrast to his emotionally charged dreams, these political messages receive an alienated smirk from Adem at the beginning of the film; he even paints over one. By the end, however, they have supplanted America/capitalism in his heart and mind: in the final scene of the movie, Adem joins in the workers' steady, collectively sung march, which contains a refrain familiar from the graffiti he had long ignored, "May 1st, workers' day." Capitalist simulacra have been replaced by Marxist reality; the worker is finally awake.

One of the most striking images in the subconscious pastiche series is the quick close-up of a young woman's bare breast, being squeezed by a disembodied hand, possibly Adem's. This image alludes to an earlier scene in the film in which Şükran, the faux-pious flirt, manipulates Adem by placing his hand over her "heart" and asking him to see how fast it beats for him. Adem blushes, mumbles indiscriminately, and makes a fool of himself by blurting out "boobs" when Şükran's mother appears. This is a typical Şaban sequence marked by sexual and linguistic misunderstandings; yet things get darker and begin to border on S&M as the movie progresses. In another sexualized scene, Adem dreams that he is a donkey being led around on all fours by the sexy secretary at the gum factory. Variations of this theme made it to the sexualized posters of the movie, with Şaban kneeling down next to the donkey or taking the place of the donkey, as the women stand tall, all dolled up in makeup and Western-style clothing.[19] This power dynamic, however, is soon reversed, thanks to Mr. Fourfoot and the imaginary American diamond. In one real-life revenge scene, Adem forces the haji and his family to dress more modernly in order to please him and Mr. Fourfoot, the representatives of America. He then calls for a casual evening stroll for the whole family, making the haji walk the streets in a suit, bowtie, and a Kemalist top hat, as his wife walks by his side in makeup and a shiny dress, with Şükran in front, in a sparkly outfit that reveals her legs and high-heeled shoes. The family is harassed and humiliated as the town's people surround them and laugh; young hoodlums whistle, praise Şükran's legs, and loudly offer to buy her for the night. To add insult to injury, Adem has been two-timing Şükran with the secretary at work. The secretary, however, also fails to translate her sexual favors to Adem into any material gain, even though she claims she has been impregnated.

The gendered and/or sexual revenge of the rugged representative of the East over pretentious upper-class or "westoxicated" women was also the theme of many 1970s Turkish sexploitation films, and it is present in milder forms in the Şaban films above. Yet such

Şaban films always ended with the reconciliation of the couple and the submission of the spoiled heroine through love, understanding, and a properly hierarchical marriage. Comedy as a classical genre has long indicated that the problems encountered within the narrative would be minor, that no one would die, and that everything would end in marriage, or at least a similar ritualistic resolution that symbolizes a return to order.[20] The resolution of structural and political conflicts at the personal and romantic levels is a staple of Hollywood romance, comedy, and drama as well. Many Şaban comedies, though not all, fit this formula; none diverges from it as significantly as *Köşeyi Dönen Adam*. Not only is the real problem revealed to be a major one (i.e., class struggle), the film ends open-endedly, with a call to action: the common man and woman are supposed to replicate Adem's actions and refuse the false bride/bribe of capitalism in order to join the worker's movement. Thus, the film contributes to the politically polarized atmosphere of 1970s Turkey, a time of intense street-level and cultural conflict between the right and the left, by casting its vote unequivocally on the side of socialism.

Unfortunately, during the 1970s, 1980s, and 1990s, few audiences in Turkey ever got to see this ending. According to the film's producer, Arif Keskiner, the day *Köşeyi Dönen Adam* was released, Turkish police raided the cinema and cut out all the portions of the film relating to the workers' struggle, including the ending. (In the approved cut, the film ends before Mr. Dörtnal's defecation, with Adem's words, "Whose turn is it for the shit watch?") The police staged yet another raid in 1980, upon seeing that an uncensored video brought from Germany was being shown publicly in a tea garden. This time, the director, the producer, and the great Kemal Sunal himself were all taken to court. The situation seemed dire until Sunal lightened the mood by pulling a clueless Şaban act, saying, "I am an actor; I act whatever script they give me," to bursts of laughter.[21] The prosecutor dismissed the three men, yet *Köşeyi Dönen Adam* continued to be seen as a threat as well as a potential cash cow. In the early 1990s, private TV channels, founded in response to calls of freedom from state censorship, made their fortunes by buying and showing old Turkish movies in bulk. On multiple occasions *Köşeyi Dönen Adam*, with its political and sexual sections censored, was the most-watched TV broadcast in the Turkey, attracting 32 percent of the viewing audience in October 1991, when there was only one private channel, and 28 percent in March 1994, a time of immense competition between multiple new private channels.[22] The overwhelming, decades-long popularity of even a crippled *Köşeyi Dönen Adam* can be explained by the film's complex and layered humor, as well as the economic realities of the Turkish film industry in the 1980s and 1990s.

During the 1970s, Turkish cities were overtaken by street and campus violence, read as paramilitary proxy wars between the Soviet Union and the United States. The political violence pulled mixed-gender and mixed-age audiences further away from movie theaters toward TV and video. On September 12, 1980, a military junta took over control of the government for three years, advancing a new conservative constitution and instituting a brutal suppression of leftist movements. The coup suffocated the Turkish cinema industry, already struggling due to the rise of TV and video, by putting an end to what had been its last resort: cheap pornographic comedies. The democratically elected center-right government that followed the junta rule liberalized the Turkish economy, initiating a post-coup privatization frenzy embodied by the alliance between President Reagan and Prime Minister Ozal. The Turkish movie industry fell further into a slump as the 1988 Law on Foreign Capital allowed Hollywood companies to absorb and displace local companies inside Turkey. From the mid-1980s until the late 1990s, Hollywood films dominated the market, with most Turkish-made films never seeing the light of day or going straight to video. In this cultural desert, Kemal Sunal took a decade-long break from film acting, completing a master's thesis in media studies in 1998.[23]

Turkish TV audiences, however, watched Yeşilçam movies over and over on the new private channels, which needed cheap fodder for their round-the-clock schedules. A new cultural lingo emerged in which audiences developed a semi-parodic affection and appreciation for classical Yeşilçam movies, with their foolish Şabans, contrived melodramatic plots, blind singers, and golden-hearted fallen women. Şener Şen emerged as a cultural icon, providing two successful comic films that helped audiences make sense of Yeşilçam-dominated TV and Hollywood-dominated theaters. In 1988, Şen brought audiences to cinemas in a post-Yeşilçam parody of Turkish melodramas called *Arabesk* (Arabesque). Similarly, his 1993 Turkish parody of Hollywood movies, *Amerikalı* (The American), was one of the few exceptions in a bleak Turkish cinematic landscape, becoming a box office success with an audience of around 400,000, raking in eight billion in old Turkish liras ($720,850), four times what it reportedly cost to produce.[24] If the popularity of *Köşeyi Dönen Adam* on 1990s TV symbolized the frustrated yearnings of an unfinished era, this new film embodied the new era in its bizarre apolitical combination of Americanization, sex, violence, and technical mediocrity, the latter being Yeşilçam's longtime Achilles' heel.[25]

The American in this movie is Şeref the Turk (Şener Şen), a Turkish Texan millionaire who comes back to Turkey after making a fortune in the United States. Şeref is an eiron only insofar as his motives remain clouded to the other characters. He evinces little wit, unless we count the playful spring in his step, his knowing smile, and the mocking laughter with which the director has coded a youthful Americanness. The movie opens with the media speculating on why Şeref has decided to return to Turkey, thinking it might have to do with business deals. The audience, however, has already been informed via a Star Wars–like opening script that Şeref the Turk intends to take revenge from Melek (Lale Mansur), the childhood love who abandoned him, and the "friend" who married her after plying Şeref with drugs that led to his wrongful imprisonment. In the meantime, the rival has become a successful businessman, he and Melek have divorced, and she has adopted a child and become a prostitute. A series of misunderstandings ensue based on everyone's inability to recognize each other. Şeref and his fallen ex even get to re-create several recognizable Hollywood sex scenes before their identities are revealed to each other. Eventually Şeref and Melek are reconciled and they overcome a bizarre kidnapping and exhortation attempt by his rival. Soon after, however, they accidentally kill a rapist and go on the run from the police, initiating an endless chase scene. Needless to say, this muddled narrative is driven purely by the wish to reference popular Hollywood movies, including *Pretty Woman, Home Alone, Terminator, Thelma and Louise,* and *Basic Instinct*. The film, in Şeref's non-linguistic bursts of laughter, also attempts to articulate the changes the Turkish cultural landscape has experienced since the free market reforms following the coup of 1980. The trailer summarizes these two goals, containing parodies of famous Hollywood scenes layered over a pop/rap sound track:

> Bridge, tower, subway, pool
>
> Watermelons sold by the slice
>
> Burger, blue jeans, coke, ice
>
> Man, we have all become Americans.[26]

Film scholar Savas Arslan finds in this song and the movie itself "an implicit criticism of the loss of authenticity and nativity" in Turkish culture.[27] Similarly, Nezih Erdoğan and Deniz Göktürk suggest that the film parodies blockbusters in order to question "the ways in which they have been integrated into the Turkish imagination."[28] Newspaper articles from 1993 show that *Amerikalı* was indeed advertised as a satirical text, foregrounding and criticizing the drastic changes in late twentieth-century Turkish culture, including the abundance of private TV channels, sex hotlines, game shows, and the infusion of English into all levels of Turkish media.[29] Such a reading would indeed suggest parallels between the dream sequences in *Köşeyi Dönen Adam* and the parodic moments of *Amerikalı*. The two films also share a revenge plot, unfolding with the help of a fantasy America. More tangentially, Şener Şen is the son of Ali Şen, the actor playing the hypocritical haji in *Köşeyi Dönen Adam,* and Şen and Sunal have acted together in comedies before, with Şen placed in positions of braggarts and authority figures who are then undermined by Sunal's wise fool. Thus it is clear that, despite the fact that Sunal is associated with the 1970s and early 1980s and Şen with the 1990s, the two actors are not from widely different comedic schools. Yet a subversive reading of *Amerikalı* as a post-coup comrade of *Köşeyi Dönen Adam* is necessarily strained at many levels, from production to distribution to reception.

In a 1993 interview, Şerif Gören, the director of *Amerikalı,* expressed that his team's wish was purely to make audiences laugh "a hundred times," to approach the technical quality of American movies, and to capture "an American tempo."³⁰ *Amerikalı* indeed became one of only four domestic films to be listed among the fifty highest-grossing films of the 1990s in Turkey—the other forty-six were Hollywood movies. Some casual analyses even cast the film as the beginning of a renaissance in Turkish cinema.³¹ We could, therefore, read *Amerikalı*'s economic triumph as a moment of the master's tools dismantling the master's house, but the film functions more as a second-rate homage to that edifice. On a structural level, the film owes much of its success to the fact that it was the first film to be distributed by American-owned Warner Bros. after the 1988 passage of the Law on Foreign Capital. In addition, the film's marketing team used every trick that the film is supposed to be criticizing in their advertising campaigns, including scenes of sexuality, sexualized violence, famous actors, and the Turkish-English lyrics of its theme song.

There are indeed opportunities for a critique of the media cultures of U.S.-led globalization in this movie, but they never materialize. Şeref tries to escape the paparazzi and fight the overblown media hype around his return, but lo and behold one of the paparazzi turns out to be an old friend and an ally. Şeref's other close companion, on the other hand, is a Mickey Mouse puppet with whom he regularly commiserates. Much could have been done with this trope, given the importance of shadow puppetry to the development of Turkish cinema, specifically Turkish comedy. Şeref's love of Mickey, however, is not so much a critique of Hollywood's domination of world's humor as it is a sentimentalized buying-in to the system. Mickey is no Mr. Fourfoot; Şeref is no Adem. His American Dreams only come true. Şeref has mysteriously gone from rags to riches, from wrongful imprisonment in Turkey to billions in Texas, and Mickey, a symbol of the American Dream, stands as a silent, smiling witness to this success story—a dissembling eiron in his own right.

Nothing exemplifies the movie's political commitments (or lack thereof) as the scene in which Şeref's rival hires a group of men to kidnap Şeref and Melek in order to make him sign away his fortune. The four would-be terrorists, dressed as a Native American, a Nazi, a Turkish veteran of the First World War, and a bearded man with a Palestinian kuffiyeh, describe themselves as the union of terrorists organized against "The United American Idiots Empire." In fact, they are all Turkish imposters with amateurish costumes. Our blindfolded heroes are not even on a plane but in a film set. Again, this might have been a Karagöz-style moment revealing the unnaturalness of U.S. hegemony over the world's media; but the film squanders (or rejects) any possibilities for critique. Not only is all political dissent against the United States dismissed as pure evil madness, with the pseudo-Arab linked with the pseudo-Nazi, but there is no explanation as to why these characters are in costume even though the blindfolded hostages cannot see them. When Şeref finally signs the documents and their blindfolds are removed, he asks for an explanation. The rival simply says, "Doesn't the world resemble Disneyland these days?" There is no reason why Şeref, who totes Mickey Mouse around with a loyalty bordering on totem worship, would feel this resemblance is a bad thing. Are we then to identify with the villain of this movie? Even if the answer is a postmodern yes, it would be generous to read this movie within a movie as a critique of Hollywood, or to see Şeref and Melek as participants in a Plato's cave metaphor, because "Doesn't this resemble that?" is in fact the main visual refrain of *Amerikalı*.

Look at this, the movie asks, over and over: doesn't this resemble that Hollywood movie you saw two years ago? As we laugh at a kid who says he likes to be "home alone," wait breathlessly for the replication of that familiar scene from *Basic Instinct,* or watch a car fly in the air to destroy a hovering helicopter at the last minute, we become complicit in the marginalization of Turkish cinema. Particularly because of the low production values and the obviously fake Americans in the movie, Hollywood remains the ultimate signified for each uncanny yet familiar local signifier. We are not sure how to change things or whether we even should. After all, there is comfort in recognition, repetition, and in playing along. *Amerikalı* drew in audiences who might have been ambivalent about the infusion of American cultural products into the Turkish psyche, yet rewarded them with a comic sensation every time they successfully recognized a line or a scene from Hollywood. Because parody depends on audiences' familiarity with the original genre or body of texts, "the success of film parody in America testifies to a nation of moviegoers."[32] In a transnational context, however, parody's short-term financial success might underline a deep socioeconomic cost. *Amerikalı* reminds us that a parody may always be "an imitation of an imitation," but it is not always satire.[33] This is especially so if we agree with Kierkegaard that satire "entails pain, but this pain has a dialectic which gives it a teleology in the direction of a cure."[34] To use a Turkish proverbial expression, *Amerikalı* is much more interested in eating grapes than in beating the owner of the vineyard.[35] As suggested by the interview with Gören, the film is too committed to Hollywood-style entertainment (and Hollywood-level profits) to commit to neither pain nor cure.

The political ambivalence of *Amerikalı* is confirmed in the abrupt finale of the movie and echoed in the film's unexplained withholding of marriage from its hero and heroine. After surviving their car crashing into a police helicopter and faking their deaths, Şeref and Melek are joined by their adopted son. As the three members of this makeshift family hug each other in relief, Şeref's paparazzi friend appears out of nowhere and asks to take a photo; they all submit, with Şeref finally rewarding the media with a big smile. There is something deeply uncanny about this scene that has just followed the unsatisfactory "explosion" of a toy car and helicopter, followed by the unexplained disappearance of the many police cars that had been chasing the protagonists. According to the final captions, Şeref and his "lover" will simply escape from "the claws of Turkish justice" to Texas with their son. The text also suggests that a sequel might be in the works, hinting that Şeref will be battling the mafia from here on out. Melek's role in this American crime-fighting future and in this almost-nuclear family is not clear. The lack of a marriage-based resolution may imply the director's unwillingness to have Şeref officially marry a confirmed prostitute—despite the couple's previous reconciliation and their vows never to part. It may be an attempt to stay true to the action-movie prototype, in which the hero must remain unencumbered by domestic duties. It may be simply to leave the relationship unstable in case of a sequel, which, thankfully, never materialized. Either way, there is no politically conscious alternative to marriage, no painful dialectic in Kierkegaard's words that resemble the censored, subversive end of *Köşeyi Dönen Adam*.

The reactions of late twentieth-century audiences elude us, beyond our knowledge of both films' commercial success; Turkish social media, however, offers some clues as to current readings and audience memories of *Köşeyi Dönen Adam* and *Amerikalı*. Both movies may be seen in their entireties on YouTube, but *Amerikalı*'s afterlife has differed drastically from that of *Köşeyi Dönen Adam*. On the Internet, *Köşeyi Dönen Adam* is currently available with its censored parts reincorporated; under the comments section, viewers recall watching the film on TV, express indignation at its amateurish censoring, celebrate the film for its clear political commitments, and praise Sunal for being brave enough to act in it during a time of such political repression. With multiple YouTube postings advertising the censored parts, the film has gained quite a leftist-cult following and even occasioned discussions around various aspects of the workers' movement. The few YouTube comments under *Amerikalı*, on the other hand, simply attack the film for being made by America-loving crypto-Jews. "Their aim must have been to spread pro-American aspirations under the guise of comedy," claims one commentator.[36] On Sinemalar.com, the Turkish-language archive for Turkish movies, some audiences note that, even though they laughed when they first saw *Amerikalı*, they could not watch it again because of the low technical quality and the heavy-hitting allusions.[37] For such commentators, *Amerikalı* marks the long way Turkish cinema has come in terms of quality and nuance. "No imitation can be better than the original," argues one poster; another defends the film by insisting it is not an "imitation" but a "parody."[38] Certainly, many of the attacks on *Amerikalı* are far from nuanced themselves. They also contrast with the economic success of the film in its time. However, the ease with which *Amerikalı*'s "parody" can be seen as a pro-American propaganda and/or a second-rate imitation informs us that the political ambiguities of the film—its wish to have its Americanization and criticize it too—were/are not lost on lay audiences. If *Köşeyi Dönen Adam* marked an era that could still imagine an alternative cultural front, *Amerikalı* can be seen as a cynical recognition of the point of no return, distributed by a representative of the winning side, Warner Bros.

It is a truism that Turkish cinema in the twenty-first century has entered its second golden age, aided by laws implementing state support for the industry since 2005, as well as the rising stars of Turkish and European-Turkish auteurs such as Fatih Akın, Ferzan Özpetek, and Nuri Bilge Ceylan. The number of Turkish movies available in movie theaters is still weak in comparison to the number of Hollywood movies pushed by Warner Bros. and United International Pictures (UIP), a joint venture of Paramount and Universal Studios, but globalization works in complex ways.[39] In both *Köşeyi Dönen Adam* and *Amerikalı*, Turkish actors speaking English with heavy Turkish accents play the American characters. In the early twenty-first century, however, a recent crop of media, including commercials and movies, has begun to employ famous American actors. A 2004 Cola Turka commercial imagines Chevy Chase and his suburban family drinking the Turkish Coke and becoming Turkified, in a reversal of Turkey's Americanization via Coca-Cola and National Lampoon comedies. A 2012 Doritos commercial consists of the starlet Megan Fox being bullied by an old Turkish drag queen, who deems her not sexy enough to shoot a commercial for the new spicy Doritos Fritos shots. In these, and in the 2010 comedy *Ay Lav Yu* featuring Steve Guttenberg, representatives of Hollywood are made to take orders from Turkey. These famous Americans are thus domesticated and revealed to be harmless white buffoons, struggling to fit in, tripping over Turkish with their heavy American accents, and smiling at joke after joke made at their expense.[40]

Ay Lav Yu, directed by Kurdish actor/director Sermiyan Midyat, not only employs real Americans but real Kurdish villagers as well, in line with a new trend in comedy that banks upon the perceived comic implications of rural accents and speech patterns without resorting to more obvious ethnic minstrelsy.[41] Two marriages take place in the film. The first, between an educated Kurdish villager named Ibrahim, the hero of the film, and a beautiful blonde American ingénue named Jessica, who has fallen in love with Turkey's culture, is to be expected. Jessica's family's visit to the village, after all, motivates much of the culture-clash based humor of the movie, which ends with the lovers' wedding. A memorable scene is Jessica's father Christopher's (Steve Guttenberg) inability to use the Anatolian-style toilet, which consists of a simple hole in the ground over which one must squat. Guttenberg's ridiculous antics and his inability to communicate with the locals proves Americans to be harmless clowns, cultural fish out of water, a rhetorical move that can also be found in Japanese advertisements utilizing white actors.[42]

The other marriage in *Ay Lav Yu*, however, is the unplanned marriage of Ibrahim's robust, old-maid sister and Jessica's younger, muscled brother, who spends most of the movie recording events with a camcorder and working out shirtless to the delight of the village girls. Somewhat like Hollywood, the young man cannibalizes the Orient with his vision-machine and, in a telling reversal, ends up being cannibalized by it. The sister, driven mad by unfulfilled sexual desire, takes him hostage in a parody of terrorism: she agrees to release him on the condition that they get married. The uncomfortable resolution of the crisis is his forced circumcision and their wedding, in which he seems to be all smiles, inexplicably resigned to his fate. (Is it the Stockholm syndrome? a realization of subconscious desires? the irresistible allure of the savage Other?) In any case, the film represents, via adult circumcision, scatological humiliation, and a forced marriage/rape, the taming of the oppressively hilarious American, not the least by a Kurdish director—an Other to the Other. The "happy" ending of this film is thus an awkward allegory of international and multicultural peace and understanding through "love." The two marriages, jagged sutures touted as personal resolutions to unresolved international crises, are echoed in the film's manic claims to be the "first movie to feature Turkish, Kurdish, Syriac and English dialogue; first movie to show the blend of different religions in East Turkey; and first comedy with an international ensemble to look at the 9/11 attacks."[43]

The 2010 comedy *Yahşi Batı* (The Mild West, or The Ottoman Cowboys) collects similar symbolic compensation from the United States without having to humiliate overpaid American actors and force multiple marriage/rapes on them in order to make up for real cultural and political tensions. *Yahşi Batı* is a mock western depicting the adventures of two Ottomans in the Wild West who have been ordered by the sultan to bring a priceless diamond to the president of the United States in return for an earlier, unspecified gift from America. Significantly, this "historical" narrative is framed as a tall tale told by two Turkish con men trying to sell a pair of long Wellington boots to a rich Turkish dandy. Cem Yılmaz, already well known as a stand-up comic and a fast-talking urban trickster from other movies, most notably the 2005 space comedy *G.O.R.A.*, plays the con man telling the story. He also doubles as Aziz Vefa, the con man's supposed great-grandfather, an Ottoman secret service agent who is sent to the West with Lemi Galip (Ozan Güven), an agent from the treasury, played by the second, more silent con man. Aziz is a scrapper, a coarse and manly Turk; Lemi is a highly educated, multilingual Ottoman Jew, whose Jewishness is only implied with his name, westernized refinement, and profession and is never a cause for nationalist suspicion in the movie. This allows the film to reproduce Karagöz-Hacivat style conflicts between the coarse fool and the westernized pedant, even as it creates situations in which the Karagöz and Hacivat characters must forget their differences, learn from each other, and band together against the real Other.

According to the story, bandits attack the two men's carriage and steal the diamond; Aziz and Lemi then find themselves strangled in a violent Wild West filled with Hollywood and spaghetti western clichés. Along the way, they befriend a female sharp-shooter, Susan Van Dyke, whom they first suspect to be a "dyke." Instead, she turns out to be half-Native American, helps the duo retrieve the diamond along with her father, the tribal chief, and eventually falls in love with Aziz. When Aziz and Lemi finally bring the diamond to President Garfield—a chronologically inaccurate decision that nevertheless allows the team to comment on Garfield the Cat and the infusion of American culture into the Turkish comical psyche—he looks down on them for being Ottomans. He also mocks them for having lost the diamond in the first place. Repeating a joke from the beginning of the movie, Garfield asks Aziz and Lemi whether they have camels in Turkey (a pet-peeve question from Westerners for most Turks). With boisterous belly laughs, he hands them a pair of boots to take back with them, in case they get their shoes stolen on the way back. These boots are the very boots the two con men are now trying to sell to the rich dandy. When the sale falls through, the duo produce a pair of bejeweled nunchaku and begin to tell of Lemi and Aziz's adventures in China, the Beautiful East.

Returning a gift is a central trope of postcolonial protest writing, from Ariel Dorfman and Arman Mattelard's 1972 *How to Read Donald Duck,* in which the authors returned Donald Duck back to Disney, "feathers plucked and well roasted," to Malek Alloula's 1987 critical readings of French colonial postcards from Algeria that "return this immense postcard to its sender."⁴⁴ As such, it makes for a more versatile and nuanced plot than revenge. Like *Amerikalı*, *Yahşi Batı* employs familiar symbols, images, and scenes from Hollywood. While these drive the humor somewhat, they are not the point. The film is critical of racism toward blacks, Native Americans, and Middle Easterners such as the visiting Ottomans. It also questions white America's primacy, casting the success of famous American goods such as Coca-Cola and KFC as the result not of hard work, but of theft and bullying. A scene showing the characters being beaten up for trying to sell chicken sandwiches exemplifies this critical approach toward U.S. economic hegemony.

Stranded and broke in the Wild West, Aziz and Lemi begin to look for ways to make money to buy guns so they can retrieve the diamond. These schemes include their accidental invention of Coca-Cola (Cola Turka), an attempt at Ottoman-style candy-making, and a chicken sandwich stand. In the latter scene, they yell for customers in Turkish bazaar style—another nod to the Turkish vernacular—standing across from another chicken sandwich stand. Yet they are chastised by the burly men at the rival stand for their "shameful" salesmanship in raising their voices in this way. The men attack Aziz and Lemi's stand, spill their homemade Coke, and destroy their other goods. The fight ends in the bullies' favor with a gunshot fired by a likeness of Colonel Sanders, who emerges from the sheriff's office and shakes the latter's hand, signifying a deep, sinister connection between the U.S. government and American corporations worldwide. The scene is humorous on multiple levels: the incongruity created by a bazaar-style food stand in the Wild West, the burlesque of Wild West brawls, complete with extra-diegetic musical accompaniment, and the emergence of Colonel Sanders, a familiar icon for many Turks. This last moment of humor, however, is burdened with an ambiguity and self-consciousness unmatched in *Amerikalı*. Cem Yılmaz, in his role as the tale-teller, interjects his unwillingness to even say Colonel Sanders's name:

> Aziz/Con man: So they are trying to sell chicken sandwiches in Kentucky. Like they would get away with it. . . . The guys are in business there. Would they give anyone else a chance? You

recognize him?

Listener: Who do you mean?

Aziz/Con man: Who do you think? The guy on the logo. Don't make me advertise him here.[45]

With this, the director and the screenwriter mark their unwillingness to uncritically parody well-known symbols of the United States for cheap laughs. Even Aziz's supposed great grandson, an unscrupulous trickster, appears highly aware of the potential pitfall of parody and how its laughs can function as prizes handed out for recognition and even as subliminal advertising. He therefore opts for Kierkegaardian pain instead.

The film's greatest critique is specifically in relation to U.S. hegemony over humor and entertainment. In another one of their early money-making schemes, Aziz and Lemi put on a Karagöz shadow puppet show for the unimpressed Wild West locals. The heroes decide that the humor gets lost in translation, but they never stop acting. The first successful scheme they invent is pretending one of them is a wanted outlaw so the other one can bring him to a town's sheriff, collect the prize money, and then free him. They then move to another town and try the trick again. This traveling shape-shifting act works wonderfully, until they run into Susan holding target practice in a forest. Susan has vowed to kill Johnny Lesh, the outlaw Lemi is pretending to be, because he killed her mother when Susan was just an infant. Aziz and Lemi panic and try to convince her that they are harmless foreigners, not bloodthirsty outlaws. In dizzying rapidity, they act out scenes from Ottoman entertainment, including well-known royal and folk plays, switching from one character to another as she stares suspiciously at them with two guns pointed at their heads. In this scene, the frantic awareness that humorous communication with America has been one-sided and that this woman knows next to nothing about their culture becomes a matter of life and death. Only *lokum*, the Turkish delight candy, which Aziz miraculously produces out of his pocket, can save them. Susan's ingestion of the Turkish delight means they are in the clear: "I didn't get the Arab maid [a stock character from Ottoman plays], but lokum makes sense," she explains.

Like *Köşeyi Dönen Adam* and *Amerikalı*, and unlike *Ay Lav Yu*, *Yahşi Batı* resists a transparent marriage-based resolution for Aziz and Susan. In fact, the film's slowest and most strained scenes take place as Aziz tries to convince Susan of their compatibility; when she brings up the possibility that Aziz might make her one of his four wives, for example, Aziz teaches her about the Turkish folk heroine, "Hürmüz with seven husbands." The closest thing to marriage in the movie is the "wedding song," a well-known late Ottoman duet Aziz and Susan perform toward the end of the movie. The song takes place within the context of a hybrid Ottoman-Western variety show staged by the protagonists, taking this movie (a mock Wild West epic) within a movie (con men trying to sell suspicious goods) to an even deeper level of artifice. Having found out that the corrupt Sheriff Lloyd has gotten hold of the diamond, Aziz and Lemi come up with a plan that will force the sheriff's hand. They decide to stage a variety show with sharp-shooting, horseback riding, Turkish oil wrestling, and song and dance portions. They then invite the governor and announce that the prize for the oil-wrestling portion of the event will be a priceless diamond from the Ottoman Empire, awarded by the sheriff of the town. With the governor there, they believe they would be able to get the diamond without having to resort to violence. However, the plan fails when Sheriff Lloyd gives Aziz, the winning oil-wrestler, a fake diamond instead. As the wedding duet, a song that typically ended Ottoman variety shows, commences, Lemi has to ride to town and punch Lloyd's henchman in the face, retrieving the diamond out of the locked case.

The camera alternates between the wedding song and Lemi's righteously violent act of stealing back what has been stolen. This moment marks another recognition on the part of the filmmakers. The wedding song, coming at the end of the variety show but not the movie, would have allowed for a typically comedic personal "resolution" to a clash that is more socioeconomic and political than cultural or libidinal. *Yahşi Batı* rejects this option. In front of President Garfield, Aziz and Lemi are again dressed like Ottomans; Susan is wearing her sharp-shooting cowgirl outfit, and Susan's father is in his Native American clothes. Yet it is important to remember that even this is not the end of the movie. The tall tale ends here, but the sale of the boots falls through and the con men must produce a new gift and start a new story. This splitting of the narrative act between Aziz's supposed great-grandson (a con man) and the camera (an untrustworthy Hollywood device) is nothing less than what Bakhtin has identified as the "process of inner dialogization," which manifests in parodies marked by an awareness of "substantial resistance, a certain forcefulness and profundity" in their original source.[46]

With its complex, layered, and self-aware comedy, combined with cheap sexual and scatological gags, *Yahşi Batı* enjoyed immense success at the box office. The film spent two weeks at number one in Turkish cinemas, earning over $13.5 million, well over its $2 million budget.[47] Even these numbers, when compared to *Amerikalı*, show how far Turkish comedy has come in the last decade. In the early twenty-first century, the proliferation of Turkish comedies that combine higher budgets and technical expertise with elements of folkloric cultural immersion has led to many locally produced movies besting Hollywood at the box office. The year *Yahşi Batı* was released, seven out of the top ten box office hits were Turkish films; four of those were comedies and two featured Cem Yılmaz.[48]

Yahşi Batı's differences from *Amerikalı* are as interesting as its connections to *Köşeyi Dönen Adam*. At least one commentator on Sinemalar.com has noted the continuities between this film and the Kemal Sunal tradition, mentioning the similarities between Sheriff Lloyd and the corrupt haji played by Ali Şen.[49] Tellingly, Kemal Sunal himself acted in a mock western in 1979: *Umudumuz Şaban* (Şaban Our Only Hope), directed by Kartal Tibet, depicts Şaban as a fool enchanted by westerns who becomes a vigilante hero through a series of misunderstandings. However, it is important to remember that for all its cultural nationalist defiance and financial success, *Yahşi Batı* was distributed by United International Pictures within the country. Despite the presence of Turkish comedy fans within diasporic Turkish communities abroad and the rising number of western aficionados of Turkish auteurs, few Americans will ever see this movie. This is, of course, in contrast to the audiovisual and thematic elements that *Yahşi Batı* parodies: they have long been a part of vernacular imaginations worldwide. The very "forcefulness and profundity" of Hollywood's cultural and economic power motivates *Yahşi Batı*'s dialogism at the level of both content and form.

Like Lego pieces, images from U.S. media are reinterpreted, reassembled, and recombined in Turkish comedies about the United States.[50] Turkish cinema has emerged from the slump of the 1980s and 1990s, yet battle scars remain, marked by narratives of comic anxiety and by the continued Hollywood domination of film distribution inside the country and elsewhere. Even though Middle Easterners are often treated to comic representations of themselves by Hollywood, few Americans see this gift returned. In this time of paranoia about Muslim culture and straight-faced assertions that Muslims have no sense of humor, the laughter about the oppressively hilarious American may encounter, at best, a void, and at worse, a puzzled face and loaded guns.

NOTES

1. "Turkey's Movie Industry Seeks Firm Foothold," *Hürriyet Daily News,* May 3, 2011, www.hurriyetdailynews.com/default.aspx?pageid=438&n=turkeys-movie-industry-seeks-a-firm-foothold-2011-03-04, accessed September 22, 2012. All translations from Turkish are the author's, unless otherwise noted.
2. Melis Behlil, "Close Encounters? Contemporary Turkish Television and Cinema," *Wide Screen* 2, no. 2 (2010): 1–13, 6.
3. See, for example, "Turkish Romantic Comedy Gets European Release," *Today's Zaman,* December 26, 2009, www.todayszaman.com/newsDetail_getNewsById.action;jsessionid=168D7E19270082A138F32BA0B1017432?newsId=196659, accessed November 21, 2012.
4. The scarcity of popular comedies in the lineup for the spring 2012 Turkish film retrospective, titled "The Space Between: A Panorama of Cinema in Turkey" and sponsored by the American Turkish Society and the Film Society of Lincoln Center, is only a recent case in point.
5. For "critical transnationalism," see Marwan M. Kraidy, *Hybridity, or the Cultural Logic of Globalization* (Philadelphia: Temple University Press, 2005), 149.
6. Due to its historiographic bend, grounding in the political economy of cinema, and the incorporation of viewer responses, this research presents a significant analytical and archival shift. In particular, it diverges from the only full-length academic study of Americans in Turkish comedy available so far: Elif Kahraman, "Arm-Wrestling a Super Power: American Representations in Turkish Comedies" (M.A.

thesis, Kadir Has University, 2010). That work explores five other movies, all from the early twenty-first century, with exclusive methodological focus on the representation of Americans.

7. *Köşeyi Dönen Adam* (The Man Who Turned the Corner), dir. Atıf Yılmaz (Cicek Film, 1978); *Amerikalı* (The American), dir. Şerif Gören (Anadolu Filmcilik, 1993); *Yahşi Batı* (The Mild West), dir. Ömer Faruk Sorak (Fida Film, 2010).

8. Ulrich Marzolph, "'Focusees' of Jocular Fiction in Classical Arabic Literature," in *Story-Telling in the Framework of Non-Fictional Arabic Literature*, ed. Stefan Leder (Wiesbaden: Harrassowitz, 1998), 118–29, 123.

9. Nazlı Kırmızı, *Geleneksel Anlatılar ve Söylen: Türk Güldürü Filmleri Üzerine Yapısal Bir Çözümleme* (Eskişehir: Anadolu Üniversitesi Açıköğretim Fakültesi, 1990).

10. Miriam Hansen, "The Mass Production of the Senses: Classical Cinema as Vernacular Modernism," *Modernism/Modernity* 6, no. 2 (1999): 59–77.

11. Gerald Mast, "Comic Films," in *What's So Funny: Humor in American Culture*, ed. Nancy A. Walker (Wilmington, Del.: Scholarly Resources, 1998), 225–48, 226.

12. Savaş Arslan, *Cinema in Turkey: A New Critical History* (New York: Oxford University Press, 2011), 27.

13. Ibid., 79.

14. Nezih Erdoğan and Deniz Göktürk, "Turkish Cinema," in *Companion Encyclopedia of Middle Eastern and North African Film*, ed. Oliver Leeman (London: Routledge, 2001), 533–73, 534.

15. Ibid., 540.

16. Dimitri Eleftheriotis, "Turkish National Cinema," in *Asian Cinemas: A Reader and Guide*, ed. Dimitri Eleftheriotis and Gary Needham (Honolulu: University of Hawai'i Press, 2006), 220–29, 222.

17. Leo Charney, "American Film," in *Comedy: A Geographic and Historical Guide*, ed. Maurice Charney, vol. 1 (Westport, Conn.: Praeger, 2005), 78–92, 86–87.

18. Vadullah Taş, *Kemal Sunal Filmlerini Anlatıyor* (Istanbul: Esen, 2011), 140.

19. Image reproduced in ibid., 142.

20. Andrew Stott, *Comedy: The New Critical Idiom* (London: Routledge, 2005), 1.

21. Emre Baylan, "Ali Sunal: Telif Konusunda Enteresan Bir Şey Yapacağız," *Hürriyet*, October 11, 2010, hurarsiv.hurriyet.com.tr/goster/ShowNew.aspx?id=16016512.

22. "Yerliler Yabancılara Fark Attı," *Milliyet*, October 7, 1991, 21; "Telebarometre," *Milliyet*, March 18, 1994, 5.

23. Şükran Esen, introduction to *TV ve Sinemada Kemal Sunal Güldürüsü* by

Ali Kemal Sunal (Istanbul: Om, 2001), 7.
24. Füsun Dedehayır, "Amerikalı, Amerikalılarla Kapisiyor," *Milliyet,* November 17, 1993, 7; İhsan Mursaloğlu, "Amerika'dan Sevgilerle," *Milliyet,* February 21, 1993, 16.
25. Arslan, *Cinema in Turkey,* 163.
26. Ibid., 256. Arslan's and my translation.
27. Ibid.
28. Erdoğan and Göktürk, "Turkish Cinema," 7.
29. Mursaloğlu, "Amerika'dan Sevgilerle."
30. Nazğm Alpman, interview with Şerif Gören, "Hedefim Amerika," *Milliyet,* October 24, 1993, 19.
31. "Yeşilçam'da Rönesans," *Hürriyet,* December 4, 1997, hurarsiv.hurriyet.com.tr/goster/ShowNew.aspx?id=-276899.
32. Walker, introduction to *What's So Funny,* 56.
33. Gerald Mast, "Comic Films," 227.
34. Søren Kierkegaard, "Concluding Unscientific Postscript," trans. David F. Swenson, reprinted in John Morreall, *The Philosophy of Humor and Laughter* (Albany: State University Press of New York, 1987), 83.
35. In Turkish: "Maksat bağcıyı dövmek değil üzüm yemek."
36. Ulas888, untitled post, YouTube, August 2012, www.youtube.com/comment?lc=32kH0mg_Qtw2DTtqC9ODFJ9P1XApAkTItOl0-eXC45k, accessed September 16, 2012.
37. Snowboard83, untitled post, "Amerikalı," Sinemalar.com, June 29, 2011, www.sinemalar.com/film/1100/Amerikalı, accessed September 16, 2012.
38. Salyaz, untitled post, January 16, 2011; Babydoll, untitled comment, March 12, 2011, Sinemalar.com, www.sinemalar.com/film/1100/Amerikalı.
39. Behlil, "Close Encounters," 6.
40. Kahraman makes a similar argument about the "Silliness and Clumsiness" of Americans in new-generation Turkish comedies in "Arm-Wrestling a Super Power" (34–35).
41. Other examples include *Dondurmam Gaymak,* dir. Yüksel Aksu (2006), and *Entel Köy Efe Köye Karşı,* dir. Yüksel Aksu (2012).
42. Millie R. Creighton, "The Other in Japanese Advertising Campaigns," in *Occidentalism: Images of the West,* ed. James G. Carrier (Oxford: Oxford University Press, 1995), 135–60.
43. "Ay Lav Yu," Wikipedia.org, en.wikipedia.org/w/index.php?title=Ay_Lav_Yu&oldid=506573788, accessed September 17, 2012.
44. Arief Dorfman and Armand Mattelart, *How to Read Donald Duck: Imperialist Ideology in the Disney Comic* (New York: International General, 1975), 10; Malek Alloula, *The Colonial Harem,* trans. Myrna Godzich and Wlad Godzich (Minneapolis: University of Minnesota Press, 1986), 5.

45. Original English subtitles, with minor edits by the author.
46. Mikhail Bakhtin, "Discourse Typology in Prose," as quoted by Henry Louis Gates Jr. in *The Signifying Monkey: A Theory of Afro-American Literary Criticism* (New York: Oxford University Press, 1988), 112.
47. "Yahşi Batı," Box Office Mojo.com, boxofficemojo.com/movies/intl/?id=_fYAHSIBATI02&country=TR&wk=2010W2&id=_fYAHSIBATI02&p=.htm, accessed September 21, 2012.
48. Christiane Stützle, "Turkish Hollywood," Hogan Lovells.com, tllg.net/SQvr, accessed September 22, 2012.
49. PKellerman, untitled post, Sinemalar.com, www.sinemalar.com/film/39625/yahsi-bati, accessed September 20, 2012.
50. For the Lego metaphor as an explanatory tool for studying U.S. culture abroad, see Rob Kroes, *If You've Seen One, You've Seen the Mall: Europeans and American Mass Culture* (Urbana: University of Illinois Press, 1996), 104–5.

9

LAUGHTER ACROSS BORDERS

The Case of the Bollywood Film *Tere Bin Laden*

MARA MATTA

In an article published in the *Sydney Morning Herald,* the Asian British comedian Shazia Mirza recounts her journey to her family's country of origin, Pakistan, to perform stand-up comedy. Held up for six hours at Lahore customs, as she did not have a visa to enter Pakistan, she was interrogated by the customs officer:

"Are you a spy?"—No, I'm a stand-up comedian.
"What's that?"—I tell jokes.
"And will you be doing that in this country?"—Yes.
"Oh, is this the entertainment for the Taliban?" he asked, quite seriously.—No, I replied.[1]

Once allowed into the country, Shazia is again cautioned by armed security personnel before going onstage: a soldier tells her to be careful and stick to "*halal* comedy." Shazia wittily replies:

"*Halal* comedy? There is no such thing. That's like saying, I only eat *halal* bacon!"[2]

Shazia's article raises important questions related to the role of comedy and the potentially subversive role of humor in communities where hierarchical structures of power are in place and fun and laughter can be subjected to the management of joy.[3] In such situations, free expression and the performance of comedy, both in public spaces such as theaters or cinemas or in private spheres, such as on personal blogs, SMS, or Facebook/Twitter profiles, can be seen as a challenge to the power regime, be it political, religious, or both. As Asef Bayat has rightly pointed out, "Anti-*fun*-damentalism is a historical matter, one that has to do significantly with the preservation of power. In other words, at stake is not necessarily the disruption of the moral order, as often claimed, but rather the undermining of the hegemony, the regime of power on which certain strands of moral and political authority rest."[4]

And the moral and political authorities can hardly allow the masses to ridicule them through such carnivalesque humor. As Henri Bergson had also highlighted, the comic appeals to people because they can laugh at somebody else's expense, antagonizing fear and exorcising even the most terrifying regime: "However spontaneous it seems, laughter always implies a kind of secret freemasonry, or even complicity, with other laughers, real or imaginary. How often has it been said that the fuller the theatre, the more uncontrolled the laughter of the audience!"[5]

Through a linguistic and visual analysis of the Bollywood comedy *Tere Bin Laden* (which may be translated both as "Without You, Laden" and "Your Bin Laden"), I would like to appraise the role of humor, comedy, and satire in addressing sensitive issues like the global war on terror and the stereotypical representation of Muslim/Pakistani/Arab characters in Indian cinema. Popularly perceived Middle Eastern matters become a comedic target in India because it allows the average spectator to take a more distant look at a threat that is perceived as ever-incumbent. The Indian subcontinent is home to three modern nations carved out of British India in 1947, along communal and religious lines: India, Pakistan, and, later, Bangladesh. Projecting the problems of the Western (specifically the American) war on terror onto neighboring Pakistan, and yet creating an increasingly manufactured cultural distance that binds Pakistan to the Middle East (and its related issues) because of its perceived loyalty to Islamic ethos, writer and director Abhishek Sharma creates what Bergson termed "a momentary anesthesia of the heart."[6] This allows the audience a liberatory laugh and the opportunity to free itself, also momentarily, from the paranoia of terrorism and the related global war in which

India is an important Western ally. This Middle Easternization of Pakistan creates a comedic space where Bollywood can exploit the dramatic events connected to the Taliban, Al Qaeda, and the September 11 attacks, transforming them into potential material for humor. The *otherization* of these events as belonging to a different geopolitical area and the caricature of the main character of Osama Bin Laden as a simpleton who raises chickens for a living creates a further hiatus. If indifference is, indeed, the natural environment for the comic effect, as "laughter has no greater foe than emotion,"[7] then *Tere Bin Laden* craftily delivers a film setting that the Indian spectator can easily identify with. At the same time, the viewer is able to distance himself enough to be able to laugh at the unfolding events, which—after all—do not really affect him but Pakistan and the Middle East as a world "other" than South Asia.[8] The spoof idiom of humor used in this film has the express geopolitical intent to distance India as distinctly South Asian, as opposed to Pakistan, which is perceived to be aligned with the Middle East. In its explicit nod to America's unbounded global war on terror after the September 11 attacks, *Tere Bin Laden* throws into question our received notions about what constitutes the Middle East as a geopolitical, historical, and cultural category.

THE FILM SYNOPSIS AND THE FILMMAKER'S INTENTIONS: A MAD COMEDY AND A SPOOF

Tere Bin Laden (2010) stars the Pakistani pop singer Ali Zafar as Karachi-based reporter Ali Hassan.[9] The story revolves around Ali's private ambition of migrating to the United States and fulfilling his American Dream. He eventually succeeds in obtaining a visa and flies to America, but he ruins the opportunity by repeating the words "hijack" and "bomb" while recording himself on camera on his flight to New York. His visa is cancelled and he gets stuck in Karachi once again, with his old job at Danka TV. While covering a local event, Ali comes across Noora, a simpleton who raises cocks and hens for a living. Noora's resemblance to Osama bin Laden gives Ali an idea: to make a spoof video with a fake Osama bin Laden warning the West and America about the consequences of the war on terror in Iraq and

Afghanistan. He tricks Noora into unknowingly posing as bin Laden and then sells the tape to Mr. Majid, the obnoxious owner of Danka TV, hoping to use the money to obtain a new visa to the United States. The U.S. government, however, takes the tape seriously and decides to move its troops into Pakistan and bomb Afghanistan, also requesting that the Inter-Services Intelligence of Pakistan (ISI) collaborate in this new Osama-hunting campaign. Noora, in the meantime, has discovered the trick played on him and tries to hide. Ali decides to solve the situation by making another tape in which Osama would declare a ceasefire with the United States. Meanwhile, the FBI team, led by the arrogant Ted Wood and his incapable Pakistani counterpart, Usman, head of the ISI, tracks down the location of Ali and his bunch and manages to arrest all of them. During the interrogation, the truth is revealed. To free himself and to save Ted's face, Ali releases a second tape where "Osama" declares a ceasefire. The film ends with the U.S. government accepting the offer of ceasefire and Usman locked in a mental asylum.

PLOT AND SEQUENCE STRUCTURES: LAUGHING IN TERROR WHILE LAUGHING AT TERROR

In *Le rire: Essai sur le signification du comique* (1924), Bergson remarked upon the importance of the social dimension in order to unload the potential of laughter: "To understand laughter, we must put it back into its natural environment, which is society, and above all must we determine the utility of its function, which is a social one.... Laughter must answer to certain requirements of life in common. It must have a *social* signification."[10]

In *Tere Bin Laden,* however, it is worth pointing out how laughter travels across borders and is effective not just at community level, but in a transnational dimension where its "social signification" has the potential to be received by South Asian communities living in the subcontinent and in diasporic settings. Nurturing itself on Middle East–related issues and choosing as the title character an Arab terrorist, the film at the same time recontextualizes the question of terror inside very specific national borders—Pakistan—and even more precisely in a single city, Karachi. This comedy thus reveals itself to be more serious and provoking than it may seem at first: its humorous take on the life of a young Pakistani turns into a vitriolic satirical portrayal of Pakistan, revealing a controversial political agenda. The idea that Pakistan, although usually considered culturally and geopolitically affiliated with the Indian Subcontinent, may be drifting toward the area that we define as the Middle East is worth highlighting here, because it is more than a mere allegation. As Aparna Pande has argued, "For decades a majority of Pakistani policy makers, intellectuals and strategists have attempted to virtually relocate Pakistan within the Muslim Arab Middle East."[11]

If we look at Pakistan as a country that aspires to being integrated into this geopolitical and cultural frame, then we can posit that the director intended to poke fun at something disconnected from the rest of India and South Asia at large. His goal would have been a film whose comedic effects stem both from a sense of the Indian audience's superiority, a sense that their country can merrily dissociate itself from Pakistan as belonging to another geopolitical sphere, and from an aggressive humor that turns a dreadful figure like Osama bin Laden into a fool, thus vilifying him and neutralizing the threats posed by Taliban terror. Thus, the film provokes the question, what is the aesthetic status of a film that spoofs a war on terror that has claimed hundreds of thousands of lives and has destabilized the current geopolitical region known as the Middle East for future generations?

The choice of (virtually) setting the film in Karachi is quite interesting in itself. Karachi is the economic hub of Pakistan: it is the city of money, but also of mosques, muhajirs, and the MQM.[12] It is thus the most important city when it comes to issues of regional instability, national security threats, and global fundamentalism. In the Indian imaginary, it is the city that most represents this Middle Easternization of Pakistan. As an Indian production, the satire is directed toward some easily identifiable Pakistani characters and groups, set into an easily recognizable place, Karachi. This needs to be kept in mind throughout the film: the fact that *Tere Bin Laden*, despite its main actor being a Pakistani, is an Indian production shot and edited by an Indian crew working in the Mumbai Film Studios deeply affects the image of Pakistan portrayed therein. At the same time, given that India is an important ally of the United States in the region, the satirical portrayal of the United States, in the image of the FBI team leader Ted Wood,[13] is toned down: Wood is made an object of fun but does not end up being truly punished, while the ISI officer Usman is totally thrashed and exposed to utter ridicule by being locked in a mental asylum. For India, the caricatured image of a spoofy FBI leader can be acceptable, but the last, profound laughter remains directed at the ISI. In this respect, *Tere Bin Laden* may be read as an aesthetic representation of India's radical severing of its historical South Asian kinship with Pakistan.

The first sequence of the film, shot at the airport of Hyderabad,[14] introduces us to Ali Hassan. He walks confidently into the camera among a crowd of people waiting to board a flight to the United States. He is carrying a trolley with a sticker that affirms "I love Amreeka": he is quite arrogant, full of himself, and looks down on other Pakistani men dressed in traditional clothes. He clearly "is somebody who aspires to be an American."[15] Ali is more an anti-hero, a charming scoundrel who gets punished for his hubris, but whose cleverness in manipulating the Americans leads him to achieve his goal: by convincing Wood to shoot a second video where Osama bin Laden offers a ceasefire to George Bush, he finally acquires fame and a new visa to the United States, fulfilling his American Dream.

In the scene where Ali is arrested and interrogated by U.S. airport security, for example, we see three U.S. judges accusing him of being, first, a member of Al Qaeda, then of the Taliban. While the scene should have been a dramatic mirroring of the humiliation suffered by many South Asians subjected to rush controls in American airports because of their religious affiliation or because they resembled someone from the Middle East, in actuality the film delivers a comic sequence edited along the lines of its theme song, "Ullu Da Pattha," literally "son of an owl," a Punjabi way of calling somebody a fool. As Sharma comments,

> [The song] is actually a character sketch of Ali, how he feels trapped in the Third World, and how he wants to go to America so desperately. It is about his American Dream. It is about how he is misinterpreted by the Americans. Actually, the song represents the soul of the film, ... the perspective of the film. A film, which is about this character from South Asia

who is not welcomed in the America post-9/11, but he so desperately wants to go to America and he can go to any length to achieve that American dream. It also shows how frustrated he is in Pakistan, or in the Third World.[16]

The comedic effect is obtained mostly through two expedients: first, by depicting a dramatic scenario—that potentially expects every Muslim migrant moving to America in the post-9/11 era—as laughable. By preventing the seriousness of reality from sinking in and by delivering a moment of collective relief from tension, the sequence is constructed as a caricatured version of what would happen in a real interrogation room. As Kant had argued in his *Critique of Judgment* (1790), "Laughter is an effect that arises if a tense expectation is transformed into nothing."[17] The tense expectation of an empathizing audience would be the dreadfulness of such an interrogation. Instead, and this is the second expedient, the director chooses to accompany the sequence by an utterly ironic Punjabi song[18] that describes the hero of the film as a fool, thus almost marking his trial as a deserved punishment for his clumsy naiveté. This changes the spectators' perspective and disrupts the expectation of a dramatic outcome of the events. As O. J. Double has argued, the comic or the ludicrous is often obtained by "an abrupt transposition of the order of our ideas, as taking the mind unawares, throws it off guard, startles it into a lively sense of pleasure, and leaves no time for painful reflections."[19] This incongruity is what makes the audience laugh at an event that in itself is quite dramatic. It is a swinging feeling of laughing in terror while laughing at terror, a subtle pleasure of being able to ridicule an otherwise despicable occurrence that recently has had among its victims even illustrious personalities of the Bombay star system like Shah Rukh Khan, who had been detained at a New York airport by immigration officials.

THE ISI AND THE TERRORISM IN PAKISTAN: ANOTHER BIASED INDIAN FILM?

Abhishek Sharma has always maintained that his film is just a "mad comedy" poking fun at the paranoia of Americans regarding Muslims, Middle Easterners, and South Asians, often suspected of being potential terrorists merely on account of their place of birth, their physiognomy, or their religion. Then why was the film banned and why did the Central Board of Film Censors (CBFC) of Pakistan find it offensive, vulgar, and even potentially dangerous? Abdul Sattar Khokhar, acting chairman of the CBFC, openly judged the film as "anti-Islam and anti-Pakistan"[20] and warned that its screening could actually pose a security threat. Other members of the CBFC stated that the film "ridiculed Pakistani society, . . . was offensive to Muslims, portrayed bin Laden as a 'coward and ridiculous,' contained vulgar language and could fan hostility among 'fanatic and fundamentalist elements' in Pakistan."[21] In addition, Khokhar alleged that the film "mocks security agencies and the character of Osama bin Laden and the public exhibition can trigger violence."[22]

In contrast, Nadeem Madiwalla, the owner of one of the largest Pakistani film distribution companies, called *Tere Bin Laden* a "95-minute peace tape" that conveyed "a message of peace and not war"; he urged the Pakistani Minister of Culture, Pir Aftab Hussain Shah Jilani, to view the film again.[23] His plea fell on deaf ears, however, as the Minister reportedly stated that an appointed appellate board comprising senior officials prepared a statement that did not contain a "single positive angle about the Indian film,"[24] which allegedly perpetrates a negative image of Pakistan as a hub of terrorism: "Its impact is surely going to hurt Pakistan's strategic interests. US-bashing is on the extreme, while Americans are a coalition partner in the war on terror and have bailed out Pakistan on many occasions. The abusive language used against America in the film is in bad taste and cannot be justified even under the worst-case scenario."[25]

In an interview on the Al Jazeera English channel in September 2010, Abhishek Sharma and Ali Zafar had a chance to reply to such allegations and to discuss the main question surrounding the film: Is there room for humor in the war against terrorism? More specifically, the interviewer asked Ali Zafar, "Did you have any hesitation in playing in a movie that features Osama bin Laden, especially because you are, of course, Pakistani?"[26] The question is significant, because Ali Zafar is the first Pakistani actor to play a leading role in a Bollywood film, as well as one of Pakistan's most famous pop singers, especially popular among young people. [27] While he admitted to some concerns in playing the lead role in an Indian film that openly referred to Osama bin Laden even in its title,[28] he explained that once he read the whole script and discussed it with Sharma, he felt that the story "needed to be told": "I realized that the movie talks about something more and . . . I wouldn't even say it's a spoof on him [bin Laden]: it talks about a larger issue."[29]

In the course of the interview, Al Jazeera continuously projected onscreen the comments of the viewers watching the channel and interacting via Facebook. One of the messages affirmed the right of Muslims to finally laugh at American paranoia about Muslims: "Whenever a tragic situation is made into a satire, there usually is one party who is laughing while the other takes offence. For Muslims, we finally get to laugh."[30]

The comment highlights the most controversial point surrounding the film: Can we really laugh at stuff like this? Other comments were rather negative and took the same position as the Pakistani censors, declaring the theme of the film unsuitable for comedy. "Making humour out of the world's deadliest terrorist is idiotic," wrote one viewer in an email. "Imagine a comedy about the Pakistan floods, Haiti or the conditions faced by the Palestinians."[31]

Ali Zafar tried to present an apology for the comic medium: "Laughter can be sometimes the best medicine. Laughter can sometimes do what cannot be done otherwise. Sometimes, making something on a very serious note can have its limitations. But you can wave the message on a lighter tone, in a way that people can also absorb it more. So I think laughter does help. But . . . the thought is not funny. The thought is serious in itself."[32]

Charlie Chaplin also had to justify himself when he appeared on screen interpreting Hitler in *The Great Dictator* (1940). Theodor Adorno, for example, was not at all pleased with the way Chaplin addressed a serious and dramatic issue like the question of Nazi Germany and the threat that Hitler posed for Europe and the world at large;[33] he believed that the film trivialized Nazi-fascism: "[It] loses all satirical force and becomes obscene when a Jewish girl can hit a line of storm-troopers on the head with a pan without being torn to pieces. For the sake of political commitment, political reality is trivialized."[34] Nevertheless, and more importantly, Chaplin's film deeply irritated Hitler, who quickly banned it from all the Nazi-occupied countries. This point is crucial in our analysis of *Tere bin Laden* and the potentially disruptive power of humor in a fragile country like Pakistan. Even if these comedies fail to please some of the most critical spectators, there is an undeniable truth that emerges: in such carnivalesque humor, where the masses are laughing together at somebody's else expense, politics or ideologies always fail to appropriate and exploit this humor to their advantage. However, even if many Jewish viewers appreciated *The Great Dictator* for its positive portrayal of Jewish characters and its open condemnation of their persecution by the Nazis, Chaplin himself had second thoughts about the use of humor and comedy as suitable means to address these serious issues. As he wrote later: "Had I known of the actual horrors of the German concentration camps, I could not have made fun of the homicidal insanity of the Nazis."[35]

But Abhishek Sharma and the Bollywood crew are all very much acquainted with the horrible tragedies of the war on terror in Pakistan and the Middle East. So why did they not back out from such a controversial project? Was the film truly devised as a message of peace, a critique of the war on terror, and a condemnation of the Islamophobic attitude of the West? Or was it meant, instead, to be derisive of the Pakistani people, to mock the ISI's alleged involvement with the United States and some terrorist groups and, ultimately, to shame Pakistan? The construction of a parallel reality where the average Indian spectator can find a liberatory space to laugh at the tragedy of the war on terror in order to exorcize its terrible consequences,[36] while at the same time distancing himself from the Middle Easternized Pakistan, may explain India's welcoming this spoof comedy and its ban in Pakistan and the Middle East, where the issue was deemed too sensitive to be turned into comic material.

BOLLYWOOD AND THE TERRORIST FILMS ON PAKISTAN: FIGHTING THE POLITICAL IN THE CINEMATIC ARENA

In his famous work *Rabelais and His World,* Mikhail Bakhtin defines the nature of the festive, carnivalesque laughter:

It is not an individual reaction to some isolated "comic" event. Carnival laughter is the laughter of all people. Second, it is universal in scope; it is directed at all and everyone, including the carnival's participants. The entire world is seen in its droll aspect, in its gay relativity. Third, this laughter is ambivalent: it is gay, triumphant, and at the same time mocking, deriding. It asserts and denies, it buries and revives. Such is the laughter of carnival.[37]

As David Robb has argued, "There is an open-ended moment in carnivalesque humor which precludes it from being appropriated by politics or ideology. Unlike the superior humor of the satirist, the laughter of the market place embraces 'the wholeness of the world's comic aspect.'"[38] Although *Tere Bin Laden* was never officially screened and distributed in Pakistan, we can assume that it widely circulated through pirated copies in the black market. This unofficial distribution, however, prevented the "laughter of the market place" from being elicited, since people were likely forced to watch the film alone or in small groups. In this way, the subversive power of humor was curtailed, and the irony directed at the authorities was disempowered. However, *Tere Bin Laden,* unlike Chaplin's comedy, did not threaten only what Bayat calls the "power paradigm," "the discursive space that enables those in charge within a particular paradigm to maintain their position by making them . . . acceptable to their subjects";[39] it also questioned the moral integrity of the subjects themselves, depicting most of the Pakistanis either as stupid simpletons or as untrustworthy. While I do not think the film may have provoked outrage among Pakistanis or managed to offend them, we have to admit that there is no way to prove that the film has been really welcomed by the Pakistani people. What is certain is that the potential "laughter of the market place" has deeply upset the authorities, especially the ones who are the most parodied in the film: the ISI.

If *Tere Bin Laden* can be counted among those Bollywood films that aim to address geopolitics by lampooning Pakistan, we should also keep in mind that humor is not something employed only by outsiders or competitors in the area. Pakistani authors and artists are increasingly using comedy and satire to discuss their country's most serious issues. Among them, some women have been particularly successful, at home and abroad. Moni Mohsin's recently published comic novel *Tender Hooks*, for example, has been well received. Interviewed by a journalist in Mumbai, who asked her what she really wanted to say about Pakistan in such a humorous book, she replied:

> I just want to talk about how difficult it is to live there at the moment. How things have deteriorated, both politically and socially. Schools are shut every other day because of terror threats. You worry about being stuck in a traffic jam because you don't know if it's going to be a bomb or not. I wanted to talk about how difficult it is to live in a situation like that and how the people there have survived. *I didn't want to just criticize Pakistan. I wanted to talk about how normal people, outside of the privileged circle, manage.* Not everyone is so well off they don't have to think about life.[40]

When asked why she thought humor would be an effective medium, Mohsin gave a very interesting answer:

> Well, because I didn't want to write a rant. I didn't want to lecture people or say how awful things are. And people in Pakistan still have a great sense of humor, in spite of everything. Also satire has a great history in Pakistan—it's greatly appreciated.[41]

This contradicts the image of stern and serious Muslims, one especially conveyed in the aftermath of 9/11 by Western media, which have come to prefer the definition of "cultures according to their presumed 'essential' characteristics, especially as regards politics," as Mahmood Mamdani has argued.[42] And these "essential characteristics," when it comes to Pakistanis and Middle Easterners, seem to be a tendency toward seriousness and dullness, which translates into an image of unhumorous, fun-averse, almost misanthropic Muslims. Since for Western media (and consequently many Western people) Muslims are almost "pathologically humorless,"[43] it must have struck them as a big surprise that the new comedic spaces opened by a tragedy like September 11 would have been filled exactly by Muslim comedians![44]

One of the Pakistani censors' concerns about *Tere Bin Laden*, after all, was exactly the image of a "coward and ridiculous" Osama bin Laden, in total disagreement with the prescription of the hard-core Islamists, whose idea of the behavioral disposition of the "ideal man" is "heavy, austere, warrior-like, controlled, resolute, selfless, and highly emotional—in short, an extraordinary personality who stood against the expression of lightness, carefreeness, and spontaneity, in a word, ordinariness."[45] But the concern of the Pakistani Ministry of Culture was probably not related to these dogmatic considerations. We need to remember that the ties between Osama bin Laden, the ISI, some terrorist groups like Lashkar-e-Taiba, and the United States are not just allegations jeeringly put forward by a comedy film like *Tere Bin Laden*.

THE ISI, OSAMA BIN LADEN, AND LASHKAR-E-TAIBA: A THREAT TO INDIA?

Serious studies have furnished enough evidence to support the alleged connection between the ISI and Osama bin Laden. As Mamdani points out, "The idea of an Islamic global war was not a brainchild of bin Laden; the CIA and Pakistan's Inter-Services Intelligence (ISI) hoped to transform the Afghan jihad into a global war waged by Muslim states against the Soviet Union."[46] Michel Chossudovksy maintains that communication between the mujahideen and the CIA was mediated through the ISI, which became increasingly powerful, slowly but steadily moving to the center of governmental power in Pakistan. And this line of reasoning can be found even today.[47]

An analysis of the structural and semantic construction governing the comic signifiers of *Tere Bin Laden* may provide evidence that humor, in cinema, does not necessarily threaten political stability, security, and peace as long as the government is capable of guaranteeing a safe space where laughter and comedy can take place. As Nina Seja has rightly stated in her analysis of American comic film *Harold and Kumar*, comedy may contribute to creating a proximity to the "terrorist" figure and to raise important questions:[48]

THE CASE OF THE BOLLYWOOD FILM *TERE BIN LADEN*

I think there is value in looking to how comedy can also offer productive criticism of controversial political topics and perhaps offer a cathartic release from anxieties about terrorism. . . . [Humor] can signify limits and negotiations about not only the ethics of humor but social boundaries as to who 'we' are, given that humor is often based on a violation of these boundaries.[49]

The boundaries Seja talks about are the ones that fuzzily define ethnicities and national belonging of Indians, Pakistanis, Bangladeshis, Middle Easterners, and others in the post-9/11 United States, where everybody is marked as "Arab": such conflation calls up post-9/11 paranoia of conspicuous dark-skinned peoples in the United States as Arabs and/or Muslims (and therefore terrorists).[50]

Tere Bin Laden presents itself as a film that aims at negotiating the ethics of humor and at violating social and political boundaries, as it claims to be devised to make not just Pakistanis but the entire Indian subcontinent laugh at the paranoia unleashed by the war on terror. It is a "comedy of semantic confusion," to borrow a definition used by Roderic H. Davison in the 1960s to explain the conundrum around the question "Where is the Middle East?"[51] As much as we would like to explain it, the nature of the comic medium is based on a certain degree of elusiveness, which would prevent a spectator who is not very well acquainted with the culture and the ethos of Pakistan to fully appreciate the irony and the satire of the film.[52]

Would *Tere bin Laden* have caused Pakistanis simply to laugh to their hearts' content, or would they have felt misrepresented, as some officials have claimed? This is not the first film that India has produced on the topic of the war on terror, the post-9/11 paranoia, or the aftermath of the war in Pakistan and Afghanistan. In 2007, a Bollywood film titled *Kabul Express* was shot in Afghanistan: the film claimed to portray the real condition of the Afghani people in the aftermath of the war unleashed by the Americans and their allies. However, the government of Afghanistan quickly banned the film and condemned India for the biased depiction of Afghans. In 2010, a blockbuster hit titled *My Name Is Khan* was released to international acclaim. The film, starring the famous actor Shah Rukh Khan in the role of a Forrest Gump–like Indian Muslim, was devised to debunk the stereotypical depiction of Muslims as terrorists. The famous sentence that the hero finally manages to say to President Obama, "My name is Khan and I am not a terrorist," constituted the synthesis of the film's message. The film went viral, was subtitled and dubbed in many languages, and was widely distributed in South Asia and abroad. For the first time, Pakistan seemed pleased with Bollywood and the way India was portraying Muslims. However, the film was also a harsh critique of the war on terror. American policies and the war in Afghanistan and the Middle East were criticized, but nobody felt the film was doing an injustice to the United States, or that they needed to be safeguarded because they were a precious ally in the region. So why has a relatively naive comedy like *Tere Bin Laden* raised so much outrage among Pakistani officials and the government, while a serious film like *My Name Is Khan* is presented as the official vision of Muslims from South Asia? Is the comic/satirical representation of a serious reality more challenging than a dramatic narration of facts?

THE DISCOURSE OF VICTIMHOOD VS. SATIRE ON CORRUPTION, POWER GAMES, AND DYSFUNCTIONAL POLITICS

Do South Asians, and South Asian Muslims in particular, prefer to be portrayed as victims of the war on terror, or is there a space to recognize a complex net of diverse agencies and mutual responsibilities? In a very interesting article titled "Muslim Comedians and Social Criticism in Post-9/11 America," Amarnath Amarasingam notes: "After 9/11, the ability to laugh, at themselves as well as their elected leaders, became for Americans a symbol of their freedom and the value of their democracy.... Muslim comedians are inserting themselves into the dialogue, helping the Muslim community cope with the backlash brought on by 9/11, and attempting to repaint the public perception of Arab and Muslim Americans as unpatriotic and hostile to the United States."[53]

He argues that this is extremely important for the Muslim and Arab communities living in the United States, because all of a sudden comedy has become a significant cultural activity for Americans facing the trauma of post-9/11, and Americans have taken to it as a way to reaffirm the superiority of their values such as freedom of expression and of dissent, "*in opposition to the fundamentalist dogmas and joyless religious strictures* that were believed to characterize those responsible for the attacks."[54]

"Fundamentalist dogmas and joyless religious strictures" seem to be taken for granted when talking about Muslims and Arabs (in the broadest sense). They are looked upon as people who lack any capacity of laughing, and this, apparently, is not just the Western perception of Muslims. In the post-9/11 world, many look at the Muslim communities as a serious challenge to security and democratic values. Recently, Riaad Moosa, a South African comic and actor of Indian heritage and Muslim faith who has become famous in Cape Town for poking fun at Islamic stereotypes, declared during an interview with CNN: "When I started out it was around the whole 9/11, Islamophobia was just sort of hitting a second wind.... Obviously that informed a lot of my humor and it influenced a lot of what I was talking about on stage because it was extremely relevant at the time. I would just speak about how people perceived Muslims and how scared they are of Muslims."[55]

Islamophobia, according to Moosa and other Muslim comedians, can be efficiently debunked through humor and comedy, and the stereotypical representation of Muslims and Arabs as inherently unhumorous people can be shown to be just a prejudice due to misplaced fears of terrorism or violent extremism. Discussing whether Islam is truly a "religion, which is tolerant and open to comedy,"[56] Bayat has pointed out that "the fear of fun is not restricted to Islamists and Islam but extends to most religions."[57] This fear is rooted, more than in a doctrinal question, in historical perspective: because of what humor, comedy, laughter, and, ultimately, cracking jokes and poking fun at somebody/something might cause—a potential disruption of the moral order and a serious undermining of political authority, for example[58]—the religious and political authorities have begun discouraging it. In Umberto Eco's novel *The Name of the Rose,* a series of murder/suicides in a fourteenth-century Benedictine monastery is hinged on Aristotle's lost treatise on comedy and the power of subversive laughter. Humor-phobia is not a pathological feature of Muslims, but it affects any ideological system that bases itself on the uncritical acceptance of its rules and dogmas. Cinema and comedy can be potentially as disruptive in a country such as Afghanistan under the Taliban regime as they would be in Communist China or in army-administered Burma.

"Fun, just like any exercise of freedom, has the potential to become a social problem if individual and social responsibilities are not recognized."[59] And, as Walter Benjamin has observed, "there is no better start for thinking than laughter. And, in particular, thought usually has a better chance when one is shaken by laughter than when one's mind is shaken and upset."[60] Thus the artist, the writer, and the filmmaker have a responsibility when crafting their work of art: they must feed their audience food for thought; they must open up venues of critique; they must fuel ideas capable of leading to social (and even political) change.

What seemed more disturbing, then, to the censors in Pakistan is the threat that *Tere Bin Laden* posed as a comic narration of the reality of Pakistan, opening for the viewers, through the liberating power of laughter, a venue for expressing criticism and discontent, for venting their disappointment at being forced to live in fear of those same people who should guarantee them protection and security. What the film challenges the most, as we have repeatedly noticed, is in fact the role of the ISI. Another disturbing feature of the film, for those in charge of curtailing criticism, is the lack of a clear-cut demarcation between those who are laughing and those who are laughed at: it is not a question of Muslims poking fun at Americans, or Americans ridiculing Islam, Arabs, or Muslims. Here the most obvious dichotomy is between those who usually become victimized and those who usually are glorified. It would then seem that the film is trying to pit powerful Pakistan against the powerless "Paranoidistan,"[61] as the Pakistani scholar Ayesha Jalal has called her country, compelled to live in a perennial state of crisis, on the verge of being declared a failed country and disappearing at the bottom of the Human Development Index (developed, ironically, in 1990 by a Pakistani economist, Mahbub ul Haq, in collaboration with his Indian colleague Amartya Sen).[62]

I suspect that the unwillingness to let the common man finally laugh at the failure of his own country, at the people who have determined a perennial status of paranoia, and at the army and the ISI intelligence officials that keep Pakistan under their grip is perhaps the real cause of the censorship. In a carnivalesque twist of the events, the hegemonic structures that rule Pakistan are turned into ridiculous and gullible objects of gaze, satire, and amusement. An unforgivable condemnation was then expected by the government of Paranoidistan, because allowing the common man to laugh at the big men would have deeply undermined that hegemony and cause a humanization—and thus a weakening—of the sanctity of national and religious institutions.

TERE BIN LADEN OR TERE BIN, LADEN: WHEN A COMMA REALLY MAKES A DIFFERENCE

The title of the film is in itself quite provocative, depending on which translation we base our analysis on, and in which language we decide to read it. *Tere Bin Laden* plays, in fact, on a subtle game of words: if we read the title as it is written, without any comma, the translation comes across as "Your Bin Laden," thus giving away the fact that the film aims at presenting a spoof version of Osama bin Laden. However, if we place a comma between the second word *bin* and the third word *laden*, the meaning changes, and we get a mixed sentence where the first two words are in Hindi-Urdu, *tere bin*, meaning "without you," while the last one is a loanword from English that means "heavily loaded, weighed down" (Oxford English Dictionary) or "burdened, oppressed" (Collins Dictionary). So if we insert a comma, the title of the film becomes "Without you, [I'm] laden," which means "Without you, [I'm] in trouble." Though the English verb "laden" is pronounced with a diphthong [ei] rather than the low-back vowel sound of the Arab surname Laden, the role bin Laden has played in the global war on terror, particularly in Iraq, Afghanistan, and Pakistan, cannot be disputed. Thus the title "Without you, Laden" could begin a series of predicates for the future: if there were no "Laden," what would the world have been like?

While this potential double meaning is lost if we write the title in Hindi or in Urdu, the semantic ambiguity is obvious in the English transcription of the title, where the word "laden" stands out as a clear loanword with a peculiar meaning. The use of a comma would have restricted the reading to a single, unequivocal one. The director chose instead to play with the ambiguity of the sentence and create, from the beginning, a funny and intriguing title loaded with a double meaning, summarizing in this clever way the topic of the film: a presentation of a unique bin Laden, as you have never seen him, and the warning that, without him, without the *real* Osama bin Laden, we are all in trouble, as there is no scapegoat to accuse, no excuse to bomb Afghanistan and to dispatch thousands of soldiers to the remotest areas of the Middle East.

Such a reading of the title becomes obvious in some of the sentences that Osama/Noora is made to utter during the recording of the spoof video, such as, "How long can you use me as an excuse to go oil hunting?"

CAN HUMOR PROVIDE A SPACE FOR REFLECTION ON THE PARANOIA OF THE WAR ON TERROR?

Dismantling the image of Pakistan as a poor victim of the U.S. game in South Asia and the Middle East and reclaiming responsibility for poor governance, lack of accountability, human rights abuses, and thriving fundamentalism in Pakistan, the film does not really deliver a "message of hope." It is more a sarcastic take on the reality of the American Dream among the young South Asians and the recognition that the clever one always gets it all.

Instead of addressing the problems, things are solved—in the film, at least—by conveniently scapegoating the ISI, in a twist that unmistakably betrays the Indian genesis of the comedy. Even so, again, the ones who have a clear understanding of the historical events and are not keen on maintaining the status quo must be confined in the middle of nowhere and accused of being lunatics. Although they speak the truth, the others plainly reject their utterances as nonsensical. The reality must stay backstage. It should not be part of the show where the United States keeps fueling Islamophobia while Pakistan nurtures the victim complex and shuts down whoever tries to find a voice and says to the United States, together with Noora: "Damn your mother... damn your dad... damn your plans... go to hell."

As Shuja Nawaz, director of the South Asia Center at the Atlantic Council in Washington, has put it, "Both countries need to address their concerns frankly and in detail rather than continue a charade that misinforms their own people about what they are doing and why."⁶³ Maybe a comedy like *Tere Bin Laden,* born from the fantasy of an Indian director and spawning its own geopolitical agenda, rather than a self-referential comedy of a Pakistani artist, is not the best way to do so, but it certainly helps to debunk some of that paranoia that has been engulfing Pakistan and the Middle East for so long.

NOTES

1. Shazia Mirza, "Sex Is No Laughing Matter in Pakistan," *Sydney Morning Herald,* April 18, 2010, available at www.smh.com.au/opinion/society-and-culture/sex-is-no-laughing-matter-in-pakistan-20100417-sleb.html.
2. Ibid.
3. Asef Bayat, "Islamism and the Politics of Fun," *Public Culture* 19, no. 3 (2007): 433–59.
4. Ibid.
5. Henri Bergson, *Le rire. Essai sur la signification du comique* (Paris: Éditions Alcan, 1924). Translated into English as *Laughter: An Essay on the Meaning of the Comic* (Rockville, Md.: Arc Manor, 2008), 11. Also available at the Gutenberg Project Organization website: www.gutenberg.org/ebooks/4352
6. Ibid.
7. Ibid., p. 10.
8. In a recent and very interesting article addressing the issue of racialization of South Asians in the United States after 9/11, Sangay Mishra has pointed out: "The racial hostility towards South Asians and Arabs of all religious and national backgrounds started immediately after the 9/11 attacks, and the process of lumping of a broader segment of South Asians started with descriptors such as Muslim, terrorist, Middle Easterner, Arab, etc. . . . The killings and attacks on Muslims, Sikhs, Hindus, and others in the initial days clearly pointed to the hostility faced by all South Asians irrespective of their religion, nation of origin, and other distinctions. It also pointed to a process where people of South Asian origin were racialized through lumping, and the Muslim religious identity was being used as a broader descriptive category for all members of the group." See Sangay Mishra, "Race, Religion, and Political Mobilization: South Asians in the Post-9/11 United States," *Studies in Ethnicity and Nationalism* 13, no. 2 (2013): 124.
9. The official website is www.terebinladen.com.
10. Bergson, *Laughter: An Essay on the Meaning of the Comic,* 12 (emphasis in the original).

11. Aparna Pande, research fellow at the Hudson Institute's Center on Islam, Democracy, and the Future of the Muslim World in Washington, D.C., has analyzed this political agenda carried out by some Pakistani leaders and intellectuals in the past decades in her book *Explaining Pakistan's Foreign Policy: Escaping India* (New York: Routledge, 2011). For the cited quotation, see www.huffingtonpost.com/aparna-pande/is-pakistan-part-of-south_b_803654.html.
12. The MQM was founded by Altaf Hussain in 1978 under the name of All Pakistan Muhajir Students Organisation (APMSO). Its main objective was to provide political representation to the muhajir community, the community of Urdu-speaking Muslims (mostly Punjabis) who had migrated from India to Pakistan during Partition (1947) and that even today comprises a large part of the population of Karachi. The organization was elevated to a political party in 1985 and renamed the Muhajir Qaumi Movement. It became the Muttahida Quami Movement in 1997, and its Manifesto (1998) states:

    > Muttahida Quami Movement (MQM) believes in Realism and Practicalism. Acceptance of reality with an open heart is Realism, a concept based upon the philosophy of its Founder and Leader Mr. Altaf Hussain. Based on Realism positive achievement made through ideologically supported pragmatic programs is called Practicalism.
    >
    > The short history of Pakistan will show that the country has been ruled throughout history by feudal lords, *waderas* and bureaucrats belonging to the two percent privileged population of the country. This class dominates the country's political life, the administrative services, the military establishments, the economy and the general decision making process, while the 98 percent under-privileged population is denied its rightful share in the exercise of political and economic power in running the affairs of the state. . . . As a consequence, it remains perpetually deprived and alienated.

    See the MQM website, www.mqm.org/manifesto/manifesto-1998-ideology.htm. See also Moonis Ahmar, "Pakistan: The Sindhi-Mohajir Conflict," in *Searching for Peace in Central Asia*, 2002, available at www.conflict-prevention.net/page.php?id=40&formid=73&action=show&surveyid=15/.
13. The character of the FBI officer, Ted Wood, is played by the famous theater director Barry John, a British national who moved to India in the 1960s, establishing in Delhi the Imago Media Company, a prestigious acting school that has become famous for having bred great Bollywood actors such as Shah Rukh Khan and Abhishek Bachchan. Barry John moved to Mumbai in 2007, where he established his new acting school in the heart of Bollywood.

14. This information is provided by the filmmaker in the DVD of the film, distributed in 2010.
15. Ibid.
16. Ibid.
17. Immanuel Kant, *Critique of Judgment*, trans. J. H. Bernard (New York: Hafner Press, 1951), 177.
18. Throughout the film, it is extremely interesting to point out how the use of the regional language, Punjabi, is mainly restricted to the theme song "Ullu Da Pattha" and for the swearing words uttered by the Osama-look alike Noora. English and Arabic are, instead, reserved for the serious register of official speeches, such as the ones by Ted Wood and the spoof videos of Osama. Hindi/Urdu are the neutral languages of ordinary dialogues. The Bollywood frame of production justifies the choice of Hindi as the main language of the film, since it is the only one that can guarantee the wider circulation of a commercial film in the Indian subcontinent, and among the South Asian communities living abroad.
19. Oliver John Double, "An Approach to Traditions of British Stand—Up Comedy" (Ph.D. diss., University of Sheffield, 1991). Available at etheses.whiterose.ac.uk/1873/.
20. "Pakistan Delays Review Decision on 'Tere bin Laden,'" *Express Tribune*, July 16, 2010, available at tribune.com.pk/story/28263/pakistan-reviews-ban-on-bollywood-bin-laden-film/.
21. Ibid.
22. Ibid.
23. Pak Film Distributors Want 'Message of Peace'; 'Tere Bin Laden' Ban Lifted," Available at www.thefreelibrary.com/Pak+film+distributors+want+'message+of+peace'+'Tere+Bin+Laden'+ban...-a0231770197.
24. Jamal Shahid, "Tere Bin Laden Hangs between Desire and the Undesirable," *Pakistani Press Foundation*, July 24, 2010, available at www.pakistanpressfoundation.org/news-archives/36175.
25. Ibid.
26. "'Tere Bin Laden': Looking at a Satirical Spin on the US-led 'War on Terror' We Ask If Comedy Can Be Used to Fight Violence," *Riz Khan*, Al Jazeera, September 6, 2010, last modified on September 7, 2010 (emphasis added). Available at www.aljazeera.com/programmes/rizkhan/2010/09/2010968455534861.html.
27. Ali Zafar's position is, in fact, quite sensitive and his opinion is certainly significant, as he is both the main actor of a Bollywood commercial film, made and distributed in India, and also one of the most famous Pakistani pop singers, largely popular in his own country, especially among young people.

28. It is interesting to note that the Pakistani distributors had decided to change the title and to release the film, in Pakistan, as simply *Tere Bin*, which in Hindi/Urdu means simply "Without You," leaving out the word "Laden" and avoiding the word game that had created so much fuss among the censors. However, even with this clever change, the film was not cleared for screening.
29. Ibid.
30. The message was signed Jamila Keenadiid, presumably the name of a Muslim woman.
31. This email came from Rogert Ntongo, presumably a Nigerian man.
32. Ibid.
33. Jennifer Lynde Barker, *The Aesthetics of Antifascist Film: Radical Projection* (New York: Routledge, 2012), 92–93.
34. Ibid.
35. Ibid.
36. Sangay Mishra, "Race, Religion, and Political Mobilization: South Asians in the Post-9/11 United States," *Studies in Ethnicity and Nationalism* 13, no. 2 (2013): 115–37.
37. Mikhail Bakhtin, *Rabelais and His World,* trans. Helene Iswolsky (Bloomington: Indiana University Press, 1984), 11–12.
38. David Robb, "Carnivalesque Meets Modernity in the Films of Karl Valentin and Charlie Chaplin," in *Remapping World Cinema: Identity, Culture and Politics in Film,* ed. Stephanie Dennison and Song Hwee Lin (London: Wallflower Press, 2006), 95; Bakhtin is quoted from *Rabelais and His World,* 12.
39. Bayat, "Islamism and the Politics of Fun," 456.
40. Shilpa Jamkhandikar, "Book Talk: The Humorous Side of Pakistan's Troubles," *Mumbai,* May 5, 2011, available at www.reuters.com/article/2011/05/05/us-books-author-mohsin-idUSTRE74427V20110505, emphasis added.
41. Ibid.
42. Mahmood Mamdani, "Good Muslim, Bad Muslim: A Political Perspective on Culture and Terrorism," *American Anthropologist,* n.s. 104, no. 3 (September 2002): 766.
43. Waleed Aly, "In a Comedy of Terrors," *Sydney Morning Herald,* July 6, 2006, available at www.smh.com.au/news/arts/in-a-comedy-of-terrors/2006/07/06/1152158275617.html.
44. Ibid.
45. Bayat, "Islamism and the Politics of Fun," 438.
46. Mamdani, "Good Muslim, Bad Muslim," 766.
47. Michel Chossudovsky, "Who Is Osama bin Laden?," *Montreal: Centre for Research for Globalisation,* 2001, available at globalresearch.ca/articles/CHO109C,html.
48. Nina Seja, "No Laughing Matter? Comedy and the Politics of the Ter-

rorist/Victim," *Continuum: Journal of Media and Cultural Studies* 25, no. 2 (2011): 228.
49. Ibid., 232.
50. Ibid.
51. Roderic H. Davison, "Where Is the Middle East?" *Foreign Affairs* 38, no. 4 (1960): 665–75.
52. It is, instead, not too difficult to see how complex the position of Pakistan is in terms of geopolitical and sociocultural positioning. As Davison had noted, "International crisis is one of the best teachers of geography." After Partition, in 1947, and even more after September 2001, Pakistan has been projected more and more to the east of the fuzzy line, which divides South Asia from West Asia (or the Middle East, as it is more commonly defined). "Yet the fact remains that no one knows where the Middle East is, although many claim to know. Scholars and governments have produced reasoned definitions that are in hopeless disagreement. There is no accepted formula, and serious efforts to define the area vary by as much as three to four thousand miles east and west. There is not even an accepted core for the Middle East" (ibid.).
53. Amarnath Amarasingam, "Laughter the Best Medicine: Muslim Comedians and Social Criticism in Post-9/11 America," *Journal of Muslim Minority Affairs* 30, no. 4 (2010): 464.
54. Andrew Stott, *Comedy* (New York: Routledge, 2005), 103, emphasis added. Quoted in Amarasingam, "Laughter the Best Medicine," 464.
55. Robyn Curnow, "Comic Talks Muslim Humor and Islamophobia," *CNN*, November 13, 2012, edition.cnn.com/2012/11/13/world/africa/riaad-moosa-south-africa/index.html.
56. Ibid.
57. Bayat, "Islamism and the Politics of Fun," 434.
58. Ibid., 435.
59. Ibid., 441.
60. Walter Benjamin, "The Author as Producer," 1934, reprinted in *New Left Review* 62 (July–August 1970). Available at freeunit.files.wordpress.com/2007/10/benjamin-the-author-as-producer.pdf.
61. See the essay by Ayesha Jalal, "Past and Present," in *Pakistan: Beyond the Crisis State*, ed. Maleeha Lodhi (London: Hurst, 2011), 7–20.
62. In 2011, according to the Human Development Index, Pakistan was listed among the Low Human Development countries and positioned at 145 on a total of 187 countries. See the 2011 UNDP Human Development Statistical Annex at hdr.undp.org/en/media/HDR_2011_EN_Tables.pdf.
63. Shuja Nawaz, "Feeding Pakistan's Paranoia," *New York Times,* May 9, 2011, available at www.nytimes.com/roomfordebate/2011/04/12/when-pakistan-says-no-to-the-cia/feeding-pakistans-paranoia.

BIBLIOGRAPHY

Abbassi, Driss. *Quand la Tunisie s'invente: Entre Orient et Occident, des imaginaires politiques*. Paris: Éditions Autrement—collection Mémoires/Histoire, 2009.

Ahmad, Aijaz. "Jameson's Rhetoric of Otherness and the 'National Allegory.'" *Social Text* 17 (1987): 3–25.

Ahmar, Moonis. "Pakistan: The Sindhi-Mohajir Conflict." *Searching for Peace in Central Asia*, 2002.

Al Arabiya. "Pakistan Reviews Ban on Indian 'Bin Laden' Film." *Al Arabiya*, July 16, 2010. www.alarabiya.net/articles/2010/07/16/114015.html

Al-Maghout, Muhammad. *Al-Athar Al-Kamila*. Beirut: Dar Al-'Awda, 1981.

——. *Sa'akhun Watani: Hadhayan fi al-Ru'b wal-Huriyya*. London: Riyad al-Rayyis lil-Kutub wal-Nashr, 1994.

Al-Malih, W. *Tareekh al-Masrah al-Suri Wamudhakkarati*. Damascus: Dar al-Fikr, 1984.

Al-Sayyid, Y. "Al-Shi'r al-Hadathi Yuharib Tawahin al-Hawa." *Al-Jumhuriyya*, March 2, 1989, 14.

Al-Zobaidi, Sobhi. "Tora Bora Cinema." *Jump Cut: A Review of Contemporary Media* 50 (Spring 2008). Available at www.ejumpcut.org/archive/jc50.2008/PalestineFilm/index.html. Accessed April 6, 2014.

Al-Zubaidi, Kais. *Palestine in Cinema*. Beirut: Institute for Palestine Studies, 2006.

Ali, Abdul. *Arab Legacy to Humour Literature*. Delhi: M. D. Publications, 1998.

Alloula, Malek. *The Colonial Harem*. Trans. Myrna Godzich and Wlad Godzich. Minneapolis: University of Minnesota Press, 1986.

Alpman, Nazım. Interview with Şerif Gören. "Hedefim Amerika." *Milliyet*, October 24, 1993.

Aly, Waleed. "In a Comedy of Terrors." *Sydney Morning Herald*, July 6,

2006. Available at www.smh.com.au/news/arts/in-a-comedy-of-terrors/2006/07/06/1152158275617.html.

Amarasingam, Amarnath. "Laughter the Best Medicine: Muslim Comedians and Social Criticism in Post-9/11 America." *Journal of Muslim Minority Affairs* 30, no. 4 (2010): 463–77.

Ames, Roy. *Arab Filmmakers of the Middle East: A Dictionary.* Bloomington: Indiana University Press, 2010.

Anderman, Nirit. "The Book of Rachel." *Haaretz*, April 11, 2010.

Anderson, Benedict. *Imagined Communities: Reflections on the Origin and Spread of Nationalism.* 1983. Rev. ed. London: Verso, 1991.

Anouar, Hatem. *The New Iranian Cinema: Politics, Representation and Identity.* New York: I. B. Tauris, 2002.

Arasoughly, Alia, ed. *Screens of Life: Critical Film Writing from the Arab World.* Quebec: World Heritage Press, 1996.

Armburst, Walter, ed. *Mass Mediations: New Approaches to Popular Culture in the Middle East and Beyond.* Berkeley: University of California Press, 2006.

Arslan, Savaş. *Cinema in Turkey: A New Critical History.* New York: Oxford University Press, 2011.

Aṭri, Abd al-Gani. *Adabuna al-dahik.* Beirut: Dar an-Nahar, 1970.

Avery, Helen. *Thèmes de l'humour arabe: les anecdotes des 8e–13e siècles.* Genève: Association Suisse-arabe, 1989.

Awadah, Ridadib. *Qutuf Min Adab al-Dahik fi al-Sharq wa al-Gharb.* Beirut: Dar al-Hikayat, 2004.

"Ay Lav Yu." Wikipedia. Available at http://en.wikipedia.org/w/index.php?title=Ay_Lav_Yu&oldid=506573788. Accessed September 17, 2012.

Azoulay, Ariela. "Cartography of Resistance." *Afterimage* 34, nos. 1–2 (2006): 80–81.

Bajoghli, Nargess. "The Outcasts: Reforming the Internal 'Other' by Returning to the Ideals of the Revolution." 23rd Annual Middle East History and Theory Conference. May 9, 2008.

Bakhtin, Mikhail. *Problems of Dostoevsky's Poetics.* Ed. and trans. Caryl Emerson. Introduction by Wayne C. Booth. Minneapolis: University of Minnesota Press, 1984.

———. *Rabelais and His World.* Trans. Helene Iswolsky. Bloomington: Indiana University Press, 1984.

Ball, Anna. "Between a Postcolonial Nation and Fantasies of the Feminine: The Contested Visions of Palestinian Cinema." *Camera Obscura* 23, no. 3 (2008): 1–33.

Baloch, Bilal. "The Role of Leadership and Rhetoric in Identity Politics: Muttahida Qaumi Movement (MQM), a Case Study." *Al-Nakhlah—Online Journal on Southwest Asia and Islamic Civilization* (Winter 2012): 1–13.

Bardenstein, Carol. "Cross/Cast: Passing in Israeli and Palestinian Cinema." In *Palestine, Israel and the Politics of Popular Culture*, ed. Rebecca L. Stein and Ted Swedenburg, 99–125. Durham, N.C.: Duke University Press, 2005.

Barker, Jennifer Lynde. *The Aesthetics of Antifascist Film: Radical Projection.* New York: Routledge, 2012.

Barreca, Regina. *The Penguin Book of Women's Humor.* New York: Penguin, 1996.

Barsamian, David. *Culture and Resistance: Conversations with Edward Said.* London: Pluto, 2003.

Bayat, Asef. "Islamism and the Politics of Fun." *Public Culture* 19, no. 3 (2007): 433–59.

Baylan, Emre. "Ali Sunal: Telif Konusunda Enteresan Bir Şey Yapacağız." *Hürriyet.* October 11, 2010. hurarsiv.hurriyet.com.tr/goster/ShowNew.aspx?id=16016512.

Bayyumi, Muṣṭafa. *Al Fukahah inda Najib Mahfouz.* Al-Jizah: Al-Sharikah al-Miṣriyah al-'Alamiyah lil-Nashr, Lunjman, 1994.

Beaumont, Daniel. *Love and Hope and Sex and Dreams: Comic Narratives in Classical Arabic Literature.* Princeton, N.J.: Princeton University Press, 1991.

——. "A Mighty and Never Ending Affair: Comic Anecdote and Story in Medieval Arabic Literature." *Journal of Arabic Literature* 24, no. 2 (1993): 139–59.

——. "Parody and Lying in al-Bukhala." *Studia Islamica* 74 (1994): 27–49.

Behlil, Melis. "Close Encounters? Contemporary Turkish Television and Cinema." *Wide Screen* 2, no. 2 (2010): 1–13.

Béji, Hélé. *Nous, décolonisés: Essai.* Paris: Arléa, 2008.

Ben David, Abraham. *Humor judéo-arabe et autre.* Ivry: A. Lasry, 1995.

Benjamin, Walter. "The Author as Producer." *New Left Review* 62 (July–August 1970). Available at newleftreview.org/I/62/walter-benjamin-the-author-as-producer.

——. "The Work of Art in the Age of Mechanical Reproduction." In *Illuminations*, trans. Harry Zohn, 217–51. New York: Schocken, 1968.

Berger, Peter. *Redeeming Laughter: The Comic Dimension of Human Experience.* New York: Walter de Gruyter, 1997.

Bergson, Henri. *Laughter: An Essay on the Meaning of the Comic.* Trans. Clousdesley Brereton and Fred Rotwell. New York: Macmillan, 1912.

Blincoe, Nicholas. "Shoot and Run—Palestinian Cinema Is Not All Suffering and Martyrdom." *New Statesman*, July 21, 2003, 38.

Bloom, Harold, and Drake Hobby, eds. *Dark Humor*. New York: Bloom's Literary Criticism, 2010.

Boskin, Joseph, and Joseph Dorinson. "Ethnic Humor: Subversion and Survival." *American Quarterly* 37 (1985): 81–97.

Bourlond, Ann. "A Cinema of Nowhere: An Interview with Elia Suleiman." *Journal of Palestine Studies* 29, no. 2 (2000): 95–101.

Bresheeth, Haim, and Haifa Hammami, eds. "The Conflict and Contemporary Visual Culture in Palestine and Israel." Special issue of *Third Text* 20, nos. 3–4 (2006).

Bronstein, Phoebe. "Paradise Now." *Jump Cut* (Summer 2010).

Büchel, Christoph et al. *The Hugo Boss Prize 2008*. New York: Guggenheim Museum, 2008.

Burt, Clarissa. "The Tears of a Clown: Yusuf Idris and the Postrevolutionary Egyptian Theater." In *Images of Enchantment: Visual and Performing Arts in the Middle East*, ed. Sherifa Zuhur. Cairo: American University of Cairo Press, 1998.

Butler, Judith. *Precarious Life: The Powers of Mourning and Violence*. New York: Verso, 2006.

———. "What Shall We Do without Exile." Sixth Annual Edward Said Memorial Lecture, American University in Cairo. Available www.youtube.com/watch?v=MLgIXtaF6OA. Accessed November 30, 2010.

Butler, Linda. "The Occupation (and Life) through an Absurdist Lens." *Journal of Palestine Studies* 32, no. 2 (2003): 63–73.

Camau, Michel, and Vincent Geisser. *Le syndrome autoritaire: Politique en Tunisie de Bourguiba à Ben Ali*. Mayenne: Presses de Sciences Po, 2003.

Castel, Robert, et al. *Encyclopédie internationale du rire: Le tour du monde en 4000 histoires drôles*. Paris: Mengáes, 1979.

Chan, Felicia. "What Dreams May Come: (Palestinian) Cinema/Nation/History." *Variant* 30 (2007): 8–9.

Chapman, A. J., and H. C. Foot, eds. *Humor and Laughter: Theory, Research and Applications*. New York: Wiley, 1976.

Charaf, Abdal-Aziz. *Al Adab al Fukahi*. Beirut: Maktabat Lubnan, 1992.

Charney, Leo. "American Film." In *Comedy: A Geographic and Historical Guide*, ed. Maurice Charney, 1:78–92. Westport, Conn.: Praeger, 2005.

Chelala, Rania. "Border-Crossing Laughter: Humor in the Short Fiction of Mark Twain, Mikhail Naimy, Edgar Allan Poe, and Emile Habiby." Ph.D. diss., University of North Carolina, Chapel Hill, 2010.

BIBLIOGRAPHY

Chelkowski, Peter J. *Staging a Revolution: The Art of Persuasion in the Islamic Republic of Iran*. London: Booth-Clibborn Editions, 2000.

Chossudovsky, Michel. "Who Is Osama bin Laden?" *Montreal: Centre for Research for Globalisation* (2001). Availableat globalresearch.ca/articles/CHO109C.html.

Creighton, Millie R. "The Other in Japanese Advertising Campaigns." In *Occidentalism: Images of the West*, ed. James G. Carrier, 135–60. Oxford: Oxford University Press, 1995.

Critchley, Simon. *On Humour*. London: Routledge, 2002.

Dabashi, Hamid. *Close Up: Iranian Cinema Past, Present and Future*. London: Verso, 2001.

———. *Dreams of a Nation: On Palestinian Cinema*. New York: Verso, 2006.

———. "Paradise Delayed: With Hany Abu-Assad in Palestine." *Third Text* 24, no. 1 (2010): 11–23.

Darwish, Mustafa. *Dream Makers on the Nile: A Portrait of Egyptian Cinema*. Cairo: American University in Cairo Press, 1998.

Davison, Roderic H. "Where Is the Middle East?" *Foreign Affairs* 38, no. 4 (1960): 665–75.

Dedehayır, Füsun. "Amerikalı, Amerikalılarla Kapisiyor." *Milliyet*, November 17, 1993.

Déjeux, Jean. *Djoh'a: Héros de la tradition orale arabo-berbère: Hier et aujourd'hui*. Sherbrooke, Québec: Naaman, 1978.

Dickinson, Kay. "The Palestinian Road (Block) Movie: Everyday Geographies of Second Intifada Filmmaking." In *Cinemas of the Periphery*, ed. Dina Jordanova et al., 201–27. Detroit: Wayne State University Press, 2000.

———. "Report on the First Ramallah International Film Festival." *Screen* 46, no. 2 (2005): 265–73.

Dickinson, Peter. *World Stages, Local Audiences: Essays on Performance, Place, and Politics*. Manchester: Manchester University Press, 2010.

Dönmez-Colin, Gönül. *The Cinema of North Africa and the Middle East*. London: Wallflower Press, 2007.

Dorch, T. S., ed. *Classical Literary Criticism*. Harmondsworth: Penguin, 1965.

Dorfman, Ariel, and Armand Mattelart. *How to Read Donald Duck: Imperialist Ideology in the Disney Comic*. New York: International General, 1975.

Ebied, R. Y., and Michael M. J. Young, eds. *An Anthology of Arab Wit and Wisdom*. Piscataway, N.J.: Gorgias Press, 2003.

Eleftheriotis, Dimitri. "Turkish National Cinema." In *Asian Cinemas: A Reader and Guide*, ed. Dimitri Eleftheriotis and Gary Needham, 220–29. Honolulu: University of Hawai'i Press, 2006.

Elena, Alberto. *The Cinema of Abbas Kiarostami*. Trans. Belinda Coombes. London: Saqi, 2005.

Elkhadem, Saad. *An Egyptian Satire about a Condemned Building*. Fredericton, N.B.: York Press, 1996.

Erdoğan, Nezih, and Deniz Göktürk. "Turkish Cinema." In *Companion Encyclopedia of Middle Eastern and North African Film*, ed. Oliver Leeman, 533–73. London: Routledge, 2001.

Esen, Şükran. "Introduction." In *TV ve Sinemada Kemal Sunal Güldürüsü*, ed. by Ali Kemal Sunal. Istanbul: Om, 2001.

Fakhredin, Ali. "The Satellite Subversives." *New York Times*, February 24, 2002.

Fandis, Ahmad. *Al-Himar khanah*. Cairo: Shams lil-Nashr wa-al-Tawzi', 2008.

Farrokhzaad, Foroogh. *A Rebirth*. Costa Mesa, Calif.: Mazda Publishers, 1997.

Fawal, Ibrahim. *Youssef Chahine*. London: British Film Institute, 2001.

Fayad, Mona Shafik. "The Impact of the Absurd on Modern Arabic Literature: A Study of the Influence of Camus, Ionesco and Beckett." Ph.D. diss., University of Illinois at Urbana-Champaign, 1986.

Feinstein, Howard. "Laila's Birthday." *Screen International*, September 7, 2008.

Fenoglio, I., and F. Georgeon, eds. *L'humour en Orient*. Paris: Edisud, 1996.

Figueroa-Dorrego, Jorge et al., eds. *A Source Book of Literary and Philosophical Writings about Humour and Laughter*. Lampeter, Wales: Mellen, 2009.

Fir'aun, al-Husaini'Ali. *Ad-dahik wa fann al-idhak*. Cairo: Maktab ad-Dimyati, 1980.

Foucault, Michel. *The History of Sexuality, Volume I: An Introduction*. New York: Vintage, 1990.

———. "Of Other Spaces." Trans. Jay Miskowiec. *Diacritics* 16, no. 1 (1986): 22–27.

Freud, Sigmund. *Collected Papers*. Vol. 5. Ed. James Strachey. New York: Basic Books, 1959.

———. *Jokes and Their Relation to the Unconscious*. New York: Norton, 1960.

Frye, Northrop. *Anatomy of Criticism*. Princeton, N.J.: Princeton University Press, 1957.

Gates, Henry Louis Jr. *The Signifying Monkey: A Theory of Afro-American Literary Criticism*. New York: Oxford University Press, 1988.

Gershenson, Olga, and Dale Hudson. "New Immigrant, Old Story: Framing Russians on the Israeli Screen." *Journal of Film and Video* 60 (2008): 25–41.

Gertz, Nurith, and George Khleifi. *Palestinian Cinema: Landscape, Trauma and Memory.* Bloomington: Indiana University Press, 2008.

Gertz, Nurith. "Space and Gender in the New Israeli and Palestinian Cinema." *Prooftexts* 22, no. 1–2 (2002): 157–85.

Ghitany, Gamal. *L'appel du couchant.* Trans. Valérie Creusot. Paris: Seuil, 2004.

———. *The Zafarani Files.* London: Arabia, 2009.

Ginsberg, Terri, and Chris Lippard. *Historical Dictionary of Middle Eastern Cinema.* Lanham, Md.: Scarecrow Press, 2010.

Gliouïz, Azaiez. *L'humour, miroir caché de la société: Étude sur la presse humoristique en Tunisie.* Tunis: Or du Temps, 1995.

Golamkani, Hushang. "Ranandegi-ye Batrili-ye Hijdah: Goftogu Ba Masoud Dehnamaki Darbare-ye Ekhrajiha." *Māhnāmeh-ye Sinemāi-ye Fīlm* 365 (2007): 169–76.

Griffin, D. H. *Satire: A Critical Reintroduction.* Lexington: University Press of Kentucky, 1994.

Grimm, Reinhold, and Jost Hermand. *Laughter Unlimited: Essays on Humor, Satire, and the Comic.* Madison: University of Wisconsin Press, 1991.

Grugeau, Gérard, and André Roy. "Les cinémas face à la mondialisation." *24 Images* 121 (Spring 2005): 10–12.

Gruner, Charles R. *The Game of Humor: A Comprehensive Theory of Why We Laugh.* New Brunswick, N.J.: Transaction Publishers, 2011.

Gugler, Josef. *Film in the Middle East and North Africa: Creative Dissidence.* Austin: University of Texas Press, 2011.

Habiby, Emile. *The Secret Life of Saeed the Pessoptimist.* Northampton, Mass.: Interlink 2002.

Habreich-Euvrard, Janine. *Israéliens, Palestiniens: Que peut le cinéma?* Paris: Éditions Michalon, 2005.

Haddawy, Husain. *The Arabian Nights II.* London: Norton, 1996.

Hakim, Tawfiq. *The Prison of Life: An Autobiographical Essay.* Cairo: American University of Cairo Press, 1992.

Hamdan, Masud. *Poetics, Politics and Protest in Arab Theatre: The Bitter Cup and the Holy Rain.* Brighton: Sussex Academic Press, 2006.

Hamzaoui, Hamid. *Histoire du cinema Égyptien.* Marseille: Éditions Autres Temps, 1997.

Hansen, Miriam. "The Mass Production of the Senses: Classical Cinema as Vernacular Modernism." *Modernism/Modernity* 6, no. 2 (1999): 59–77.

Hartog, François. *Régimes d'historicité. Présentisme et expériences du temps.* Paris: Seuil, 2003.

Hazbun, Waleed. "Images of Openness, Spaces of Control: The Politics of Tourism Development in Tunisia." *Arab Studies Journal* 15, no. 2/16, issue 1 (2007/2008): 10–35.

Heidegger, Martin. "The Origin of the Work of Art." *Poetry, Language, Thought*. Trans. Albert Hofstadter. New York: Harper and Row, 1971.

Hibou, Béatrice. "Domination and Control in Tunisia: Economic Levers for the Exercise of Political Power." *Review of African Political Economy* 108 (2006): 185–206.

———. *The Force of Obedience: The Political Economy of Repression in Tunisia.* Trans. Andrew Brown. Cambridge: Polity Press, 2011.

Hillauer, Rebecca, et al. *Encyclopedia of Arab Women Filmmakers.* Cairo: American University Press of Cairo, 2005.

Hodgart, M. J. C. *Satire.* London: Weidenfeld and Nicolson, 1969.

Hodson, Gordon, Cara MacInnis, and Jonathan Rush. "Prejudice-relevant Correlates of Humor Temperaments and Humor Styles." *Personality and Individual* 49, no. 5 (2010): 546–49.

Holden, Stephen. "Navigating Ramallah, an Eye Out for the Absurd." *New York Times,* May 27, 2009.

Horton, Andrew, and Joanna Rapf. *A Companion to Film Comedy*. Hoboken, N.J.: Wiley, 2012.

Horton, Andrew. *Comedy/Cinema/Theory*. Berkeley: University of California Press, 1991.

Hutcheon, Linda. *A Theory of Parody: The Teachings of Twentieth-Century Art Forms*. Urbana: University of Illinois Press, 2000.

"An Iranian Sitcom Barareh: Why Was It So Popular?" *Monitoring Middle East, BBC,* April 10, 2006.

"Iranians Watch Four Hours of TV a Day, and Like Comedy." *Monitoring World Media, BBC.* March 4, 2008.

"Iran's Top 20." *Newsweek,* June 1, 2009, 36-37.

Irvine, A. K. et al. *A Miscellany of Middle Eastern Articles in Memoriam Thomas Muir Johnstone 1924-83.* Harlow: Longman, 1988.

Iskarbit, Rubir. *Al-Fukaha.* Cairo: Dar al-Mustaqbal al-'Arabi, 1992.

Jalal, Ayesha. "Conjuring Pakistan: History as Official Imagining." *International Journal of Middle East Studies* 27 (1995): 73–89.

Jalal, Ayesha. "Past and Present." In *Pakistan: Beyond the Crisis State*, ed. Maleeha Lodhi, 7–20. London: Hurst, 2011.

Jameson, Fredric. *The Political Unconscious: Narrative as a Socially Symbolic Act*. Ithaca, N.Y.: Cornell University Press, 1982.

———. "Third-World Literature in the Era of Multinational Capitalism." *Social Text* 15 (Autumn 1986): 65–68.

Jamkhandikar, Shilpa. "Book Talk: The Humorous Side of Pakistan's Troubles." *Reuters*, May 5, 2011.

Jayyusi, Salma Khadra et al., eds. *Tales of Juha: Classic Arab Folk Humor*. Northampton, Mass.: Interlink, 2007.

Jeong-A, Kim. *Al Bukhala Satires by Al-Jahiz*. Tokyo: Islamic Area Studies Project, 1998.

Jordan, Thomas H. *The Anatomy of Cinematic Humor*. New York: Revisionist Press, 1975.

Jordanova, Dina et al. *Cinema at the Periphery*. Detroit: Wayne State University Press, 2010.

Joyard, Olivier. "Dans l'œil d'Elia Suleiman le nomade: Palestine, *Intervention divine*." *Cahiers du Cinéma* 572 (October 2002): 12–16.

Juni, Samuel, and Bernard Katz. "Self-Effacing Wit as a Response to Oppression: Dynamics in Ethnic Humor." *Journal of General Psychology* 128 (2001): 119–42.

Kahraman, Elif. "Arm-Wrestling a Super Power: American Representations in Turkish Comedies." M.A. thesis, Kadir Has University, 2010.

Kant, Immanuel. *Critique of Judgment*. Trans. J. H. Bernard. New York: Hafner Press; London: Collier Macmillan, 1951.

Karamcheti, Indira. "Minor Pleasures." In *Postcolonial Discourse and Changing Cultural Contexts: Theory and Criticism*, ed. Gita Rajan and Radhika Mohanram, 59–68. Westport, Conn.: Greenwood Press, 1995.

Kellerman, P. Untitled post on Sinemalar.com, September 20, 2012. Available at http://www.sinemalar.com/film/39625/yahsi-bati. Accessed September 22, 2012.

Khatib, Lina. *Filming the Modern Middle East: Politics in the Cinemas of Hollywood and the Arab World*. New York: I. B. Tauris, 2006.

Khouri, Malek. *The Arab National Project in Youssef Chahine's Cinema*. Oxford: Oxford University Press, 2010.

Kierkegaard, Søren. "Concluding Unscientific Postscript." Trans. David F. Swenson. Reprinted in John Morreall, *The Philosophy of Humor and Laughter*. New York: State University of New York Press, 1987.

King, Geoff. *Film Comedy*. New York: Wallflower, 2002.

Kishtainy, Khalid. *Arab Political Humour*. New York: Quartet Books, 1985.

Kırmızı, Nazlı. *Geleneksel Anlatılar ve Söylen: Türk Güldürü Filmleri Üzerine Yapısal Bir Çözümleme*. Eskişehir: Anadolu Üniversitesi Açıköğretim Fakültesi, 1990.

Kojeve, Alexandre. *Introduction to the Reading of Hegel: Lectures on the Phenomenology of the Spirit*. Trans. James J. Nichols Jr. Ithaca, N.Y.: Cornell University Press, 1969.

Kraidy, Marwan M. *Hybridity, or the Cultural Logic of Globalization*. Philadelphia: Temple University Press, 2005.

Krichtafovitch, Igor. *Humor Theory: Formula of Laughter*. Denver: Outskirts Press, 2006.

Kritzman, Lawrence D., ed. *Realms of Memory: Rethinking the French Past. Volume I: Conflicts and Divisions*. Trans. Arthur Goldhammer. New York: Columbia University Press, 1996.

Kroes, Rob. *If You've Seen One, You've Seen the Mall: Europeans and American Mass Culture*. Urbana: University of Illinois Press, 1996.

Landau, Jacob M. *Études sur le théâtre et le cinéma arabe*. Paris: Larousse, 1965.

Lefebvre, Henri. *The Production of Space*. Trans. Donald Nicholson-Smith. Oxford: Blackwell, 1991.

Lewis, Libby. "Are Some Countries Abusing Interpol?" *CNN Online*, July 18, 2011. Available at www.cnn.com/2011/WORLD/europe/07/18/interpol.red.notices/index.html. Accessed April 6, 2014.

Lindsey, Ursula. "As Told by Chahine: Was the Best-Known Arab Film-Maker Also the Best?" *The National*, May 14, 2010. Available at www.thenational.ae/arts-culture/as-told-by-chahine-was-the-best-known-arab-film-maker-also-the-best#ixzz2IU2RJBx7. Accessed April 6, 2014.

Lippitt, Jonathan. "Humour and Incongruity." *Cogito* 8, no. 2 (1994): 147–53.

Longinus. *On the Sublime*. Available at www.gutenberg.org/files/17957/17957-h/17957-h.htm. Accessed January 28, 2013.

Loshitzky, Yosefa. *Identity Politics on the Israeli Screen*. Austin: University of Texas Press, 2001.

Lunacharsky, Anatoly. *On Literature and Art*. Moscow: Progress Publishers, 1965.

MacFarquhar, Neil. "Exiles in 'Tehrangeles' Are Split on Iran." *New York Times*, May 9, 2006.

Mamdani, Mahmood. "Good Muslim, Bad Muslim: A Political Perspective on Culture and Terrorism." *American Anthropologist* 104, no. 3 (2002): 766–75.

Manto, Saadat Hasan. "Chacha Sam ke Nam Chutha Khat" (Fourth letter to Uncle Sam). In *Manto Rama*, 393–94. Lahore: Sang-e-Meel, 1990.

———. *Letters to Uncle Sam*. Trans. Khalid Hasan. Lahore: Alhamra, 2000.

———. "Toba Tek Singh." Available at www.sacw.net/partition/tobateksingh.html. Accessed April 6, 2014.

Marmysz, John. *Laughing at Nothing: Humor as a Response to Nihilism*. Albany: State University Press of New York, 2003.

Marzolph, Ulrich. "'Focusees' of Jocular Fiction in Classical Arabic Literature." In *Story-Telling in the Framework of Non-Fictional Arabic Literature,* ed. Stefan Leder, 118–29. Wiesbaden, Germany: Harrassowitz, 1998.

Marzouk, Waleed. "Love, Anger and Song: Remembering Youssef Chahine, Egypt's Most Eminent Filmmaker." *Ahram Online,* July 15, 2011. Accessed January 10, 2012.

Mast, Gerald. "Comic Films." In *What's So Funny: Humor in American Culture,* ed. Nancy A. Walker, 225–48. Wilmington, Del.: Scholarly Resources, 1998.

Mehr. www.mehrnews.com/fa/newsdetail.aspx?NewsID=1364288. Accessed September 2012.

Mehrabi, Massoud. "The History of Iranian Cinema." Available at www.massoudmehrabi.com/articles.asp?id=659039788. Accessed September 16, 2012.

Midani, Akram. "Modern Arabic Literature: The Allegory and the Absurd." In *Critical Perspectives on Modern Arabic Literature,* ed. Issa J. Boullata, 327–31. Washington, D.C.: Three Continents, 1980.

Moaveni, Azadeh. "900 Channels of the Great Satan." *Foreign Policy* 188 (September/October 2011): 1–4.

Morreal, John, ed. *The Philosophy of Laughter and Humor.* Albany: State University of New York Press, 1986.

Moura, Jean-Marc. *Le sens littéraire de l'humour.* Paris: Presse Universitaire de France, 2010.

Mroueh, Ali. *An Anthology of Humour in Arab Literature.* London: Riad El-Rayyes, 1987.

Mu'allimi, Ahmad Abd al-Rahman. *Qisas sakhirah.* Beirut: Dar Maktabat al-Hayah, 1987.

Mursaloğlu, İhsan. "Amerika'dan Sevgilerle." *Milliyet,* February 21, 1993.

Muruwah,'Ali. *Mawsu' al adab al-dahik.* London: Riyad al-Rayyis lil-Kutub wa-al-Nashr, 1987.

Naaman, Dorit. "Elusive Frontiers: Borders in Israeli and Palestinian Cinemas." *Third Text* 20 (2006): 511–21.

——. "Unruly Daughters to Mother Nation: Palestinian and Israeli First-Person Films." *Hypatia: A Journal of Feminist Philosophy* 23, no. 2 (2008): 17–32.

Nachmann, R. "Can't Stop the Slingshot: Hip Hop Arises in Palestine." *Tikkun* 20, no. 3 (2005): 65–79.

Naficy, Hamid. *An Accented Cinema: Exilic and Diasporic Filmmaking.* Princeton, N.J.: Princeton University Press, 2001.

———. *Home, Exile, Homeland: Film, Media and the Politics of Place.* Routledge, 1998.

———. *The Making of Exile Cultures: Iranian Television in Los Angeles.* Minneapolis: University of Minnesota Press, 1993.

———. "Palestinian Exilic Cinema and Film Letters." In *Dreams of a Nation,* ed. Hamid Dabashi, 90-104. New York: Verso, 2006.

———. *A Social History of Iranian Cinema.* Durham, N.C.: Duke University Press, 2011.

Nahhas al-, Hashim, ed. *Al insan al misri 'ala al-shasha* (The Egyptian on the Screen). Cairo, 1986.

Nahum, André. *Humour et sagesse judéo-arabes: Histoires de Ch'ha proverbes et contes.* Paris: Desclée de Walter de Gruyter, 1997.

Nawaz, Shuja. "Feeding Pakistan's Paranoia." *New York Times,* May 9, 2011. Available at www.nytimes.com/roomfordebate/2011/04/12/when-pakistan-says-no-to-the-cia/feeding-pakistans-paranoia. Accessed April 6, 2014.

Ne'eman, Judd. "The Death Mask of the Moderns: A Genealogy of 'New Sensibility' Cinema in Israel." *Israel Studies* 4, no. 1 (1999): 100–128.

Nice, Pamela. "Alexandria Trilogy." *Al Jadid* 6, no. 32 (Summer 2000).

Nora, Pierre, ed. *Les Lieux de mémoire.* 3 tomes. Tome 1: *La République* (1 vol., 1984); Tome 2: *La Nation* (3 vols., 1987); Tome 3: *Les France* (3 vols., 1992). Paris: Éditions Gallimard.

Norris, H. T. "Review of Fedwa Malti Douglas's *Structures of Avarice: The Bukhala in Medieval Arabic Literature.*" *Bulletin of the School of Oriental and African Studies* 51, no. 1 (2006): 131-32.

Pahlavi, Pierre. "Understanding Iran's Media Diplomacy." *Israel Journal of Foreign Affairs* 7, no. 2 (2012): 21–33.

Palmer, Jerry. *Taking Humour Seriously.* London: Routledge, 1993.

"Paper Slams Iranian Comedy Series for Ridiculing Afghans." *Monitoring South Asia, BBC.* October 31, 2007.

Pappé, Ilan. *The Modern Middle East.* New York: Routledge, 2005.

———. "Post-Zionism and Its Popular Cultures." In *Palestine, Israel and the Politics of Popular Culture,* ed. Rebecca L. Stein and Ted Swedenburg, 77–95. Durham, N.C.: Duke University Press, 2005.

Peleg, Yaron. "From Black to White: Changing Images of Mizrahim in Israeli Cinema." *Israel Studies* 13, no. 2 (2008): 122-45.

Perfetti, Lisa. *Women and Laughter in Medieval Comic Literature.* Ann Arbor: University of Michigan Press, 2003.

Pisters, Patricia. *The Matrix of Visual Culture: Working with Deleuze in Film Theory.* Stanford, Calif.: Stanford University Press, 2003.

Porton, Richard. "Notes from the Palestinian Diaspora: An Interview with Elia Suleiman." *Cineaste* 28, no. 3 (2003): 24–27.
Powers, John. "'A Separation' of Hearts, Minds and Ideas in Iran." *Fresh Air*, National Public Radio, January 17, 2012.
Rancière, Jacques. *Dissensus: On Politics and Aesthetics*. Ed. and trans. Steven Corcoran. London: Continuum, 2010.
Robb, David. "Carnivalesque Meets Modernity in the Films of Karl Valentin and Charlie Chaplin." *Remapping World Cinema: Identity, Culture and Politics in Film*. Ed. Stephanie Dennison and Song Hwee Lin. London: Wallflower Press, 2006.
Rohter, Larry. "Che Today? More Easy Rider than Revolutionary." *New York Times*, May 6, 2004. Available at www.nytimes.com/2004/05/26/world/letter-from-the-americas-che-today-more-easy-rider-than-revolutionary.html?pagewanted=all&src=pm. Accessed May 7, 2004.
Rosenthal, Franz. *Humour in Early Islam*. Leiden: Brill, 1956.
Ruoff, Jeffrey. "The Gulf War, the Iraq War, and Nouri Bouzid's Cinema of Defeat: *It's Scheherazade We're Killing* (1993) and *Making Of* (2006)." *South Central Review* 28, no. 1 (2011): 18–35.
Sabir, Majdi. *Min al-Adab al-Sakhir: Al-Sukut min Dahab*. Cairo: Hay'ah al-Misriyah al-'Ammah lil-Nashr, 2002.
Sadan, Yusuf. *Al-Adab al-Arabi al-Hazil wa-Nawadir al Thuqala*. Tel Aviv: Jami'at Tel Abib, 1983.
Sadoul, George, ed. *The Cinema in the Arab Countries*. Paris: UNESCO, 1966.
Said, Edward. *After the Last Sky*. Photographs by Jean Mohr. New York: Columbia University Press, 1986.
———. "The Art of Displacement: Mona Hatoum's Logic of Irreconcilables." In *The Entire World as a Foreign Land*, 7-17. London: Tate Gallery, 2000.
———. *Culture and Imperialism*. New York: Knopf, 1993.
———. *Orientalism*. New York: Pantheon, 1978.
———. "Orientalism Reconsidered." *Cultural Critique* 1 (1985): 89–107.
———. *Reflections on Exile and Other Essays*. Cambridge, Mass.: Harvard University Press, 2000.
Saloul, Ihab, and Aniko Imre. "'Performative Narrativity': Palestinian Identity and the Performance of Catastrophe." *Cultural Analysis* 7 (2008): 5–39.
Samarkani, Mohamad Habib, ed. "Créations palestiniennes: Roman, nouvelle, poésie, récit, art contemporain." *Horizons Maghrébins: Le droit à la mémoire* 57 (2007).
Sanbar, Elias. *Figures du Palestinien: Identité des origines, identité de devenir*. Paris: Gallimard, 2004.

Santayana, George. *The Sense of Beauty: Being the Outlines of Aesthetic Theory.* New York: Scribner's, 1902.
Sassen, Saskia, ed. *Deciphering the Global: Its Scales, Spaces, and Subjects.* New York: Routledge, 2007.
Schmidt, Jean-Jacques. *Le livre de l'humour arabe.* Arles: Actes Sud, 2005.
Schweinitz, Jörg. *Film and Stereotype: A Challenge for Cinema and Theory.* Trans. Laura Schleussner. New York: Columbia University Press, 2011.
Scott, A. O. "ABC Africa: Film Review. A Darkness Cast upon Childhood." *New York Times,* May 3, 2002. Available at http://movies.nytimes.com/movie/review?res=9902E4DA1331F930A35756C0A9649C8B63&partner=Rotten%20Tomatoes.
———. "Youssef Chahine, Egyptian Filmmaker, Dies at 82." *New York Times,* July 28, 2008.
Sedagatnejad, Jamshid. "Dast o Bal-e Ma Baste Ast." *Soureh Cinema* 23 (2008): 42.
Seja, Nina. "No Laughing Matter? Comedy and the Politics of the Terrorist/Victim." *Continuum: Journal of Media and Cultural Studies* 25, no. 2 (2011): 227–37.
Shadid, Anthony. "Yearning for Respect, Arabs Find a Voice." *New York Times,* January 29, 2011. Available at www.nytimes.com/2011/01/30/world/middleeast/30arab.html?_r=1&hpw. Accessed January 30, 2011.
Shafik, Viola. *Arab Cinema: History and Cultural Identity.* Cairo: American University in Cairo Press, 2007.
———. *Popular Egyptian Cinema: Gender, Class, and Nation.* Cairo: American University in Cairo Press, 2007.
Shahid, Jamal. "Tere Bin Laden Hangs between Desire and the Undesirable." *Pakistani Press Foundation,* July 24, 2010. Available at www.pakistanpressfoundation.org/news-archives/36175.
Shehata, Samer. "The Politics of Laughter: Nasser, Sadat and Mubarek in Egyptian Political Jokes." *Folklore* 103, no. 1 (1992): 75–91.
Shemer, Yaron. "Trajectories of Mizrahi Cinema." In *Israeli Cinema: Identities in Motion,* ed. Miri Talmon and Yaron Peleg, 120–33. Austin: University of Texas Press, 2011.
Shohat, Ella. *Israeli Cinema: East/West and the Politics of Representation.* 2nd ed. London: I. B. Tauris, 2010.
———. "Post-Third Worldist Culture: Gender, Nation, and Cinema." In *Feminist Genealogies, Colonial Legacies, Democratic Futures,* ed. M. Jacqui Alexander, 183–209. New York: Routledge, 1996.
———. *Taboo Memories, Diasporic Voices.* Durham, N.C.: Duke University Press, 2006.

Smith, G. Rex. "Ibn al-Mujawir's 7th/13th Century Arabia: The Wonderous and the Humorous." In *Colors of Enchantment: Theater, Dance, Music, and the Visual Arts of the Middle East*, ed. Sherifa Zuhur. Cairo: American University of Cairo Press, 1998.

Snir, R. "The Literary System in Syria." *Hamizrah Hehadash* 38 (1996): 165–82.

Soja, Edward W. *Thirdspace: Journeys to Los Angeles and Other Real-and-Imagined Places*. Cambridge, Mass.: Blackwell, 1996.

Soja, Edward. "Keeping Space Open." *Annals of the Association of American Geographers* 89, no. 2 (1999): 348–53.

Stam, Robert. "Third World Cinema." *Journal of Film and Video* 36 (Spring 1984): 50–61.

Stein, Rebecca L., and Ted Swedenburg. *Palestine, Israel, and the Politics of Popular Culture*. Durham, N.C.: Duke University Press, 2005.

Stott, Andrew. *Comedy: The New Critical Idiom*. New York: Routledge, 2005.

Stützle, Christiane. "Turkish Hollywood." Available at www.hoganlovells.com/files/Publication/77a8982a-930c-43bc-9559-1d8f1f7d71a7/Presentation/PublicationAttachment/a61315f2-a6ba-45bd-b98c-299a4335627a/ProMedia_Turkish%20Hollywood%20_English_%20_2_.doc.pdf. Accessed September 22, 2012.

Suleiman, Elia. "Illusions nécessaires." Trans. Hélène Frappat. *Cahiers du Cinéma* 560 (September 2001): 54–56.

Talmon, Miri, and Yaron Peleg, eds. *Israeli Cinema: Identities in Motion*, 30–40. Austin: University of Texas Press, 2011.

Taş, Vadullah. *Kemal Sunal Filmlerini Anlatıyor*. Istanbul: Esen, 2011.

Tawil, Helga. "Coming into Being and Flowing into Exile: History and Trends in Palestinian Film-Making." *Nebula* 2, no. 2 (June 2005): 113–40.

———. "Where Is the Political in Cultural Studies?" *International Journal of Cultural Studies* 14, no. 5 (2011): 467–82.

Taylor, Ella. "Laila's Birthday Is Mashrawi's Day in the Life of Ramallah." *Village Voice*, May 27, 2009.

Tcheuyap, Alexie, "Comedy of Power, Power of Comedy: Strategic Transformations in African Cinemas." *Journal of African Cultural Studies* 22, no. 1 (2010): 25–40.

"Telebarometre." *Milliyet*, March 18, 1994.

"Turkey's Movie Industry Seeks Firm Foothold." *Hürriyet Daily News*, May 3, 2011. Available at www.hurriyetdailynews.com/default.aspx?pageid=438&n=turkeys-movie-industry-seeks-a-firm-foothold-2011-03-04. Accessed September 22, 2012.

"Turkish Romantic Comedy Gets European Release." *Today's Zaman,* December 26, 2009. Available at www.todayszaman.com/newsDetail_getNewsById.action;jsessionid=168D7E19270082A138F32BA0B1017432?newsId=196659. Accessed November 21, 2012.

Ulas888. Untitled web post. *YouTube,* August 2012. Available at www.youtube.com/comment?lc=32kH0mg_Qtw2DTtqC9ODFJ9P1XApAkTI-tOl0-eXC45k. Accessed September 16, 2012.

Varzi, Roxanne. *Warring Souls: Youth, Media, and Martyrdom in Post-revolution Iran.* Durham, N.C.: Duke University Press, 2006.

Ventura, Elbert. "Ghost World." *Pop Matters,* February 20, 2003.

Vira, Varun, and Anthony H. Cordesman. *Pakistan Violence vs. Stability: A National Net Assessment. A Report of the CSIS Burke Chair of Strategy.* Washington, D.C.: Center for Strategic and International Studies, 2011.

Wassef, Magda, ed. *Egypte: 100 ans de cinéma.* Paris: Institut du monde arabe, 1994.

West, Dennis, and Joan M. West. "Coming to Amreeka: An Interview with Cherien Dabis." *Cineaste: America's Leading Magazine on the Art and Politics of the Cinema* 35, no. 1 (2009): 22-26.

Whitaker, Sheila. "Youssef Chahine: Egyptian Filmmaker Who Championed Nationalism and Arab Concerns with an Independent Eye." *Guardian,* July 28, 2008.

White, Rob. "Sad Times: An Interview with Elia Suleiman." *Film Quarterly* 64, no. 1 (2010): 38-45.

"Yahşi Batı." Box Office Mojo. Available at http://boxofficemojo.com/movies/intl/?id=_fYAHSIBATI02&country=TR&wk=2010W2&id=_fYAHSIBATI02&p=.htm. Accessed September 21, 2012.

Yaqub, Nadia. "The Palestinian Cinematic Wedding." *Journal of Middle East Women's Studies* 3, no. 2 (2007): 56-85.

——. "Paradise Now: Narrating a Failed Politics." In *Film in the Middle East and North Africa: Creative Dissidence,* ed. Josef Gugler, 219-27. Austin: University of Texas Press, 2011.

Yehudai, Nir. "Creating a Poetics in Exile: The Development of an Ethnic Palestinian-American Culture." In *Creativity in Exile,* ed. Michael Hanne, 192-203. Amsterdam: Rodopi, 2004.

"Yerliler Yabancılara Fark Attı." *Milliyet,* October 7, 1991.

"Yeşilçam'da Rönesans." *Hürriyet,* December 4, 1997. Available at http://hurarsiv.hurriyet.com.tr/goster/ShowNew.aspx?id=-276899.

Yosef, Raz. *Beyond Flesh: Queer Masculinities and Nationalism in Israeli Cinema.* New Brunswick, N.J.: Rutgers University Press, 2004.

———. "Homoland: Interracial Sex and the Israeli-Palestinian Conflict in Israeli Cinema." *GLQ* 8, no. 4 (2002): 553–79.

Yusufzai, Rahimullah. "Pashtoons and the Terrorist Film." *Himal South Asia* (November 2003).

Zuhur, Sharifa, ed. *Images of Enchantment: Visual and Performing Arts of the Middle East*. Cairo: American University in Cairo Press, 2001.

FILMOGRAPHY

"Abbas Kiarostami." Firouzan Films. www.firouzanfilms.com/HallOfFame/Inductees/AbbasKiarostami.html. Accessed January 28, 2013.
Abu-Assad, Hany. *Al Janna al-'an* (Paradise Now). Burbank, Calif.: Warner Home Video, 2005.
Alexandrowicz, Ra'anan. *Masa'ot James ba-Erets ha-Kodesh* (James' Journey to Jerusalem). 2004.
Aṣghar Farhādi. *Jodā'i-e Nāder az Simin* (A Separation). 2011.
Bukaee, Rafi. *Avanti Popolo*. 1986.
Chahine, Youssef. *Bab al Hadid* (Cairo Station). 1958.
——. *Al Qahira Minawara bi Ahlaha* (Cairo as Told by Chahine). 1991.
——. *Iskindiria . . . leh?* (Alexandria, Why?). 1978.
Dayan, Asaf. *Giv'at Halfon Enah 'Onah* (Halfon Hill Doesn't Answer). 1976.
Dehnamaki, Masoud. *Ekhrajiha* (The Outcasts). 2007.
Dhouib, Moncef. *The TV Is Coming*. 2006.
Gören, Şerif. *Amerikalı* (The American). Anadolu Filmcilik, 1993.
Keret, Etgar, and Shira Geffen. *Meduzot* (Jellyfish). 2007.
Kharti al-Khassa Jiddan (My Very Private Map). 1998.
Kiarostami, Abbas. *Bad mara khahad bord* (The Wind Will Carry Us). 1999.
Masharawi, Rashid. *Eid milad layla* (Laila's Birthday). Fortissimo Films. 2008.
Modiri, Mehrān. "Nāmeh-ye Mehrān Modiri beh mardom darbāreh-ye CD-e 'Māhvāreh.'" *Tābnāk* (December-January 2010–2011). Available at www.tabnak.ir/fa/news/143147. Accessed September 2012.
"Shabhā-ye Barareh." Episode no. 8, Islamic Republic of Iran Broadcasting, Channel Three, 2005.
Revah, Ze'ev. *Tipat Mazal*. 1990.
Riklis, Eran. *Ha-Kalah ha-Surit* (The Syrian Bride). 2004.
Salmona, Mushon. *Vasermil*. 2007.
Sorak, Ömer Faruk. *Yahşi Batğ* (The Mild West). 2010.
Sharma, Abhihsek. *Tere Bin Laden* (Without You, Laden/Your Bin Laden). 2010.
Suleiman, Elia. *Sijl Ikhtifa'* (Chronicle of Disappearance). New York: Kino on Video, 2005.

———. *Al Zaman al-Baqi* (The Time That Remains). 2009.
———. *Yadun Ilahiya* (Divine Intervention). Paris: Vidéo France Télévision, 2003.
Sunal, Kemal. *Amerikalı.* 1993.
Yılmaz, Atıf. *Köşeyi Dönen Adam* (The Man Who Turned the Corner). Cicek Film, 1978.
Zarhin, Shemi. *Ha-Kokhavim shel Shlomi* (Bonjour Monsieur Shlomi). 2003.

CONTRIBUTORS

ELISE BURTON is a doctoral candidate in Middle Eastern Studies and History at Harvard University. Her primary areas of research involve the political and social relationships between biology and nationalism in the modern Middle East, particularly the construction of human genetics in Israel, Iran, and Turkey. Her major secondary interest is Israeli cultural politics, especially the ideology of marriage and the performance of ethnic identity in popular music and cinema. She has also published and presented on contemporary science education in the Middle East.

GAYATRI DEVI is Assistant Professor of English and of Women and Gender Studies at Lock Haven University of Pennsylvania, where she also coordinates the Women and Gender Studies program. She received her Ph.D. in English literature from the University of North Dakota in 1995 with a dissertation on the literary, cultural, and political ramifications of Freud's theory of humor across multiple literary, theatrical, and cinematic texts. Her writings on South Asian and Middle Eastern literatures and cinemas have been published in various scholarly journals and anthologies.

PERIN GUREL is Assistant Professor of American Studies at Notre Dame University and a fellow of the Yale Initiative for the Study of Material and Visual Cultures of Religions. She received her Ph.D. in American Studies and a graduate qualification in Women's, Gender, and Sexuality Studies from Yale University in 2010. She is currently working on her first book, *Wild Westernization: Gender, Sexuality, and the United States in Turkey*, which explores how conflicts over the concept of "westernization" in Turkey have historically influenced and continue to influence international relations, cultural production, and sexual politics.

CONTRIBUTORS

SOMY KIM is a doctoral candidate in the Department of Comparative Literature at the University of Texas, Austin. She earned her B.A. in linguistics with a minor in Near Eastern languages and cultures from the University of California, Los Angeles, and an M.A. in English Literature from DePaul University. She studied Arabic at the American University in Cairo and then continued her studies at Damascus University as a Fulbright student. Her research interests include contemporary Persian and Arabic literatures and cinema, genre theory, and cultural studies.

ROBERT LANG is Professor of Cinema at the University of Hartford. He is the author of *Masculine Interests: Homoerotics in Hollywood Film*, and the editor of *"The Birth of a Nation": D. W. Griffith, Director*. His *Le Mélodrame américain* was published in 2008 in L'Harmattan's "Champs visuels étrangers" series, and his most recent book, published in 2014, is *New Tunisian Cinema: Allegories of Resistance*.

MARA MATTA is a lecturer in the modern literatures of the Indian subcontinent at the Italian Institute of Oriental Studies (ISO) of the University of Rome 'La Sapienza,' Italy. She also teaches *Modern Tibetan Language and Literature* at the University of Naples 'L'Orientale' (UNO), where, in 2005, she was awarded her Ph.D. in South and East Asia studies with a thesis on the contemporary Tibetan prose theater and cinema in China and in the Tibetan diaspora. In order to pursue the study of Asian languages and cultures, since 1996 she has been traveling in China, Tibet, Nepal, India, and Bangladesh, where she has learned Tibetan, Chinese, Bengali, and Hindi. Beside her academic work, she is also a consultant on Asian cinema for various film festivals in Italy (Asiatica Film Mediale, Rome; Napoli Film Festival, Naples; Bolzano's Borderland Film Festival, among others). Since 2008, she has been a member of NETPAC (The Network for the Promotion of Asian Cinema), where she is the main consultant for the Himalayan Cinemas and acts as Netpac Jury Member at International Film Festivals. Currently she is conducting research on the literary and cinematic representations of indigenous people in South Asia, particularly in northeast India, southwest China (Tibetan areas), and the

CHT of Bangladesh. She is also working on a project related to Asian borderlands and indigenous people living at the crossroads of the nation-states in South and Southeast Asia (India, China, Burma, and Bangladesh).

NAJAT RAHMAN is Associate Professor of Comparative Literature at the University of Montreal, with specialties in contemporary Arabic literature and culture. Previously, she taught at James Madison University and was a Fulbright Scholar in Lebanon. She received her Ph.D. in Comparative Literature from the University of Wisconsin, Madison. She is the author of *Literary Disinheritance: The Writing of Home in the Work of Mahmoud Darwish and Assia Djebar* (2008) and co-editor of *Mahmoud Darwish, Exile's Poet: Critical Essays* (2008). She has also managed the production of the documentary *Ustura* (Legend), directed by Nizar Hassan for Mashad Cinema and TV Productions in Nazareth in 1998. She served as co-chair of the Middle East Caucus of the Society for Cinema and Media Studies from 2010 to 2012.

CYRUS ALI ZARGAR is Assistant Professor of Religion at Augustana College in Rock Island, Illinois, and the author of articles in the *Journal of Arabic Literature* and *Iranian Studies*. He received his Ph.D. in Near Eastern Studies from the University of California, Berkeley. He is also the author of *Sufi Aesthetics: Beauty, Love, and the Human Form in the Writings of Ibn 'Arabi and 'Iraqi* (2011).

INDEX

Abbassi, Driss, 66
ABC Africa (film; Kiarostami), 167, 186n21
Abdi, Akbar, 146
absurdity, 6; effects, 142; film examples, 37, 39–40, 41, 43–44, 46, 115, 170; laughter from, 173; studies, 27n13; text examples, 17–18
Abu-Assad, Hany, 20, 31, 32, 33, 48–52
adab literature, 16–17
ādamsāzi concept, 156–57
Adorno, Theodor, 222
Advancement of Documentary and Experimental Cinema (Iran), 147
advertising: corporate/product, 203, 206–7; of films, 191, 198, 199, 202
aesthetics of humor: categories, 6; laughter, 7; qualities, 5, 12, 14, 15
Afghanistan, 2, 217, 226, 227, 228, 229–30, 231
Afghan language, 102n17
aggressive humor and laughter: film scenes described, 113, 134–35, 139, 142; individual vs. group laughter, 165–66; racial attitudes and, 124n13; theory, 8–10, 12, 109, 122
Ahmad, Aijaz, 81, 99
Akın, Fatih, 202

Alexandria, Again and Forever (film; Chahine), 130
Alexandria... New York (film; Chahine), 130
Alexandria, Why? (film; Chahine), 23, 126, 130–35, 135–36
Alexandrowicz, Ra'anan, 114, 116–17, 119, 120
Algeria, 64, 205–6
al-Jahiz, 16–18
Al janna al 'an (film; Abu-Assad). *See Paradise Now* (Abu-Assad)
Al Jazeera, 221–22
al-Khatib al-Baghdadi, 16
allegory: Iranian television, 21, 79–100, 101n9; national, 81–82, 98–99, 163; *The TV Is Coming* (Dhouib), 21, 56–74
All in the Family (sitcom), 93
Alloula, Malek, 205–6
Al-Rafi'i, Mustafa Sadiq, 76n9
Al Yawm alsadis (film; Chahine), 128, 129–30
Al Zaman al-Baqi (film; Suleiman), 52
Amarasingam, Amarnath, 228–29
American Dream, 199, 216, 219–20, 232
American entertainment industry: film distribution, 25, 189, 190, 196, 199, 202–3, 209–10; Middle Eastern responses, 1–2, 24–25, 188–91, 196–210; Middle East-

ern stereotypes, tropes, and themes, 1, 205, 210
"America the Oppressively Funny: Humor and Anti-Americanisms in Modern Turkish Cinema" (Gurel), 24–25, 188–210
Amerikalı (film; Gören), 24–25, 189, 190, 197–203, 206
Amirfazli, Arzhang, 146
amusement, 7, 10
Analytic of the Sublime (Kant), 171–73
Anatomy of Criticism (Frye), 11
ancestry and homeland, 66
ancient Middle East, 67–68, 78n22
Anderson, Benedict, 73
Arabic language: comedic literature studies, 6, 16–17; as cultural cornerstone, 2, 4; official usage, 2, 235n18; Quran, 48–49; scenes and subtitles, 78n24; Tunisia, 73, 78n24
Arabs, cinematic portrayals: Egyptian cinema, 22–23, 126, 132; Indian cinema, 215–33; Israeli cinema, 106, 107, 108, 110, 112–13, 117–18
Arab society: national affiliations, 59, 67–68, 105; "traditional" idea and myth, 3–4; United States, 228–29
Arab Spring revolutions, Tunisia, 76n11
Arendt, Hannah, 78n22
Aristophanes, 11
Aristotle and Aristotelian humor theory, 12–14, 19, 138, 183; characters, 189; "lost treatise," 12, 229
arranged marriage, 67

Arslan, Savas, 198
art and politics: "the artist," role and treatment, 60–61; public art, 63–64, 77n16; theories, 32–35
artistic creative process: Kiarostami, 167–68; laughter as catalyst, 230
Ashkenazi Jews: Israeli cinema, 106, 107, 111–13, 117, 119, 125n19; Israeli history and power, 105, 109
Asian characters, Israeli films, 119–21
assimilation: Israel, 105–6, 109; power, 109
audience responses: artist awareness and management, 93, 98, 100; attention and distraction, 87, 168; Chahine films, 128, 135, 144n26; character identification, 104, 113, 147, 157; humor's engagement and effect, 93, 110, 135, 149, 153, 224; imagination, 166–67; Kiarostami films, 166, 170–71; laughter, 130, 224; social media, 202, 222; special spotlighting and inclusion, 110; the sublime, 164; "taste" questions, 149–50, 151; text/scene identification, 200, 201–2; theme identification, 148, 154, 159
authenticity: Arab culture, 3, 4; culture, communication attempts, 57, 64, 69, 77n16
autobiographical films, 131–35
Avanti Popolo (film; Bukai), 114–15, 122
avarice, 17–18

264

INDEX

Avini, Morteza, 159
Ayat Film Studio, 151–52
Ay Lav Yu (film; Midyat), 203–4, 208

Bachchan, Abhishek, 234n13
Bad mara khahad bord (film; Kiarostami), 23–24, 161, 169–71, 172–73, 179–85
Bāgh-e Moẓaffar (television program), 96
Bajoghli, Narges, 146, 153, 155
Bakhtin, Mikhail, 6, 7, 14, 17, 223–24
Barareh Nights (sitcom), 79, 90–94
Baya' al khawatim (film; Chahine), 128
Bayat, Asef, 215, 224, 229
Bayyumi, Mustafa, 6
Be-en Moledet (film; Habib), 106
Béji, Hélé, 65, 66
Ben Ali, Leïla Trabelsi, 71
Ben Ali, Zine El Abidine: regime-era cinema and satire, 21, 56–74; regime, history, 71, 75n7, 75n8–76n8, 76n13–77n13; regime, nature, 59, 62, 63, 64–65, 69–70, 73–74, 74n3, 77n20, 77n21–78n21
"Benalism," 77n21–78n21
Benjamin, Walter, 7, 163, 168, 186n5, 230
Bergson, Henri: gestures, 28n44, 53n24; humor theories, 5, 6, 14, 15–16, 28n40, 35–36, 51, 128–30, 142; laughter theory, 15, 18–19, 36, 129, 130, 144n11, 215, 217
Bitter Coffee (television program), 94–96
Bollywood films: industry and actors, 191, 220, 221–22, 227–28, 234n13, 235n27; languages, 235n18; *Tere Bin Laden* (Sharma), 25–26, 215–33
Bomb-e Khandeh (comedy segment; Modiri), 83–90
Bonjour Monsieur Shlomi (film; Zarhin), 107, 113–14, 118, 122
borders and boundaries: 20th-century changes, 2; 21st-century identity, 25, 47
Boughedir, Férid, 73
Bourdieu, Pierre, 151
bourekas films (Israel), 106–7, 109, 110, 111–14, 121
Bourguiba, Habib, 68, 70, 74n3, 76n13–77n13
Bouzid, Nouri, 74n3, 75n3
Bread and Alley (short film; Kiarostami), 173–75
British colonialism, 2
Burton, Elise, 22, 104–22
Butler, Judith, 39, 42–43

Cairo, Egypt, 140
Cairo as Told by Chahine (film; Chahine), 22, 126, 140–42
Cairo Station (film; Chahine), 22, 23, 126, 135–39
Camau, Michel, 76n13–77n13
camera work: *Alexandria, Why?* (Chahine), 132; *Bread and Alley* (Kiarostami), 174–75; *Cairo as Told by Chahine*, 141; *Divine Intervention* (Suleiman), 44, 46; *Paradise Now* (Abu-Assad), 48–50, 51; topography, 1; *The Wind Will Carry Us* (Kiarostami), 180
capitalism, critiques, 25, 99, 191–94, 195, 206–7

Carikli Milyoner (film; Tibet), 191
carnivalesque humor, 25, 109, 215, 223, 224, 230–31; carnivalesque laughter, 19
censorship: Afghanistan, 227; Egypt, 127, 135; Germany, 222–23; Iran, 84, 86, 103n38, 150, 160n11; Israel, 106; Middle East, 223; Pakistan, 25–26, 221, 223, 224, 226, 230–31, 236n28; self-, 28n40; Tunisia, 74; Turkey, 195–96, 201–2
Central Intelligence Agency (CIA), 226
Ceylan, Nuri Bilge, 188, 202
Chahine, Youssef: films, 22–23, 126, 127–42, 144n26, 144n30; life and legacy, 22–23, 126–28, 142, 142n1, 143n2, 143n9; quotations, 128, 143n10–144n10, 144n26; reviews, 127, 128, 135
Chan, Felicia, 33
Chaplin, Charlie, 137, 150, 191, 222–23, 224
characters. *See* character types; personality traits; stock characters
character types, 106–7, 110, 114, 189–90, 198
Chase, Chevy, 190, 203
Chebbi, Aboulkacem, 60, 76n9, 76n11
Chelala, Rania, 27n13
Chossudovksy, Michel, 226
Cicero, 12–13
cinema: as film element, 50–51, 141, 142; humor history, 5, 11; national histories and identities, portrayals, 21–23; storytelling structures, 11, 166–68; subjective vs. mass experience, 165–66; as Western import, 3
cinema studies, 149, 185n5–186n5
cinematography: *Alexandria, Why?* (Chahine), 132; *Bread and Alley* (Kiarostami), 174–75; *Cairo as Told by Chahine*, 141; *Divine Intervention* (Suleiman), 44, 46; *Paradise Now* (Abu-Assad), 48–50, 51; topography, 1; *The Wind Will Carry Us* (Kiarostami), 180
class differences: humor and laughter, 19–20, 23; marriage as "equalizer," 107; themes and critiques, Egyptian cinema, 126, 127, 131–32, 136, 142; themes and critiques, Iranian cinema, 146, 148–49, 150–51, 152–53, 155–56; themes and critiques, Israeli cinema, 107, 109–10, 120–21; themes and critiques, Turkish cinema, 191, 194–95
classical Arabic literature, 6
"Comedic Mediations: War and Genre in *Ekrājihā*," (Kim), 23, 145–59
comedy (*see also* ethnic humor and stereotypes; humor; tragicomedy): as art form, 4, 7, 148; defining, 7, 11, 12; film studies, 149; genre types, 148, 149, 150; literary criticism, 6; rhetorical devices, 9; traditional structures, 11
comic discovery, 11
communication process, 87
communications technology innovations: cinema, 168–69; effects on Middle Eastern diaspora, 3;

Iranian society, 96; Tunisian society, 73; West vs. Middle East, 74n2
contingency, and "radical contingency," 20, 48
creative process: Kiarostami, 167–68; laughter as catalyst, 230
cultural capital, 108, 109, 112, 151
cultural discrimination: Israel, 22, 104–22; United States, 219–20, 228–29
cultural imperialism: anti-Western sentiment, 24, 67, 192–93, 205–7; artistic responses, Turkey, 24–25, 189, 191–210; Western comedy, 188–89, 190, 196–97, 199; Western literature, 99, 100
cultural power, 104–5, 108, 122, 228–29
currency, 61, 76n11

Dabashi, Hamid, 33, 169–70
dance, in film, 133, 134, 139
dark humor: film directors/styles, 126, 128, 129, 135–36; film examples and scenes, 20, 31, 44, 46, 129, 136; "sick" humor, 28n40
Davison, Roderic H., 227, 237n52
death and death scenes, 129–30, 171, 179, 184
Dehnamaki, Masud, 23, 145–59
Deleuze, Gilles, 6
democracy: addressed, *The TV Is Coming*, 57, 58, 59–60, 63, 64–66, 74; art, 35, 43; destabilization potential, 64, 77n13; humor and laughter, 19, 20, 228–29; Middle East movements, 2, 63, 64, 76n11, 77n13, 77n20, 159n5; Middle East regional power, 77n20; shams, 58, 59, 64, 75n8–76n8; Western power and domination, 65–66, 77n16
depoliticization, Palestinian film, 34, 37
Descartes, Rene, 12–13
Destiny (film; Chahine), 144n26
Devi, Gayatri, 1–26, 23–24, 161–85
Dhoub, Moncef, 21, 56–74, 78n23
diaspora, Middle Eastern, 3; communications, 3, 86; power structures, 86–87
diasporic influences, on national identity, 3, 44, 86–87
Dirbaz, Kambiz, 146
disorientation: film scenes and methods, 39, 40, 170–71, 178, 180, 182; the sublime, 162, 163, 182
displacement: filmmaking, 33; television themes, 21
dissensus, 34, 41, 42, 52n3
Distinction: A Social Critique of the Judgment of Taste (Bourdieu), 151
Divine Intervention (film; Suleiman), 18, 20, 32, 41, 43–47; awards, 53n7; viewer critiques, 54n54
domestic space, 40, 42, 87
Dönmez-Colin, Gonul, 44
Dorfman, Ariel, 205
double meanings, 46, 215, 231–32, 236n28
Double, O. J., 220
dream/fantasy sequences, 193, 194, 198
dress customs, 194, 219
Drop of Luck, A (film; Revah), 112–13, 122

INDEX

Druze, cinematic portrayals, 117–18

Eco, Umberto, 12, 229
ego, 10–11
Egypt: history, 2, 68, 127, 131, 132; humor and political resistance, 109; Islamism, 144n30; regional power, 76n10
Egyptian characters, Israeli cinema, 110, 111–12, 115–16, 122, 125n23
Egyptian cinema, 143n2, 143n9; audience tastes, 128, 144n26; Youssef Chahine, 22–23, 126–42; humor history, 5, 126, 142; and national identity, 131–32, 140
Egyptian Story, An (film; Chahine), 130
Eid Milad Laila (film; Mashrawi). *See Laila's Birthday* (Mashrawi)
18th of Tir revolts (Iran, 1999), 146, 159n5
Ekhrājihā (film; Dehnamaki), 23, 145–59
elections: Iran, 159n5; Turkey, 196
Elena, Alberto, 178
eleventh-century literature, 16–17
Emigrant (film; Chahine), 144n30
emigration, 86; film portrayals, 131, 133–34, 219–20; Muslims, post-9/11, 219–20
emotional scenes: and humor, 129, 133, 135, 142; problem-solution films, 174–79
English language: official usage, 235n18; Turkish culture and media, 198, 199, 203, 204
Erdoğan, Nezih, 198

escapist humor, 20, 109, 126
Esegin Karnindaki Elmas (Gezen), 192
espionage, 65
ethnic humor and stereotypes: American television, 101n9; combatting Islamophobia, 229; dangers of, 28n40; forms, 122; humor as subversive, 214–15; Iran cinema, 104–22, 152; Israel types, 106–7, 108, 110, 121–22; Muslims, assumptions, 210, 225–26, 227–28, 229, 233n8; studies, 22, 108–22
"Ethnic Humor, Stereotypes, and Cultural Power in Israeli Cinema" (Burton), 22, 104–22
European finance and production: Egyptian cinema, 143n9; Palestinian cinema, 33, 55n64; plot, *The TV Is Coming* (Dhouib), 21, 56–74
European imperialism and colonialism. *See* imperialism and colonialism
Everybody Loves Raymond (sitcom), 101n9
exaggeration, in humor, 110, 115, 138, 153, 164, 166
exile: heterotopias, 92; Iranian film, 180–81; Palestinian film, 33
expatriate communities: Iranian, 21, 84–86, 89; South Asian, 235n18; Turkish, 188, 195
Experience, The (film; Kiarostami), 175
experimental film and cinema, 135, 147, 193

Fakhredin, Ali, 100n4
fantasy: and comedy, 37; *Divine*

INDEX

Intervention (Suleiman), 43–45, 46, 47, 54n52, 54n54; and laughter, 19
Farabi Cinema Foundation, 151–52
farce: film examples, 130, 131, 133–34; "of history," 23, 127
Farid, Samir, 134
Farrokhzaad, Foroogh, 161–62, 170, 182, 183
fascism, 168, 222
Fatḥ-'Ali Shāh, 95
Fayad, Mona, 27n13
fear: addressed and portrayed, films, 111, 173, 174–77, 179; laughter vs., 20, 215, 229; paranoia and Islamophobia, 25–26, 210, 215–33
Filipina characters, Israeli films, 119–21
film distribution and finance: American, 25, 189, 196, 199, 202–3, 209–10; European, 33, 55n64, 143n9; Pakistani, 236n28
filmfarsi, 23, 148–49
filmmaking. *See* cinematography; sound use and editing; specific directors
film noir, 23, 136–37
film studies, 149, 185n5–186n5
focusees, 189–90
folk music, 91, 105, 208
folk stories and culture, Turkish, 189, 191, 192, 207, 208
food preparation, 72, 118
"fool" characters, 21, 65, 180, 189, 190, 191, 193, 194, 198, 205, 209, 218, 220
Foucault, Michel: heterotopias, 21, 79, 82–83, 92–93; humor theories, 6; power theories, 105, 108, 109, 124n14
Fox, Megan, 190, 203
France, historiography, 75n5
freedom: American identity and claims, 228–29; in comedy, 28n40, 36, 127, 142; literary theme, 161–62; through laughter, 18, 19, 228–29, 230; through parody, 14, 16
French colonialism, 2, 205–6
French language, scenes and subtitles, 78n24
Freud, Sigmund, 6, 10, 29n50, 29n63, 108–9, 122
From Karkheh to Rhine (film; Hatamikia), 152
Frye, Northrop, 6, 11–12
Frye, Sigmund, 6
futurism, 168

Ganj-e Qarun (film; Yasami), 148
Gāv (film; Mehrjul), 149
Geisser, Vincent, 76n13–77n13
generational conflict, 117–18, 146, 156
genre films: Egyptian studios, 143n2; *filmfarsi*, 23, 148–49; humor potential, 148, 149, 165; Turkish, 190–91
geographical allegory, 81–82, 101n9
geopolitics: India and Pakistan, 216, 218, 233, 237n52; Middle Eastern history, 2; Middle Eastern present and identity, 2, 25, 216, 218, 219–20, 223, 224–25, 227, 233n8, 237n52; Palestine, 33, 34, 47
Gertz, Nurith, 46, 47
gestures, 28n44, 36, 53n24

269

INDEX

Gezen, Müjdat, 192
Ginsberg, Terri, 126, 143n2
Giv'at Halfon Enah 'Onah (film; Dayan), 111–12, 118, 121
Glass Agency, The (film; Hatamikia), 152
Göktürk, Deniz, 198
Golan Heights, 117
Golestan, Ebrahim, 149
Gören, Şerif, 198–99, 201
Great Dictator, The (film; Chaplin), 222–23
grief, 42–43
Gruner, Charles, 28n40, 29n63
Guattari, Félix, 6
Guevara, Che, 76n11
Gurel, Perin, 24–25, 188–210
Guttenberg, Steve, 190, 203
Güven, Ozan, 205

Habib, Nuri, 106
Habiby, Emile, 52
Hadith, 17
Ha-Kalah ha-Surit (film; Riklis), 117–18, 121
Ha-Kokhavim shel Shlomi (film; Zarhin), 107, 113–14, 118, 122
Halfaouine (film; Boughedir), 73
Halfon Hill Doesn't Answer (film; Dayan), 111–12, 118, 121
happy endings, 11, 120, 128–29, 204
Hartog, François, 66
Harun al-Rashid, 78n22
Hashemi, Javad, 146
Hatamikia, Ebrahim, 152, 159
hate crimes, 233n8
Hatoum, Mona, 35
Hayai, Amin, 146
Hazbun, Waleed, 57, 64–65

Hebrew language, 113, 119–21
Hegel, Georg, 13, 35
Herzl, Theodor, 106
Hetata, Atef, 143n2
heterochronies, 93
heterotopias, 21, 79, 82, 92–93
Hibou, Béatrice, 62, 65
high and low art: comedy and tragedy, 7, 19; film genres, 149–50, 151
high and popular culture, Arab society, 4
"*hijdah-e tir*" (Iran, 1999), 146, 159n5
history, treatments of: parody, 16; satire, 21–22
Hitler, Adolf, 222–23
Hobbes, Thomas, 12–13, 19–20
Hollywood. *See* American entertainment industry
Homayoun, Shahram, 88–90, 98, 102n27–103n27
homeland concept, 66
home, space and safety, 42, 87
homework, 176–78
Homework (film; Kiarostami), 175–76, 178, 179
horror style, 135, 136, 138, 139, 141
Horton, Andrew, 5, 19, 40, 52n1
Human Development Index, 230, 237n62
human migration, Middle East, 3
human nature and behavior: endurance/survival, 5, 40–41, 43; laughter and comedy, 15, 36, 53n25, 129, 144n11; self-preservation through humor, 8, 10–11; spatial nature, 81
human rights: Israel and Palestine, 77n20; Pakistan, 232; Tunisia,

63, 70, 77n20
"Humat Al-Hima" (Tunisian national anthem), 76n9, 76n11
humor. *See also* aggressive humor and laughter; carnivalesque humor; comedy; dark humor; ethnic humor and stereotypes; tragicomedy: cinema history, 5, 11; and emotional scenes, 129, 133, 135, 142; forms, 4, 20, 31; literary history, 16–17; media, 6; and politics, 5, 6–7, 15, 26, 35–37, 41, 142, 215, 223, 226–27, 228–33; and power, 5, 13, 14, 20, 189, 214–15, 223, 224, 229–30; research, 5, 6; for social critique, 22, 23, 104, 106, 107, 110, 114, 126–27, 136–37, 225; theory, 5–16, 18–20, 29n50, 29n51, 29n63–30n63, 30n77, 35–37, 128–30, 142, 149
"Humor" (Freud), 10
"Humor and the Cinematic Sublime in Kiarostami's *The Wind Will Carry Us*" (Devi), 23–24, 161–85
"Humor, Loss, and the Possibility for Politics in Recent Palestinian Cinema" (Rahman), 20, 31–52
humorous disposition, 9–10
Hussain, Altaf, 234n12
Hutcheon, Linda, 14, 16

"Images of Openness, Spaces of Control" (Hazbun), 57
imagination: power of, in films, 129; reader/viewer use, in novels and films, 166–67
immigrants, film portrayals, 107, 112–14, 116, 117–20
imperialism and colonialism (*see also* cultural imperialism; specific colonizing nations): film content, 131–32; Middle Eastern shared history and identity, 2–3; neocolonialism, 77n16; television content, 95; Tunisian independence, 76n13–77n13
incongruity, 8, 9, 29n51, 146, 149, 153, 173, 220
Indian music, 219–20, 235n18
Indian subcontinent, films and themes, 25–26, 215–33
indifference, 15
infinity, 172–73, 179
Institute for the Intellectual Development of Children and Young Adults, 173–74
Inter-Services Intelligence of Pakistan (ISI), 217, 219, 220–21, 223, 224, 226, 230–31, 232
interviews, in films, 176
Iran (*see also* Iranian history): cinema, 23, 103n38, 145–59, 160n25, 169; economy, 147–48; media policy, 84, 86–87, 88–89, 102n22, 103n38, 149, 150, 160n25; Middle East inclusion, 2; television and society, 21–22, 79–100; Western interests and responses, 79, 80, 97–98, 100n4, 101n9, 103n38
Iranian art and culture, 91–92, 97; cinema support and success, 80, 151–52, 169; Kiarostami theory, 169; literature, 161–62
Iranian history: cinema, 150; Islamic Republic, 145, 147, 150,

151–52; Islamic Revolution and aftermath, 145–46, 153–54, 155, 159n2; student protests, 146, 159n5; television content, 90, 91–92, 94–96
Iran-Iraq War (1980–1988), 23, 145–47, 151, 153–54, 159, 160n7
Iraq: American invasion (2003), and war on terror, 77n16, 216–17; in Iran-Iraq War (1980–1988), 23, 147, 160n7
irony: qualities, 16; use in comedy films, 44, 46–47, 69, 115, 219–20; use in television, 81
Islam: consideration of religion, 229; as cultural cornerstone, 4, 67–68; history, 147
Islamic Revolution, 145–46, 153–54, 155, 159n2
Islamophobia: artistic responses, 223, 229; sources, 228–29, 232; tenets, 229
Israel: cultural politics, 104, 105–6, 112, 117–18, 122, 123n1; democracy and power, 77n20; identity issues, 108, 109, 116, 121, 122; population history, 105–6, 107, 123n1, 124n17
Israeli cinema: ethnic humor and stereotypes, 22, 104–22; Palestinians, 107, 108, 124n17
Israeli Cinema: East/West and the Politics of Representation (Shohat), 108
Jalal, Ayesha, 230
James' Journey to Jerusalem (film; Alexandrowicz), 114, 116–17, 119, 120, 122
Jameson, Fredric, 6, 21, 79, 81, 97, 98–100

Jellyfish (film; Geffen and Keret), 119–21, 122
Jewish populations: American comedies, portrayals, 222, 223; identity, 104, 105–6, 108, 115–17; Israel, and Israeli cinema, 22, 104–22
Jilani, Pir Aftab Hussain Shah, 221
Jodā'i-e Nāder az Simin (film; Farhādi), 103n38
John, Barry, 234n13
Jokes and Their Relation to the Unconscious (Freud), 10
journey themes, 116, 178–79, 181, 185

Kabul Express (film; Khan), 227
Kant, Immanuel, 6, 9–10, 162; humor theory, 173, 175; laughter theory, 9, 149, 173, 220; the sublime, 170, 171–73, 175–76
Karachi, Pakistan, 218–19, 234n12
Kavoosi, H., 150
Keaton, Buster, 44
Keskiner, Arif, 195
Khan, Shah Rukh Khan, 220, 227–28, 234n13
Khesht o Ayeneh (film; Golestan), 149
Khleifi, George, 46, 47
Khokhar, Abdul Sattar, 221
Khoury, Malek, 131–32
Kiarostami, Abbas, 16, 23–24, 161, 166–85; film techniques, 167–68, 174–75, 178, 186n21; reviews and criticisms, 169–70, 178
Kierkegaard, Søren, 8, 201
Kim, Somy, 23, 145–59
King, Geoff, 148, 153, 155
Kitab al-Bukhala (al-Jahiz), 16–18
Kitab al-Bukhala (al-Khatib al-

Baghdadi), 16
Köşeyi Dönen Adam (film; Yılmaz), 24–25, 189, 191–96, 197, 198, 201–2, 203, 209
Krichtafovitch, Igor, 20, 26n7, 29n51, 29n63, 30n77

labor: men's, 184–85; migrant, 116, 117, 118, 119–20; socialist themes, films, 193–94, 195; women's, 119–20, 183–84
Laden, Osama bin, 216–17, 218, 219, 221–22, 226, 231–32
Laila's Birthday (film; Mashrawi), 20, 32, 37–43, 50, 54n35
Lang, Robert, 21, 56–74
language humor: misunderstandings, 91, 107, 119, 120–21, 190, 203; names, 215, 231–32, 236n28; physical, 137
languages, Middle East, 2, 4; Iran, 83, 84, 86, 178; multilingualism, 107, 119–21, 122; Tunisia, 73, 78n24; Turkey, 188, 190, 204
language theory, and comedy, 14
Laugh Bomb (comedy segment; Modiri), 83–90
laughter: audiences, 130, 224; carnivalesque, 19, 223–24; Chahine films, and discussion, 130, 134–35; humanity, 15, 36, 53n25, 129, 144n11; humiliating/mean-spirited, 15, 18, 37; humor theory, 7–8, 9, 10, 12–13, 14–16, 18–20, 27n14, 29n63, 129, 130, 149, 217; national-scale, 80, 228–29; nature of, 15, 16, 19, 23, 26n7, 36, 222, 224, 230; political power, 18–20, 23, 26, 36–37, 109–10, 122, 130, 215, 229, 230; subjects of, 12–13, 20, 23, 26, 28n40, 29n63, 37, 108–9, 222, 223, 230–31; sublime, 165–66, 173
"Laughter across Borders: The Case of the Bollywood Film *Tere Bin Laden*" (Matta), 25–26, 214–33
Laughter: An Essay on the Meaning of the Comic (Bergson), 14, 35–36, 144n11
"Laughter of Youssef Chahine, The" (Rahman), 22–23, 126–42
Law on Foreign Capital (Turkey; 1988), 196, 199
Lefebvre, Henri, 82
Leviathan (Hobbes), 20
Lewis, Michael, 100n4
Lippard, Chris, 126, 143n2
literary criticism, 6, 11
Lizard, The (film; Tabrizi), 152
location. *See* settings
Longinus, 6, 9, 24, 163–66
Los Angeles, California, 84, 85, 86, 87–88, 100n4
Loshitzky, Yosefa, 108
loss: portrayals amidst humor, 20, 32–33, 42–43; portrayals with fantasy, 47
low and high art: comedy and tragedy, 7, 19; film genre rankings/studies, 149–50; film genres, 151
Lunacharsky, Anatoly, 80–81
lūti figures, 145, 152–53, 155, 156

Madiwalla, Nadeem, 221
Mahfouz, Naguib, 144n26
Māhvāreh (comedy segment; Modiri), 83–90

Mamdani, Mahmood, 225, 226
Mansur, Lale, 197
Mard-e Hezār Chehreh (television program), 83, 84, 94
Marinetti, Filippo Tommaso, 168
marriage: conflict and conflict resolution, plots, 107, 117–18, 121, 128–29, 136, 137, 190, 195, 201, 203–4, 208; dark humor, 128, 136–38, 204; satirical portrayals, 91; traditions, 67
martyrdom: in *The Outcasts* (Dehnamaki), 146–47, 148, 153, 154, 156, 157–58, 159; theme consideration and critique, 1, 23, 49–50, 154, 159
Marzouk, Waleed, 127
Masa'ot James ba-Erets ha-Kodesh (film; Alexandrowicz), 114, 116–17, 119, 120, 122
masculinity, 70–71, 78n23, 125n22, 152–53
Mashrawi, Rashid, 20, 32, 37–43
mass experience, of cinema: vs. individual, 165–66; political power, 168
master-slave dialectic, 13, 185
Matta, Mara, 25–26, 214–33
Mattelard, Armand, 205
"mechanical inelasticity," 5, 15, 36, 128–29, 137
media representations (*see also* television): of America by Middle East, 25, 189, 192–94, 196–210; of Middle East by West, 1–2, 100n4, 101n9, 140, 210, 225–26; national-level image-making, 57, 72–73; satirical films, 21, 56–74, 74n2, 198; satirical television, 21, 79, 83–90

Meduzot (film; Geffen and Keret), 119–21, 122
Mehrjui, Dariush, 149
melodrama: Iranian cinema, 146, 147, 148, 149–50, 152, 153, 159; Turkish cinema, 190–91, 196–97
memory: national identity, 66–67, 75n5, 87; themes in films, 44
Merchant of Venice, The (Shakespeare), 114–15, 116
Meredith, George, 36
Middle East: diaspora, 3; history and identity: humor methods, 16; history and identity: imperialism and colonialism, 2–3; history and identity: regional differences, 2–4, 25, 68; nations/regions included, 2, 25, 216, 218, 219–20, 223, 227, 233n8, 237n52; "traditional Arab society" myth, 3–4
Midyat, Sermiyan, 203–4
migrant labor, 116, 117, 118, 119–20
migration, Middle Eastern, 3
Mirza, Shazia, 214
Misaqiyeh, Mehdi, 150
Mishra, Sangay, 233n8
Mizrahi Jews: Israeli film portrayals, 106–7, 108, 111–14, 117, 125n19; Israeli history and population, 105–6, 109, 110, 123n2, 125n25
Moaveni, Azadeh, 79, 98
"mock-modest man" character, 189
Modern Times (film; 1936), 191
Modiri, Mehrān: acting and characters, 88–90; programs, 21–22, 79–100; ratings and reviews, 102n18; Western critiques, 79, 80, 98

Mohallel (film; Karimi), 150
Mohsin, Moni, 225
monocultures myth, 3–4
Moosa, Riaad, 229
morality and immorality: films, judgment and criticism, 11–12, 169–71, 224; humor and laughter, 12–13, 14, 18, 19; moral development and martyrdom, 156; politics' power to shape, 50, 51, 65, 66, 215; satirical content about, 85–87
Moroccan Jews, 112–14
mourning, 42–43, 184
multilingualism, films, 107, 119–21, 122
music: film uses, 134, 136–37, 140, 174, 219–20, 235n18; folk, 91, 105, 208; national anthems, 76n9, 76n11; television themes, 91–92, 95
"Muslim Comedians and Social Criticism in Post-9/11 America" (Amarasingam), 228–29
Muslim populations: humor assumptions, 210, 225–26, 229; race/ethnicity assumptions, 227–28, 229, 233n8; representation, Indian cinema, 215, 216, 218, 219–33; self-representations, in films, 67–68; "traditional" idea and myth, 3–4; United States, 219–20, 228–29
Muttahida Qaumi Movement (MQM; Pakistan), 218, 234n12
My Name Is Khan (film; Johar), 227–28
mysticism, 9, 16

Nablus, Palestine, 48, 50, 55n64

Naficy, Hamid, 33, 47, 53n8, 84–85
nakba (Palestine, 1948), 33, 44
naksa (Palestine, 1967), 33
Name of the Rose, The (Eco), 12, 229
names, 38, 215, 231–32
Nan va kuche (short film; Kiarostami), 173–75
Nasrallah, Yousry, 143n2
national allegory, 81–82, 98–99, 163
national anthems, 76n9, 76n11
national identity: defining national culture, 105; diasporas and, 3, 44, 86–87; Egyptian, 131–32, 140; geographical allegory, 81–82; Iranian, 79, 81–82, 87–88, 97, 99, 100, 103n38; Israeli, 108; multiple identities, 81, 87; Palestinian, 44, 45, 46, 47; state planning and control, and satire, 21, 57, 60–61, 63–64, 72; territory and memory, 66–68, 75n5, 87; Tunisian pluralism, 65, 78n24
national space, 21, 66, 79, 81, 87
Nawaz, Shuja, 232–33
Nazi regime, 222–23
"Negotiating Table" (Hatoum), 35
Neo-Destour Party (Tunisia), 68
new wave cinema: Iran, 148–49; Tunisia, 74n3–75n3
Nice, Pamela, 130
nonverbal communication: gestures, 28n44, 36, 53n24; humor, 137
Nora, Pierre, 57, 66, 75n5
novels, 166–67

obscenity: language humor, 190; sexual humor, 16–17, 194, 199; "sick" humor, 28n40; television content, 85–86

occupation, absurd humor representing, 44; Palestinian filmmaking, 20, 33, 52; Palestinian film representations, 32, 37, 38, 39–40, 42, 44, 47, 48–51; political, 2, 3. *See also* imperialism and colonialism
Omar (film; Abu-Assad), 33
One Thousand and One Nights (collection), 16, 78n22
On the Sublime (Longinus), 9
Orhonsay, Meral, 192
Osivand, Alireza, 146
Oubine, David, 178
Outcasts, The (film; Dehnamaki), 23, 145–59
Özal, Turgut, 196
Özpetek, Ferzan, 202

"painful" laughter and humor, 8, 13, 14, 28n40, 142
"painless ridicule," 12
Pakistan: freedom issues, 230–31, 232; history and war on terror, 2, 215–16, 217–22, 226, 230–31, 232, 234n12, 237n52; national comedy and self-reflection, 25–26, 215–16, 223, 224–25, 230–31
Palestinian art, 35, 50–51
Palestinian cinema: essays and studies, 20, 31–52, 124n17; specific films, 20, 31–33, 34, 37–52; themes and methods, 31–33, 34, 38–41, 43–47, 48–52
Palestinian history and identity, 33, 41, 42; films, 33, 44, 46, 47, 48, 51; human rights, 77n20; symbols, 46
Pande, Aparna, 218, 234n11
Pappé, Ilan, 106, 110

Paradise Now (film; Abu-Assad), 20, 31, 32, 41, 48–51, 53n7
paranoia and Islamophobia, 25–26, 210, 215–33
parody, 16, 200–201; of American film and culture, 24, 25, 189, 190, 197–210; film examples, 20, 45, 46, 131, 138, 139, 197–203; freedom, 14, 16; of Iranian politics and culture, 85, 88–90; names, 38; text examples, 16, 18
Partition, India/Pakistan, 1947, 234n12, 237n52
patriotism: as political tool, 60, 63; United States, 228–29; war movies, 159
Pāvarchin (television program), 90
Pence, Jeffrey, 185n5–186n5
performance examples: *Paradise Now* (Abu-Assad), 48–49; *The TV Is Coming* (Dhouib), 56, 57–74
Persian language and speakers, 83, 84, 86
personality traits: humor and parody, 16–18; Muslim stereotypes, 210, 225–26, 229
Personal Status Code, Tunisia, 77n20
Phenomenology of the Spirit (Hegel), 13
Philebus (Plato), 7–8
photography, in films, 48–49
"pierogi films," 107
pirated media, 84, 86
Plato, 7–8, 12, 13, 14, 19, 200
pleasure of laughter, 19, 166
pluralism, Tunisia, 65, 78n24
poets and poetry, 60–61, 76n9, 76n11, 161–62, 170, 178, 182, 183
police forces, Tunisia, 65, 76n11

INDEX

politics and art: "the artist," role and treatment, 60–61; public art, 63–64; theories, 32–35

politics and humor, 5, 6–7, 15, 35–37, 41, 142, 228–33; aggressive humor, 108–10, 122; ethnic humor, 22, 104–22, 214; laughter, 18–20, 23, 26, 36, 122, 130, 215, 223, 229, 230; Palestinian cinema, 20, 31–35, 42; political control, 214–15, 228–29; trivializing or addressing political realities, 222–23, 226–27

politics, defining, 34–35, 41–42

power structures: applications of humor, 5, 11–12, 13, 14, 20, 22–23, 108–10, 189, 223, 224; assimilation, 109; ethnic identities and cultural power, 104–5, 108, 109–10, 122, 230; humor as subversive, 214–15, 224, 229–30; laughter's action, 18–20, 23, 26, 36–37, 109–10, 214–15, 229; legitimacy of individuals/groups, 41–42, 230–31; national, 22, 42, 57, 86; order of consensus, 36–37, 41, 47, 52n3

prayers, 176–77

problem-solution films, 174–79

product placement, 203

propaganda: Iranian television, 79–80, 97, 98; Iranian wars, 145–46, 154

psychic energy, 10

psychosocial mechanism of humor, 12–13

public art, 63–64, 77n16

public relations, political, 21, 57, 60–61, 63–64, 72–73

Punjabi music, 219–20, 235n18

Qahveh-ye Talkh (television program), 94–96

Qāsemkhāni, Paymān, 81, 94

Qeysar (film), 153

quest and journey themes, 116, 178–79, 181, 185

Rabelais and His World (Bakhtin), 223–24

racial profiling, 219–20, 220–21, 227, 233n8

"radical contingency," 20, 48

Rahman, Najat, 1–26; "Humor, Loss, and the Possibility for Politics in Recent Palestinian Cinema," 20, 31–52; "The Laughter of Youssef Chahine," 22–23, 126–42

Rancière, Jacques, 6, 7, 20, 32, 34–35, 43; politics as *dissensus*, 52n3; quotations, 37–38, 41–42, 51

Rapf, Joanna, 40, 52n1

Rażaviyān, Javād, 102n18

RCD Party (Tunisia), 59, 68, 69, 75n7, 78n23

reading vs. watching experience, 166–67

Reagan, Ronald, 196

reality: differences, spaces, 82, 101n11; different/double versions, in films, 46, 47; films, and ideas about, 23–24, 163, 168, 170, 178–79; films, imagination vs. reality, 129

Recep İvedik (comedy series), 188

Recess (film; Kiarostami), 175

reformation and transformation, personal: *The Outcasts,* 156–57, 158; *The Wind Will Carry Us,* 171, 180, 185

relief theory, 149
religions, Middle East, 2, 4
religious exclusivity, 78n24
religious humor, 85, 147, 150, 154–55
religious martyrdom. *See* martyrdom
repetition, as film technique, 24, 49, 178
representation: of American film and culture, 24–25, 189, 190, 191; breakdown, 49, 155; Indian film, Muslim representations, 215, 216, 218, 219–33; Iranian film, and politics, 155; Israeli film, ethnic humor, 108; methods, 39, 43–44, 45–46; Palestinian film, and politics, 20, 31–33, 38, 39
Revah, Ze'ev, 112–13
revenge plots, 54n54, 153, 194, 197, 198
reversal, as humor technique, 18, 108, 109, 120, 166
the ridiculous, 7–8, 12, 13
Riklis, Eran, 107, 117–18
Ring Seller, The (film; Chahine), 128
rire: Essai sur le signification du comique, Le (Bergson), 217
ritual: film scenes, 178, 185; humor about, 85, 91, 147, 154; Islamic, 147, 154, 156; patriarchal, 184–85; prayers, 154, 176–77
ritual bondage, 11–12, 14
Robb, David, 224
Rohter, Larry, 76n11
romances, comedic, 148
Ruoff, Jeffrey, 74n3–75n3
Russian characters and stereotypes, Israeli films, 106–7, 113–14, 117–19

Şaban (character, Turkish cinema), 190, 191–95, 196, 209
Sadan, Joseph, 6
Said, Edward, 33
Salaam (newspaper), 159n5
Salak Milyoner (film; Egilmez), 191
Sallah Shabati (film; Kishon), 114, 117
Samad series (Iran), 152
Santayana, George, 8–9
Satellite (comedy segment; Modiri), 83–90
satellite television, 84–90, 98, 102n22
satire: cultural assumptions, 100n4; film examples, 21, 25–26, 37, 56–74, 198, 215, 218–19, 222; history, 16–17; national attitudes, 225, 228–29; purposes and methods, 12, 13, 16, 74, 78n22, 97, 98, 201, 222; television examples, 21, 79, 80–81, 83–90, 90–94, 97–100, 102n18; text examples, 9, 16–18, 225
"Satiric Traversals in the Comedy of Mehrān Modiri: Space, Irony, and National Allegory on Iranian Television" (Zargar), 21–22, 79–100
Sayyad, Parviz, 152
Schweinitz, Jörg, 110, 122
Scott, A. O., 186n21
Sedagatnejad, Jamshid, 150
Seja, Nina, 226–27
self-censorship, 28n40
self-filming, 48–49, 51
self-preservation through humor, 8, 10–11
Şen, Ali, 192, 198, 209
Sen, Amartya, 230
Şen, Şener, 24–25, 189, 190, 196–203

INDEX

Separation, A (film; Farhādi), 103n38
Sepehri, Sohrab, 178
sequels, 23, 130, 201
seriousness: balance with humor, 44, 129–30; vs. laughter, 7, 14, 134, 222
settings: *Al Janna al 'an (Paradise Now)*, 31; Karachi, Pakistan, 218–19; national places and displacement themes, 21–22, 37; story and art direction, 178
sexualization, 189, 194–95, 199
Shabhā-ye Barareh (sitcom), 79, 90–94
Shabneshini dar Jahannam (film; Khachikian and Sarvari), 150
Shafik, Viola, 3
Sharifinia, Mohammad Reza, 146
Sharma, Abhishek, 25–26, 215–33
Shelley, Percy Bysshe, 36
Shi'i Islam, 147
Shohat, Ella, 108, 109–10, 132
Shylock (literary character), 114–15, 116
"sick" humor, 28n40
sitcoms: Iran, 21, 79, 80–82, 83, 88, 90–94, 94–96, 97–100; social power, 80–81, 83; Turkey, 188, 191; United States, 93, 97–98, 101n9, 188
Six Day War (1967), 115
Sixth Day, The (film; Chahine), 128, 129–30
slapstick comedy: bourekas films, 106, 111, 113, 115; scenes described, 97, 128; Turkish series, 188, 191
slaves, 13
social class. *See* class differences

social conformity and social laughter, 12, 15, 18–19, 36–37, 165–66
social connection through humor, 127, 139, 140–41, 142, 144n17, 217, 224
social critique via humor, 22, 23, 104, 106, 107, 110, 114, 126–27, 136–37, 225
social media, 84, 201–2, 215, 222
Soja, Edward, 81, 82–83, 101n13
Sosyete Şaban (film; Tibet), 191
sound use and editing, 127, 128, 140, 141. *See also* music
South Asia: "Middle East" overlap/inclusion, 2, 25, 216, 218, 219–20, 223, 227, 237n52; populations, lumping and hostility, 219–20, 220–21, 227, 233n8; regional portrayals, Indian films, 25–26, 215–33
Soviet Union, 226
space: heterotopias, 21, 79, 82, 92–93; human nature and behavior, 81; national space and identity, 21, 66, 79, 81, 87; possibility, 81, 82–83, 101n11, 101n13; pseudo-public space, planning and control, 57; and time, 81, 82, 91–93, 95
Stam, Robert, 132
stand-up comedy, 214–15, 229
statelessness, 33, 34
stereotypes, 28n40, 106, 107, 108, 110, 121, 122. *See also* ethnic humor and stereotypes
stinginess, 17–18
stock characters, 110, 112, 189, 190, 207
"stranger" motif, 81
"Strategies of Subversion in Ben

Ali's Tunisia: Allegory and Satire in Moncef Dhouib's *The TV Is Coming*" (Lang), 21, 56–74
student protests, 146, 147, 159n5
studios, local: Egypt, 143n2; Iran, 151–52
subjectivity: in art viewing, 163, 165–66; political, 6–7, 13
the sublime: cinematic, 23–24, 163, 170, 171, 175, 177, 178–79, 182, 185; communication qualities, 164–65; Kantian theory, 171–72, 173, 175–76; laughter, 165–66, 173; theory and writings, 9, 10, 24, 162, 163–65
subtitles, 37
suffering, defenses, 10–11
suicide missions, stories, 20, 31, 32, 48–51
Suit for a Wedding, A (film; Kiarostami), 175
Suleiman, Elia, 18, 20, 32, 43–47, 52, 54n54
Sunal, Kemal, 24–25, 189, 190, 191–96, 198, 202, 209
"superiority" and humor, 12–13, 29n51, 29n63–30n63, 30n77, 93, 149
symbols: political invention and manipulation, 60–61, 63–64, 76n11, 147; use in film, 25, 46, 77n16, 189, 193, 199–200, 206–7
syndrome autoritaire: Politique en Tunisie de Bourguiba à Ben Ali, Le (Camau and Geisser), 76n13–77n13
Syrian Bride, The (film; Riklis), 117–18, 121
Syrians, portrayals, 117–18, 121

taboo subjects: Nazism, 222, 223; parody in literature, 17; terrorism and debate, 215, 218, 221–22, 226, 227, 228–29
talk shows, 85, 98
taste, 151. *See also* audience responses
Taş, Vadullah, 193
Tati, Jacques, 44
technology, communications: cinema, 168–69; effects on Middle Eastern diaspora, 3; Iran, 96; Tunisia, 73; West vs. Middle East, 74n2
Tehran, Iran: film content and treatments, 145, 156, 169; national identity and international attention, 96, 99, 100; television content and treatments, 21–22, 80, 82, 87–88, 94–96
Tel Aviv, Israel, 50
television: American, 93, 97–98, 101n9; films about, 56–74; Iranian, 21–22, 79–100; Palestinian, 52; personalities, 88–90; profit, 80; reach and power, 87; satellite programming, 84–90, 98; Turkey, 195–96, 197
Tender Hooks (Mohsin), 225
tension release: laughter, 9, 149, 173, 220; uncomfortable topics/scenes, 227
Tere Bin Laden (film; Sharma), 25–26, 215–33, 236n28
terrorism: questions of laughter and taboo, 215, 218, 221–22, 226, 227, 228–29; war on terror themes and spoofs, 25–26, 215–24, 225–33
theater, 7, 11
Theory of Parody: The Teachings of

Twentieth-Century Art Forms, A (Hutcheon), 14
"third-world literature," 81, 97, 98–100
thrift, 17–18
thug characters, 152–53, 155, 156
Tibet, Kartal, 209
time and space, 81, 82, 91–93, 95
Tipat Mazal (film; Revach), 107
topography, aerial shots, 1
Topol, Haim, 114
tourism: Tunisia, 56, 57, 65; Turkey, 188
traditional foods, 72, 118
tragedy: comedy taboos, 222, 223; as high art, 7, 19
tragicomedy, 5, 28n40, 107, 112–14, 136–37
Tramp, The (short film; Chaplin), 191
transformation, personal. *See* reformation and transformation, personal
translation (humor), 126
translation (language): films, 37, 125n19, 215, 228; literature, 99
Traveller, The (film; Kiarostami), 175
trickster characters, 189, 190, 204, 207
Tunisian cinema, 21, 56–74, 74n3–75n3
Tunisian history and politics: ancient, 78n22; considered, *The TV Is Coming*, 21, 56–57, 59, 60, 62, 64–65, 68, 69–70, 73–74; independence, 76n13–77n13; political parties and systems, 75n8–76n8, 77n21–78n21; regime change, 74n3, 77n13; regional power, 76n10, 77n20
Turkey: economy, 25, 189, 192, 196, 197–98; folk stories and culture, 189, 191, 192, 207, 208; Middle East inclusion, 2
Turkish cinema: comedies, 24–25, 188–210, 210n4; history, 24–25, 188, 189, 190–91, 195, 196, 199, 202–3, 210; industry, 188, 189, 190–91, 195–97, 199, 202–3, 209, 210
TV Is Coming, The (film; Dhouib): characters, 58–60, 61–64, 65, 66, 67–69, 70–72; plot/themes, 21, 56–74
Twain, Mark, 29n63

ul Haq, Mahbub, 230
Umudumuz Şaban (film; Tibet), 209
unemployment, 147–48
L'Union Nationale des Femmes Tunisiennes (UNFT), 68
United States (*see also* American entertainment industry): foreign and economic policy, and critiques, 25–26, 192–93, 199–200, 206–7, 219, 221, 223; immigration, in films, 131, 133–34, 219–20; war on terror, 25–26, 215–33

Varzi, Roxanne, 154
Vasermil (film; Salmona), 121–22
veterans, 146, 147, 149, 151, 153–54, 159
victimization and identity: Iran, 89; Israel, 108, 109, 116, 121, 122; South Asian Muslims, 228–29, 230–31, 232, 233n8
violence: humor as replacement, 108–9, 122; representations in cinema, 20, 169

war movies, 155–56, 159. *See also*
    Alexandria, Why?; *The Outcasts*
war on terror: film critiques,
    25–26, 215–33; planning and
    execution, 221, 226
weddings. *See* marriage
Western art: "canon" literature,
    99, 100; cinema as, 3
Western cinema studies, 185n5–
    186n5
Western cultural imperialism. *See*
    cultural imperialism
Western representations: Middle
    Eastern responses, 1–2, 24–25,
    140, 188–91, 196–210; stereo-
    types, tropes, and themes, 1,
    205, 210
westerns, comedic, 148, 191,
    204–5, 206–9
Where Is the Friend's House? (film;
    Kiarostami), 175–76, 177–79
Wind Will Carry Us, The (film; Ki-
    arostami), 23–24, 161, 169–71,
    172–73, 179–85
"Wind Will Carry Us, The" (Far-
    rokhzaad), 161–62, 170

"wise fool" character, 189, 190, 198
wit, 8–9, 10, 29n63
women's labor, 183–84
women's rights, Tunisia, 58, 68–70,
    71
"Work of Art in the Age of Me-
    chanical Reproduction, The"
    (Benjamin), 168–69
World War II–era films, 131–35
Yadun Ilahiyya (film; Suleiman). *See*
    Divine Intervention (Suleiman)
Yahşi Batı (film; Sorak), 24–25, 189,
    190, 204–10
Yeşilçam (Turkey), 191, 196–97
Yılmaz, Atıf, 24–25, 193
Yılmaz, Cem, 24–25, 189, 190,
    204–10
YouTube, 84, 202
Zafar, Ali, 216–17, 218, 221–22,
    235n27
Zargar, Cyrus Ali, 21–22, 79–100
Zarhin, Shemi, 113–14
Zeyghami, Niousha, 146
Zionism, 105, 106, 123n1
Zobaidi, Sobhi al-, 47

www.ingramcontent.com/pod-product-compliance
Lightning Source LLC
Chambersburg PA
CBHW071814230426
43670CB00013B/2452